D1598820

Law and the Transformation
of Aztec Culture, 1500–1700

Law and the Transformation of Aztec Culture, 1500–1700

by Susan Kellogg

UNIVERSITY OF OKLAHOMA PRESS : NORMAN AND LONDON

This book is published with the generous assistance of Edith Gaylord
Harper and of the University of Houston.

Book designed by Bill Cason

Library of Congress Cataloging-in-Publication-Data

Kellogg, Susan.
    Law and the transformation of Aztec culture, 1500–1700 / by
Susan Kellogg.
        p.   cm.
    Includes bibliographical references and index.
    ISBN: 0–8061–2702–3
    1. Law, Aztec—History.   2. Indians of Mexico—Legal status,
laws, etc.—History.   I. Title.
KDZ480.K45   1995
325'.3146'09720903—dc20   94–43104
                                                          CIP

The paper in this book meets the guidelines for permanence and
durability of the Committee on Production Guidelines for Book
Longevity of the Council on Library Resources, Inc. ∞

1   2   3   4   5   6   7   8   9   10

To Steve

We make out of the quarrel with others, rhetoric.

— W. B. YEATS

If it is true that the imperialists study their colonial charges, it is equally true that the charges study their masters — with great care and much cunning. Who shall say which understands the other more?

— WOODROW BORAH, *Justice by Insurance*

Contents

Illustrations

FIGURES

MAP

TABLES

Abbreviations

AC, Actas de Cabildo
AGI, Archivo General de Indias
AGNBN, Archivo General de la Nación, ramo Bienes
  Nacionales
AGNC, Archivo General de la Nación, ramo Civil
AGNHi, Archivo General de la Nación, ramo Historia
AGNH, Archivo General de la Nación, ramo Hóspital de
  Jesús
AGNI, Archivo General de la Nación, ramo Indios
AGNT, Archivo General de la Nación, ramo Tierras
AGNV, Archivo General de la Nación, ramo Vínculos y
  Mayorazgos
Bancroft/MM, Bancroft Library, Mexican Manuscript
BNMAF, Biblioteca Nacional de México, Archivo
  Franciscano
BNP, Bibliothèque National de Paris
CeI, Cedulario Indiano
CK, Códice Kingsborough
CMa, Codex Magliabecchiano
CM, Codex Mendoza
CO, Códice Osuna
FC, Florentine Codex
LAL/FSC, Latin American Library (Tulane), France Scholes
  Collection
NL/Ayer, Newberry Library, Ayer Collection

Preface

The subjects of this book, the "Aztecs," or more properly, the Mexica population of Tenochititlán and Tlatelolco, have often been treated as exotic and unique. I see them instead as a people who fashioned a fascinating society, one that is comprehensible in the context of Mesoamerican and North American indigenous societies but with its own particular characteristics. What has interested me most about this society is how those generations who lived during and soon after the Spanish Conquest dealt with that event and its aftermath and how they bequeathed to later generations a colonial society, born out of chaos.

Although this book was written primarily for historical and anthropological specialists in pre-Hispanic and colonial Mesoamerica, the story it tells—how Spanish law served as an instrument of cultural transformation and adaptation—is of broader significance. For students of colonialism, it is the story of how Spanish authorities used legal institutions to help create a colonial state that would last three hundred years. For students of law, it is a story of how court records can provide an index to changes in cultural meanings, family and kinship relationships, and inheritance practices. For students of gender, it is a story of how shifts in gender roles both underlay and signaled other significant social changes. And for students of social theory, it is the story of how Spain achieved hegemony over an indigenous population through an intricate process involving active decision making, accommodation, and compromise. To make my findings accessible to a broader audience, I have sought as much as possible to avoid jargon. Where a more specialized language is necessary (as in discussing kinship), I have tried to use it in the clearest way possible.

While authors often compare writing a book to the process of giving birth to a child, the analogy is, in fact, misplaced. After all, a child is born nine months after conception, but a book is years in the making. A more apt analogy, it seems to me, is a marathon. Now, standing at the finish line, it is a pleasure to acknowledge those who provided support and guidance along the way.

I was introduced to Aztec ethnohistory by Edward Calnek, who I first heard speak when I was an undergraduate. He is as compelling a teacher and mentor as he is a speaker. His elegant reasoning and writing remain a model for me as well. Also at the University of Rochester, I had the great fortune to study with René Millon. Exacting and challenging, René remains the most learned anthropologist I know.

Many friends and colleagues have been generous with suggestions and support over the years. Louise Burkhart, Edward Calnek, Pedro Carrasco, Susan Deeds, James Lockhart, and Patricia Seed all offered helpful advice, not all of which I was always able to use. Douglas Cope, Paul Hart, Ana Pérez, and Dan Slive each provided information crucial for finishing the manuscript. Woodrow Borah and an anonymous reader for the University of Oklahoma Press offered enormously valuable suggestions.

I have had the good fortune to teach in several anthropology departments—Oberlin College, Sweet Briar College, the University of Houston, and Rice University—where I learned a lot from my colleagues and received many helpful suggestions. My greatest fortune, however, has been to find a place in a history department and to have colleagues who find ethnohistory reasonably interesting. All of my colleagues at the University of Houston have been wonderful. If I single out a few, it is only because they have gone above and beyond the call of duty. Cheryll Cody has been a supportive friend. Sarah Fishman and Kenneth Lipartito have answered occasional questions or asked me questions that provoked a lot of thought. James Jones gave my manuscript a most careful reading and clarified the expression of many essential ideas, for which I am very grateful.

My colleagues in Latin American and Mexican-American history have been an enormous blessing. Deeply knowledgeable as well as possessing endless reserves of humor, John Hart, Thomas O'Brien, Guadalupe San Miguel, and Emilio Zamora have made writing this book a happier experience. I also thank John Hart and Tom O'Brien for their detailed readings of the manuscript. Along with Joseph Glatthaar and Steven Mintz, they also have been helpful as chairs of the department. Thanks are due as well to Lorena Garcia who, as departmental administrator and friend, helped with many matters large and small.

Several institutions have provided financial support or access to research materials. The Archivo General de la Nación in Mexico City and the John Carter Brown Library in Providence, Rhode Island, allowed access to the most important documents used in this study, and each was a wonderful place to work. In Mexico, Roberto Beristáin, Kathryn Josserand, Nicholas Hopkins, Teresa Rojas, the late Thelma Sullivan, and Arturo Soberón generously gave assistance. The Newberry Library (Chicago), the Bancroft Library (University of California, Berkeley), the Benson Library (University of Texas), and the Latin American Library at Tulane University were also places where I found important materials. I thank the staff at each institution for their interest and help. The Doherty Foundation, the University of Rochester, the Bunting Institute (which also provided a marvelous working atmosphere and many wonderful friends and colleagues), the National Endowment for the Humanities, and the University of Houston have provided generous financial support. Thanks are also due to John

Drayton, Mildred Logan, Sheila Berg, and all the staff at the University of Oklahoma Press.

My greatest debts are to four special friends and to my family. Not only are John Hart, Ross Hassig, George Marcus, and Patricia Seed brilliant practitioners of their special areas of interest but they will always be in my heart, for reasons they know. To my families of birth and marriage (especially Marian Kellogg, Melissa Kellogg McCullough, Esther and Marvin Mintz, and Cathy and Julie Mintz), I offer thanks for many years of aid and support. To my children, Seth and Sean Mintz, words can hardly express what a wonderful, joyful presence you are in my life. Your high spirits and good humor animate my work every day. Finally, I thank my husband, Steve Mintz, for the support and help he has offered. Dedicating this book to him is only a small repayment for so many years of love, friendship, and joy.

SUSAN KELLOGG

Houston, Texas

INTRODUCTION

Law and the Transformation
of Aztec Culture

In 1847, more than three centuries after the Spanish
Conquest, several officials and residents of Santiago
Tlatelolco offered an intriguing justification for why
they should be allowed to sell certain lands held by the
community. In a letter to the Mexican minister of justice, they based their property rights on a grant from the
"*cacique* Cuatimoc" [*sic*]—the last native ruler, or *tlatoani,*
prior to the conquest—who "wanted to show his fond-
ness for the courageous defenders of Tlatelolco who
fought to the last drop of blood defending the Mexican
empire" (letter quoted and translated in Lira-González
1982: I:195). By the mid-nineteenth century, such an
argument must have seemed somewhat quaint and anach-
ronistic, though the appeal to the precolonial past doubt-
less resonated with the surging nationalism of an independent Mexico at war with an expanding United States.
Yet the notion of tracing property rights to the preconquest era in fact had deep roots in Mexico's legal history.

During the sixteenth century, indigenous[1] litigants
frequently made such legal arguments. They often in-

[1]In accordance with recent usage, I will generally use "Nahua" (rather than
the more common "Aztec") to refer to the Mexica and other Nahuatl-speaking
peoples who inhabited central Mexico. According to ethnohistorical texts, the
Mexica migrated from the northern regions of Mesoamerica around A.D. 1100
and founded a permanent settlement, Tenochtitlán, in the Valley of Mexico in
A.D. 1325. Tlatelolco, Tenochtitlán's sister city, located on a nearby island, was
founded in A.D. 1337 and conquered by Tenochtitlán in 1473. I shall treat these
two cities as a single unit, using "Tenochtitlán" to refer to both places during the
pre-Hispanic period and "Mexico City" during the colonial period. When I refer
specifically to the pre-Hispanic inhabitants of Tenochtitlán, I will use the term

xvii

voked memories of the imperial period before Spanish courts. Beyond their cultural significance, such memories represented legal attempts to confirm preconquest ownership. Such ownership thereby established the right of possession at the time of conquest and thus a right to "current" ownership (unless modified by Spanish order). But by the mid-seventeenth century, these claims had already declined in frequency, reflecting Indians' increasing reliance on Spanish definitions of property rights. In the changing patterns of legal arguments made by Indian property owners lie an important series of clues about how Native Americans adjusted to colonial rule.

In explaining how a relatively small number of Spaniards created a colony that lasted three hundred years, scholars have stressed factors such as the introduction of disease, Spain's success in exploiting divisions within the indigenous population, and the importance of Spanish technology and military might.[2] Yet such medical or technological determinism is not sufficient to explain the strength and persistence of Spanish colonial rule in this region. One might simply note that even at the nadir of demographic decline (ca. 1620), the native population still vastly outnumbered the Hispanic and *casta* (or mixed-race) sectors of the population (Borah 1983: 26–27).

"Tenochcan Mexica." For the postconquest sixteenth century, I use the terms "Nahua," "Mexica," or "indigenous" (depending on context). For the seventeenth century, I rely more on the term "Indian," which reflects both a declining sense of ethnic identity and the more fluid nature of urban Indian life. "Indian" also appears where it reflects the terminology of legal documents or Spanish chroniclers.

Useful general works on colonial Mexico City include Boyer (1973), *Ciudad de México* (1978), *Ensayos sobre el desarrollo urbano de México* (1973), Maldonado López (1976, 1988), Marroquí (1900–1903), Porras Muñoz (1982), Rojas (1986), and Valle-Arizpe (1949).

[2]The clearest articulation of the connections between the introduction and spread of disease and sociocultural collapse among Indians in New Spain is to be found in Borah (1951). A dispassionate consideration of tactical and technological issues is contained in Hassig (1988: chap.16). See Todorov (1984) for a very different type of explanation focusing on forms of communication and writing. Note also that in places this introduction draws on Kellogg (1992).

And even though this population became increasingly dispirited and socially disorganized in the face of population decline, evident in high rates of alcoholism and murder (Taylor 1979: chaps. 2–3), in other respects, the population proved resilient and capable of protecting itself. Far from simply being the passive victims of the Spanish Conquest, the Mexica and other central Mexican groups proved to be significant social actors who helped shape the history of the early colonial state. Clearly, medical or technological explanations are inadequate in and of themselves to explain the particular form that Spanish colonialism assumed.

This book—a study of the role of law in the transformation of Mexica culture—suggests an alternative explanation that shifts the emphasis from the conquest itself to Spain's success in achieving cultural hegemony over Nahuatl-speaking Indians. By "hegemony" I refer not to domination based simply on the threat of force but on subtler, less spectacularly violent, yet more pervasive forms of social control. These can appear to be self-regulating (at least to some degree) on both the individual and the community levels. Hegemony develops not because people collaborate in their own subjugation but because a dominating power has been able to institute practices and beliefs that rational people choose to adhere to, often because of coercive threats, but that over time come to appear normal, even natural.[3] In Mexico

[3]Discussions of hegemony are numerous and rooted in Antonio Gramsci's comments that contrast domination ("rule") with hegemony, or the "'spontaneous' consent given by the great masses of the population to the general direction imposed on social life by the dominant fundamental group" (1971: 12). Some uses of the concept of hegemony emphasize consent and acceptance of a variety of forms of inequity (e.g., Gaventa 1980 or Genovese 1972); others emphasize hegemony as interlocking sets of ideas, rules, and values that, as Raymond Williams put it, "as they are expressed as practices appear as reciprocally confirming" (1977: 110; also see Laitin 1986; Comaroff and Comaroff 1991). Criticisms of the concept focus on the idea of "false consciousness" (see esp. Scott 1985: 38–41, 304–50; 1990: chap.4). While Scott's observations about how subjugated peoples do have clear understandings of the power relations in which they are enmeshed are tremendously important, studies of slavery,

City, hegemony was not something that was simply imposed from without. Rather, it was accommodated from within as the product of an intricate process of conflict, negotiation, and dialogue.

To understand how Spaniards succeeded in achieving a degree of cultural hegemony over the Mexica, I look at legal records, especially property records, from sixteenth- and seventeenth-century Mexico City. I show how the social upheavals of the early colonial era generated frequent civil litigation and how the court records reveal profound changes in Mexica cultural meanings and social arrangements.

During the first two centuries of Spanish rule, many within Mexico City's indigenous population came to rely on Spanish courts and use Spanish notions of private property rights. Legal records disclose the ways that Indians restructured their patterns of gender relationships and family lives. The new cultural forms that emerged were not crude imitations of Spanish models; at once, they represented a response to a rapidly changing social and material world and a process of syncre-

---

colonialism, and domination show two characteristics of social life that are also worthy of understanding: one is that small numbers of people *can* rule over much larger numbers and frequently have throughout human history; the second is that while resistance and rebellions were more common than past historians (or anthropologists studying colonial situations) recognized, these activities punctuate longer periods of time and everyday life in which upheaval is not the norm (though less dramatic forms of resistance may be). Other useful discussions of the concept of hegemony include Anderson (1976–77: 5–28); Femia (1981); Laclau (1979); Adamson (1980); Lears (1985); and Hall (1991). A related literature considers the psychological effects of colonial relations; see Fanon (1963, 1967), Memmi (1965), and Balandier (1966). For a discussion of hegemony in a Latin American colonial context, see Stern (1982: 43–44, 187–89). He places a heavy emphasis on the role of native elites in establishing the colonial hegemonic system. In this book, I deemphasize the idea of hegemony solely as an elite-imposed process and argue that the concept should be rooted in the daily realities of subjugated peoples through which cognitive and social structures are reshaped. Also see Michael T. Taussig's comments on hegemony, in which he argues that we must "push the notion of hegemony into the lived space of realities in social relationships, in the give and take of social life" (1987:288) This goal is admirably achieved in Nancy Scheper-Hughes's brilliant work on present-day Brazil, *Death Without Weeping* (1992).

tism, a complex blending of Spanish and Mexica values and practices resulting in a new synthesis. Yet it is also clear that these forms played a critical role in perpetuating Spanish rule by defusing and channeling dissent (also see Stern 1982: chap. 5).

Over the course of two centuries, the Mexica population of Mexico City came to accept the state's authority to mediate disputes, resolve conflicts, and impose decisions and punishments. A sense of separate and distinct Mexica sovereignty and identity declined. At the same time, other social collectivities—especially supracommunity institutions—that might have provided a basis for challenging Spanish cultural identity withered away. Likewise, an earlier conception of the family as an extended, complex unit embedded in a larger network of kin gradually disappeared. The decline of larger kin units and networks had political implications as well because these networks provided an important means for high nobles to gather supporters. In the final analysis, Spanish cultural hegemony provided a far stronger and more secure source of control than direct coercion ever could.

In its stress on the importance of negotiation, dialogue, and cultural accommodation, this book provides an alternative to the dominant paradigms for conceptualizing the history of New Spain's Nahua population. One view—associated most closely with George Kubler (1948), George M. Foster (1960), François Chevalier (1963), Robert Ricard (1966), Woodrow Borah (1951, 1983), and culminating with Charles Gibson (1964)—holds that the conquest profoundly transformed and rapidly Hispanicized the Nahua and other central Mexican groups, radically restructuring virtually every aspect of Nahua society from the organization of work to religion and the class structure.[4] The other perspec-

---

[4]Placing Gibson within a paradigm is difficult, partly because of the relentless empiricism of his work and partly because he intuitively understood the

tive—associated with James Lockhart and his students—stresses cultural continuities and survivals, arguing that despite broad structural shifts, Indians succeeded in maintaining a separate culture with many distinctive cultural values and behaviors (e.g., Cline 1986; Haskett 1991; Lockhart 1992).[5]

In contrast, this book emphasizes a process of cultural transformation in which Indians drew on both pre-Hispanic traditions and practices and Spanish values and practices to create a new cultural synthesis. It focuses on law as an arena of cultural conflict and accommodation and as a catalyst of cultural change and adaptation. Law has been a relatively understudied aspect of the colonial Mexican experience[6]—in contrast to such subjects as demography, disease, labor, politics, and religion—even though legal sources (cases, decisions, and compendiums of laws) have proved useful as sources of "facts" to be "mined" by countless ethnohistorians and historians. Yet law played a pivotal role in spurring cultural changes, especially changes in property relations, political organization, and the use of Nahuatl as a written language. It also played an important role in providing models for the restructuring of Indian family life and gender relations. Moreover, it became a key battleground in which indigenous and Hispanic values competed for cultural dominance.

Spain was more successful in establishing a hegemonic sociocultural system in central Mexico than in other parts of its New World empire. In the Andes,

---

strength and persistence of Indian community and political organization (Lockhart 1991: 169–71). But the strong emphasis on change throughout the book marks Gibson's interpretation as clearly different from that of many subsequent scholars.

[5]The art historians Ellen Baird (1993) and Jeanette Favrot Peterson (1993) write from a similar perspective. Also see Gruzinski (1992).

[6]In addition to Borah (1983), significant studies of Spanish colonial legal systems include Ots Capdequí (1941), Ballesteros (1945), Góngora (1951), Lira-González (1982), and MacLachlan (1974). Important ethnographic studies of law in Mexico include Collier (1973), Nader (1967, 1990), and Parnell (1978, 1988).

where local populations were less urbanized and less nucleated, indigenous institutions and leaders played a more significant role in mediating Spanish rule (Stern 1982; Spalding 1984; Larson 1988). This would also appear to be the case in the Yucatán and other Maya regions (Farriss 1984; Jones 1989; Gosner 1992).

Several factors help account for the degree of native accommodation in the Valley of Mexico: the acute devastation wrought by the conquest itself; the accompanying demographic and social disintegration; and the relatively high density of the Spanish population, which encompassed Indians in a vast net of religious, economic, and other social institutions and relationships. In the Valley of Mexico, the indigenous population then became more fragmented than elsewhere and more litigious, with individuals more likely to define themselves socially through nuclear families and non-kinship-based groups rather than through larger extended family or kinship-based communal units.

Unlike the Maya in southern Mexico — many of whom fled or abandoned their traditional homelands (Farriss 1984: chap. 7) — the indigenous people of the Valley of Mexico actively engaged the colonial system. Many Indians used the Spanish judicial system to assert or defend land claims and other property rights.[7]

The Spanish Conquest intensified — and triggered — bitter conflicts within Indian communities over a wide range of issues that often manifested themselves as conflicts over real property. For example, the Spanish legal system provided the Nahuas, for the first time, with a mechanism, other than rebellion, for directly challenging the political and legal authority of Indian officials and communal groups. But implicit in indigenous litigation was what James C. Scott (1985, 1990) has called the "hidden transcript." Among the issues that provoked bitter legal disputes were the nature of property rights

---

[7]See Borah (1983: chap. 5) on the range of civil cases.

(Who could inherit property? Who could alienate it?) and the nature of cultural authority—especially that rooted in gender, kinship, or local relations—internal to the Indian community. Nahuas also used law as an instrument for placing limits on a variety of Spanish policies on land, labor, and political process (Borah 1983: chap. 5).

Yet even when Indians used law to challenge Spanish policy, their reliance on colonial courts tied them firmly to Spanish rule (also see Stern 1982: 132–37). Instead of accepting the decisions of indigenous officeholders, Nahuas repeatedly appealed adverse decisions to colonial legal officials, undermining the power and legitimacy of indigenous officials and institutions and giving Spanish judges the task of sorting out complex disputes. This reliance on the judges and courts of the conquerors lay at the root of Spain's hegemonic colonial system. But Indians sometimes won important legal victories over Spanish officials, individuals, and institutions (also see Osborn 1973; Coy 1968; Borah 1983: chap. 5; Martin 1985; Ouweneel and Miller 1990; Lipsett-Rivera 1992; Prem 1992). These victories, in turn, established restraints on the authority of Spaniards.

As the indigenous population of the Valley of Mexico adopted Hispanic legal forms and increasingly employed the colonial legal system, some groups benefited more than others. Nahua communities, small property owners, and Nahua women were particularly adept at utilizing these legal procedures to assert property interests, often against Spaniards or elite Indians. Yet over time, each of these groups saw their legal rights diminished as the colonial legal system increasingly promoted Hispanic conceptions of property ownership, gender roles, and family and kinship structures.

No part of Spain's New World empire underwent a more visible or dramatic transformation than the Mexica capital, Tenochtitlán. The Spaniards' initial reaction to the

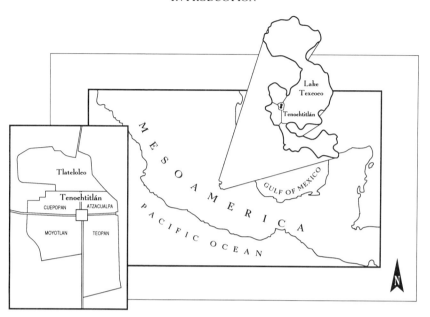

Location and layout of Tenochtitlán. The inset showing the location of Tenochtitlán is based on a map in Berdan (1982: xii); the inset showing the layout of Tenochtitlán and its relationship to Tlatelolco is based on a map in Calnek (1976: 293).

city's appearance was one of stunned amazement.[8] Situated within a lake, divided into four quarters, and linked by causeways to the mainland, Tenochtitlán possessed architecture, wealth, physical beauty, and population rivaling that of any European city. Yet within two years,

[8]The most famous descriptions are in Cortés (1932: I:56–57) and Díaz del Castillo (1955: I:333–43). Also see Conquistador Anónimo (1941). Useful general overviews of Mexica and Nahua culture in the late pre-Hispanic period include Berdan (1982), Caso (1958), Clendinnen (1991), Davies (1980), Rodríguez (1990a), and Soustelle (1961).

Spaniards had destroyed extensive parts of the city and
much of its population lay dead.

The conquerors built a new city atop these ruins. The
imperial center and ceremonial district of Tenochtitlán
became the *traza*, the seat of the colonial royal government, while the outer portions of the city became the
Indian *barrios* of San Juan: Santa María Cuepopan, San
Sebastian Atzacualco, San Pablo Zoquipan, and San
Juan Moyotlan. To the north lay the other major Indian
sector of Mexico City, Santiago Tlatelolco (Gibson 1964:
370–71). While Spaniards had transformed the city, the
Indian presence remained substantial. Even at the beginning of the nineteenth century, on the eve of Mexican
independence, Indians still constituted a fourth of Mexico City's population, numbering about 33,000 (Humboldt 1966: II:82; also see Carrasco 1975: 177).

The law also bore witness to the process of destruction and reconstruction. Between 1519 and 1700, the
legal system in the Valley of Mexico was transformed as
Spain imposed new legal institutions on top of local-
level institutions.[9] Although the Nahua and Spanish
legal systems contained certain superficial similarities,
they differed in profound ways.[10] While both systems

[9]Indigenous courts continued to function for some period after the conquest
(Offner 1983: 86), though with the decapitation of many of the councils and
institutions through which tlatoani ruled, it is unlikely that high-level courts—
especially in the Mexico City region—continued to function for very long.
Lower-level officials, especially at the ward and *calpulli* levels, continued to play a
significant legal role even when these officials began to be referred to by Spanish
titles (Haskett 1991: chap. 4; also see Borah 1983: 43). The best description of an
indigenous, pre-Hispanic legal system is to be found in Offner (1983). This work
concentrates on Texcoco, partly because many of the richest sources on pre-
Hispanic law come from this region (e.g., Ixtlilxochitl [1975–77]; Motolinía
[1971]; Torquemada [1975]; and "Estas son las leyes . . ." [1941]). Other important sources on law that reflect Tenochcan legal practices to a greater degree
include the "Historia de los mexicanos por sus pinturas" (1941), Durán (1967:
II:26:211–14), and the *FC* (1950–82: VIII:chaps. 14, 17). Berdan (1982: 96–98,
104–5) contains a brief but especially clear summary of the higher levels of
judicial administration in Tenochtitlán. Clendinnen (1991: 49) has a useful
description of the lower, local levels.
[10]See chap. 1 for a more extensive description of the Spanish legal system.

were concerned with maintaining social order, were hierarchical and allowed appeals, and relied on strict punishments applied in ways meant to instill terror and conformity, the two legal systems differed in structure and in the purview of the law.

Structural differences headed the list. While pre-Hispanic Nahuas did have courts and a formal judicial system, these represented only a small part of the broader mechanisms of social control, which relied heavily on supernatural sanctions and on families, neighborhoods and wards, work sites, and craft groups to teach and enforce rules and resolve disputes.[11] During the late pre-Hispanic period, the foundation of the Tenochcan Mexica legal system rested at the local level, with families, ward officials, and officials of young men's houses holding particular responsibilities (*FC* 1950–82: VI, VIII, X; Durán 1967: I:20:184–85, II:26:213).[12] Merchants and presumably craft groups also exercised judicial authority over their members (*FC* 1950–82: IX: 5:23). In those instances when these mechanisms failed to resolve a conflict, a case might be brought before the royal courts. The judges of the *teccalli* tried commoners' cases (ibid., VIII:14:42). The judges of the *tlacxitlan* decided cases involving nobles and cases involving especially serious offenses, particularly those that carried death as the punishment (ibid., 41). The tlacxitlan also handled appeals from the teccalli (ibid., 17:55). In addi-

---

[11]See Durán (1967: I:16:155–57) for examples of supernatural sanctions for behavior, especially those aimed at actions that ran counter to religious proscriptions such as carrying out rituals improperly. See the *FC* (1950–82: III:2:11–12) for examples of violations of taboo practices at various times of the year, especially the breaking of fasts or transgressing proscriptions of sexual abstinence. Supernatural punishments often entailed the giving of disease and ailments. Not only did these offer discomfort to the transgressor, they physically and visually symbolized the transgressions that had threatened social order. On the rhetorical methods characteristic of Nahua socialization, see *CM* (1992: III), *FC* (1950–82: VI), and Kartunnen and Lockhart (1987).

[12]The *Florentine Codex* and Duran's *Historia* are cited by volume and chapter number as well as page number.

tion, high officials accused of offenses might be tried before the councils on which they had served (ibid., 14:42–45). Pictorial records of judicial proceedings were kept, at least at the higher levels of the judicial system (Motolinía 1971: 354, 359; *FC* 1950–82: VIII:17:55).

But the Mexica system was less bureaucratic than the Spanish system that followed, affording fewer opportunities for appeal. Under the pre-Hispanic judicial system, unlike the colonial one, judges reached decisions rapidly and their rulings were more often definitive (Zorita 1942: 54–55). The Spanish legal system, for all of its reliance on written law, was in fact more flexible. Judicial venues abounded, and decisions were frequently appealed (Kagan 1981; Borah 1983). Moreover, because Spanish judges were encouraged to base legal decisions on native traditions (insofar as these did not conflict with Christian belief or practice [Puga 1945: fol. 54r–54v; *CeI* 1596: II:167; Konetzke 1953–62: I:529; also see Borah 1983: 33–35]), a new type of indeterminacy that further encouraged litigation was introduced. Because these judges were well versed in neither indigenous customs nor languages, sorting out the alternative conceptions of pre-Hispanic customs and beliefs that Indians frequently presented proved difficult. Reaching decisions under such circumstances must have been trying, and many decisions may thus have appeared arbitary.

The pre-Hispanic and colonial legal systems also differed in the definition of law's proper operation and domain. The Nahuas conceived of the law as a verbal set of commands to be followed and, more metaphorically, as a snare or trap that was an "engulfing, overpowering force" (Offner 1983: 243). But law was only one means among many through which the Nahua peoples enacted their cultural concerns with order, moderation, and balance (Burkhart 1989: 35–38).[13] Households, local-

---

[13]There is, however, some indication that Nahuas were not always rigorously

level groupings based on residence and work, local nobles, and temples and schools all played very strong roles
in the enforcement of customary practices, rules, and
law for Nahuas. In comparison, the Castilian legal system was more bureaucratic, more flexible, and while
rooted in both divine and royal authority (Haslip 1980:
76),[14] ultimately less punitive.

The colonial legal system became, I argue, a powerful
tool of acculturation, profoundly altering Mexica and
Nahua conceptions of family, property, and gender. And
it played a critical role in establishing and maintaining
Spanish cultural hegemony.

In this book, I have set myself two tasks: first, to examine why the Tenochcan Mexica turned to the colonial
legal system and how they used the Spanish colonial
courts, especially the Real Audiencia, and second, to
explain what colonial civil legal records tell us about
broader changes in Mexica conceptions of family, gender, and property. The book's organization reflects those
concerns. Part One is concerned with sources and texts.
Chapter 1 examines the social identities of the litigants,
witnesses, scribes, lawyers, and judges who took part in
Indian litigation. It demonstrates that a broad array of
Indians of varying occupations and class positions and
both genders appeared before the Real Audiencia.

---

ordered and could be contentious. Note the following explanation of the
Nahuatl expression, "My task is to guard turkeys. Shall I peck at those who peck
at one another?" Sahagún's informants explained this adage in the following
way:

It is said concerning this: The turkeys, when they preen, constantly peck at
one another. The turkey guardian does not bring it about that turkeys
constantly peck at one another, for they simply fight among themselves as
they constantly peck at each other. Hence it may well be said when common
folk contend, when they fight among themselves over perhaps their lands,
their houses, or something. The leaders do not stir them up; the commoners
purely of their own accord contend among themselves, fight among themselves. (FC 1950–82: VI:41:227)

[14]See Goody (1986: chap.4) on the influence of writing on the conception
and practice of law. Also see Hill (1991).

Chapter 2 treats the lawsuits as texts that demand the same interpretation and analysis as any cultural artifact. Implicit within these legal narratives are fundamental disputes over issues such as the nature of ownership and the proper social bases of property rights. This chapter stresses the notion that the arguments used in property disputes were not static.[15] On the contrary, the Mexica who went to court employed arguments at once dynamic and changing, reflecting profound shifts in Nahua values.

These chapters rely heavily on the extant records of seventy-three cases heard by the Real Audiencia from the 1530s through 1700. My interest in these cases first developed out of a desire to learn about pre-Hispanic household and kinship patterns among the Tenochcan Mexica (Kellogg 1980). The cases proved especially interesting because of the extensive testimony included and the large number that contained Nahuatl documentation. But over time I became intrigued by the question of what these cases had to say about Indians during the colonial period and the social conflicts and situations that ensnared the litigants.[16] The focus on property suits came from the fact that these documents constitute among the earliest and most complete legal case records for Indians, as opposed to the administrative and judicial decrees making up the bulk of the somewhat later materials from the Juzgado General de Indios (Borah 1983: 125–26). While in theory the *audiencia* served as a court of first instance for Indians (Markov 1983: 41–47), in fact the endless lower-level legal wranglings that took place before hapless and no doubt frustrated indigenous

[15]See Borah (1983: 120–21) for a general statement of stability in legal proceedings involving Indians from the founding of the Juzgado General de Indios.

[16]This interest was further stimulated by a burgeoning literature on law, colonialism, and a wide array of non-Western peoples written primarily by cultural anthropologists. Representative works are Cohn (1989), Dirks (1987), Moore (1986), and Starr and Collier (1989). For a recent review of anthropological literature on law, see Merry (1992).

officials are quite apparent in the texts of these lawsuits (see chap. 2). Most of the extant suits heard by the audiencia are today housed in the *ramo Tierras* of the Archivo General de la Nación in Mexico City. I selected lawsuits that included Indians as litigants on at least one side. These individuals were resident in the Indian barrios that were part of either San Juan Tenochtitlán or Santiago Tlatelolco, and the cases date from 1536 to 1700.[17] Legal materials from other branches of the AGN and other archives have added to the number of cases and supporting legal documents (especially wills and property transfers).[18] The bulk of the case material, fifty-five cases, comes from the sixteenth century, while eighteen cases come from the seventeenth century (as a result of the shift of most Indian lawsuits into the Juzgado General de Indios [see chap. 1]).

By looking very intensively at these cases, as an ethnographer would, it is possible to learn a great deal about how the indigenous population of Mexico City interacted with and helped shape an evolving colonial legal system. While I make no claim that the individuals who participated in these cases are statistically representative of the broader indigenous population of colonial Mexico City, I do believe their quarrels were representative of the types of issues and conflicts that developed and that these extant records represent only some portion of the actual number of cases heard by the audiencia. Furthermore, it should be noted that the procedures used and the narrative structures (see chap. 2) of these

[17]See Cope (1994) for some discussion of the experience of seventeenth-century Indians resident in the traza.

[18]Other *ramos* of the AGN with useful materials include *Vínculos y Mayorazgos, Hóspital de Jesus, Indios, Bienes Nacionales, Civil,* and *Historia.* Materials from the *Justicia, México,* and *Patronato* sections of the Archivo de las Indias in Seville (consulted primarily through the France Scholes Collection of the Latin American Library at Tulane), the Viceregal and Ecclesiastical Mexican Collection at the Latin American Library at Tulane, the Ayer Collection at the Newberry Library, and scattered manuscripts at the Bibliothèque National de Paris and the Bancroft Library also have been helpful.

suits are similar to those that would be found in criminal proceedings (see, e.g., Taylor 1979; Cope 1987; Lozano Amendares 1987; Haslip 1980; Scardaville 1977), marital oppositions and conflicts (Seed 1988; Gutiérrez 1991), and Inquisition and other Church inquiries and proceedings (Alberro 1988; Gruzinski 1989a; Greenleaf 1969). A guiding theme and assumption of this work is that anger and conflict are fully part of the normal spectrum of human behaviors, especially in societies experiencing stress and rapid change (Nader and Todd 1978: xiii).

Part Two treats the case records more as sources in colonial Mexica cultural and social history and emphasizes the examination of gender, inheritance, and family life and kinship. These aspects of everyday life formed areas of semiautonomy (at least from civil governance) for Indian societies that experienced Spanish rule and thus should prove especially instructive for assessing continuity and change. In these chapters, case materials are supplemented by a wide array of other primary source materials, especially chroniclers' accounts, legal compilations and other published documentary sources, and parish records.[19] Chapter 3 traces the declining status of Mexica women. Evolving forms of property transmission are the subject of chapter 4. Chapter 5 examines transformations in Mexica family and kinship patterns. Each of these illustrates a gradual, incremental, but nonetheless profound process of social transformation that reconstituted and reconstructed pre-Hispanic cultural meanings and social patterns.

Every chapter is concerned with time and chronology. In demonstrating the kinds of cultural shifts that occurred during the early colonial period, I emphasize the

---

[19]Especially valuable for this part of my research was the opportunity to consult many works in early editions—especially confessionals and other materials by priests working in and around Mexico City—held by the John Carter Brown Library.

years from 1550 to 1650. It has proven useful, however, to consider at certain points the period preceding 1550 (including the very late pre-Hispanic period) and the fifty years after to more fully describe the flow and dynamics of change. It also proved necessary to divide legal materials into subperiods based on the changing narrative structures of these texts (see chap. 2). Broadly, I see the period from the 1530s to the early 1580s as one in which Nahuas predominantly rooted their rhetoric in what they argued were customary cultural practices. The years from 1585 to the mid-seventeenth century constituted a period when such arguments were far fewer in number and basic changes in the legal strategies and language of Indians took place. These rhetorical transformations were accompanied by certain social transformations as well. After 1650, further changes in narrative structures developed as the rhetoric and actions of Indians in legal contexts reflected the emergence of a more firmly grounded colonial Indian culture.[20]

In the final analysis, Spanish rule did not rest solely on Spanish arms. Nor could European microorganisms reduce Indians to subjugation. So, too, internal divisions among the Indian population offer an insufficient explanation for the stability of Spanish rule in the central regions of New Spain. Instead, the explanation lies in something more subtle: a cross-cultural process of accommodation and negotiation that forged cultural hegemony.

[20]For an important discussion of the periodization of change, see Kartunnen and Lockhart (1987). Both schemas are similar, the primary difference being that my second stage begins later in the sixteenth century. While Kartunnen and Lockhart's work shows persuasively the changes occurring in Nahuatl (especially in the area of Spanish loanwords), I would only add that Nahuatl-language texts and other Nahua actions and activities indicate attempts to conform to pre-Hispanic cultural patterns *where possible* but that these goals had largely shifted by the 1580s when a colonial culture began to emerge and became more fully realized after 1650.

PART ONE

Sources and Legal Texts

CHAPTER 1

Actors in the Archive

The court records of the Real Audiencia are a valuable source of information about the social and cultural history of the indigenous peoples of early colonial central Mexico. Not only do these documents humanize the history of early colonial Mexico by allowing us to recover the lives and voices of individuals but they also reveal a series of fundamental transformations in Indian society between the sixteenth century and the eighteenth century which have been inadequately appreciated: shifts in gender roles, property ownership, and kinship and family structure.

Obviously, legal records, like any form of historical documentation, must be used with proper caution. The number of extant cases is relatively small, and many, though by no means all, litigants came from elite families. One must be careful, therefore, in extrapolating from individual cases to the broader Mexica population. Nevertheless, the court records contain testimony from a surprisingly wide range of litigants and witnesses, including many women, and the documents are filled with valuable and otherwise inaccessible information about household size and composition, kinship relationships, gender roles, and other relatively understudied aspects of colonial Indian life. Above all, the cases underscore the kinds of conflicts generated by the imposition of Spanish colonialism and shifting Indian responses.

Anthropologists, ethnohistorians, and social historians have used legal records in many different ways. They have viewed law as a system of rules, a means of conflict resolution, a system of social control, a form of

3

rhetoric and argument,[1] and a repository of factual information.[2] While rooted in an approach to law that stresses rhetorical, narrative, and textual issues,[3] this book also approaches law from some rather different perspectives: as an arena of cultural conflict in which changing conceptions of family, gender, and property were contested; as a school in interethnic relations; and as an instrument of Spanish cultural hegemony.

As a mechanism of cultural conversion, the Real Audiencia promoted a series of new values, including the privatization of property, the primacy of the nuclear family, and the growth of male privilege. Litigation also served as a powerful instrument of cultural hegemony, as lawsuits divided the indigenous population and diverted its attention from broader issues of exploitation and injustice (also see Stern 1982: 135). Although colonial courts served as a focal point for Indian resistance and protest, by the seventeenth century's end, the colonial legal system had played a critical role in the pacification, transformation, and acculturation of this indigenous population. In this chapter, I explore the court as a stage and the legal participants as dramatis personae who participated and helped to shape an enduring legal record still read and used for a variety of purposes today.

[1] In giving examples of anthropological and historical approaches to law, I am confining myself here to Latin American examples. On law as a system of rules that reveal fundamental aspects of culture, see Offner (1983). On law as a means of conflict resolution, see Collier (1973), Nader (1969, 1990), and Nader and Todd (1978). Seed (1988) uses church cases and marital disputes to study the rhetoric of family conflict. This book uses civil cases to study the rhetoric of property ownership and changing social practices and structures. See Kellogg (1992) on colonial law as a form of social control.

[2] The literature on colonial Latin American history that uses legal cases as repositories of fact to be mined is large. A few recent examples, secular and religious, coming from work by historians on the central areas of New Spain are Behar (1987), Chance (1989), Gruzinski (1989a), Martin (1985), Taylor (1979), and Van Young (1981).

[3] On legal texts, narrative structures, and rhetorical forms, see Fuller (1967), Posner (1988), White (1985), and special issues on law, discourse, and narrative in *History and Anthropology* (1985), the *Journal of Legal Education* (1990), and *Representations* (1990).

4

LAW AS SOCIAL DRAMA

The legal disputes that took place in the Real Audiencia involved more than private quarrels. They were also, to use Victor Turner's concept, "social dramas," which embodied broader social and cultural themes.[4] The disputes not only arose out of particular social contexts; the arguments and strategies that litigants employed also reflected broader cultural themes and styles. A late sixteenth-century property dispute (BNP 112, 1593) illustrates the legal mechanisms and strategies available to Indians in Mexico City; it also involves two conflicting lines of argument, one in which indigenous family histories and cultural concepts were used to explain actions taken and another in which Spanish cultural influences provided rhetorical support.

The colonial legal system in New Spain, like the legal order in Castile itself, was a "hodgepodge of confused laws and competing jurisdictions that crafty litigants exploited to their own advantage" (Kagan 1981: 31). The legal system, characterized by multiple loci of power and authority, subtly encouraged parties in disputes to plead their cases before a variety of indigenous and royal officials.[5] This practice resulted in conflicting decisions,

[4]Victor Turner used the concept of "social drama" in his work on conflict in small-scale African communities to describe the way conflicts that, at first glance, can seem both bitter and highly idiosyncratic actually are *social* occurrences that have regularized forms and are recurrent. Turner later extended the concept to written texts, describing ancient Icelandic epics, filled with conflict and dramatic overtones, as also having a socially based, patterned form. He wrote that in these texts

the individual parties would be more than mere names but . . . [they would] become characters in the round whose motives would become intelligible not only in terms of personality or temperament, but also in terms of the multiple roles they occupy simultaneously or at different times in the social structure or in transient factional groupings. In all this there was the notion that social events are spun into complex patterns over time by custom and will, and especially by conflicts of customs and wills and collective wishes and needs to resolve those conflicts. (1971: 352)

[5]This complex and malleable Spanish legal system of the late fifteenth and early sixteenth century was transmitted in similar form to the New World. This

a multiplicity of lines of argument, and extensive written records—documents that provide ethnohistorians with a unique window on indigenous cultural and social practices and how they changed over time.

In May 1593, Pero Díaz Agüero, the *procurador general de los indios,* appeared before the Real Audiencia on behalf of Diego Francisco. According to the statement made by Diego Francisco to Díaz Agüero, Diego's father, Gaspar López, had died in 1588. He left his son, Diego, and Diego's illegitimate half-brother, Felipe de Santiago, a house site and a few *chinampas* (raised or floating garden plots) in San Juan Tecpancaltitlán. While Diego was imprisoned in a textile workshop, or *obraje,* Felipe sold several rooms on the site to another Indian for seventy *pesos.* Claiming that he was his father and mother's true heir, Diego asked for restitution of the property. To substantiate this claim, Díaz Agüero introduced a will made by Diego's mother, Beatriz, in which she left the house site to Diego and two sisters (see fig. 1).

That same month, Felipe offered his story before another official, don Antonio Mendoza, an Indian *alcalde* of the audiencia. He claimed the house site was his on three grounds: that he was the eldest son; that he had inherited the property from his father and mother, his father's first wife, Inés; and that the house site was part of his family's ancient patrimony that he had inherited from his great-grandparents, Ixtlilteohuan Tecpanecatl and Hueticitl. To support his claim, he offered the testimony of four Indian witnesses, who provided extensive genealogical information indicating that Felipe had inherited the property through his mother from a group of siblings who were all children of this ancestral couple. Mendoza upheld the original sale.

---

legal system may be understood as consisting of institutional bodies that made and interpreted laws, officials who made and carried out laws, and legal codes themselves. Laws were expressed as both *fueros,* or general statements of the customary privileges granted to territories and social groups (Kleffens 1968: 125–31), and "theoretical law codes" such as the *Siete Partidas* (Kagan 1981:24).

A month later, in June 1593, Diego raised his claim a second time, now before don Antonio Valeriano, the native governor of Tenochtitlán. He asked Valeriano to order Felipe to appear before the governor to explain his sale of the property. In addition, he requested the governor to place the property in his possession. In August, the governor placed the property in the possession of Andres de las Casas, a young relative of Diego Francisco.

Litigation had still not concluded. In November 1593, Licenciado Gasco de Velasco, a lawyer of the audiencia, argued that Felipe should receive the houses because they had been owned by his great-grandparents and had also been part of his mother's dowry. There, the case documents end with no record of a final decision.

Spanish officials regarded the Indians of central Mexico as a peculiarly litigious people (Zorita 1942: 42–46; also see Borah 1983: 40–43). Under colonial law, Indians could bring their disputes before the Real Audiencia, using it either as a court of first instance or as a court of appeal, or alongside lower-level indigenous authorities. Before the audiencia, Mexica tended during the sixteenth century to use two alternative styles of argumentation: one based on Spanish legal codes and one based on indigenous concepts. In seeking to substantiate his case, Diego Francisco drew on more acculturated notions of inheritance of dowry property from his mother. And supported by her will, he went first to the audencia, and emphasized how he had been forcibly kept in an obraje. In contrast, Felipe de Santiago, like many Indians prior to the 1580s,[6] traced ownership back into the pre-Hispanic period and couched ownership in the language of inheritance through at least three generations of kin relations. Felipe initially turned not to the Real Audiencia, like Diego, but to an indigenous official. Although he defended his right to sell

6See chap. 2 for a discussion of the development of and changes in legal narrative styles.

Fig. 1
Source: BNP 112, 1593

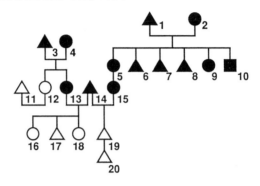

1 Ixtlilteohuan Tecpanecatl	11 Pedro de las Casas
2 Hueticitl	12 Francisca de Riberol
3 Juan Tepuso	13 Beatriz Papan (*d. ca.* 1570)
4 Catalina Xoco	14 Gaspar López (*d. ca.* 1588)
5 Ana Tiacapan	15 Inés
6 Pedro Poliuhtoc	16 María
7 Pedro Cochpin	17 Diego Francisco
8 Miguel Lázaro	18 Juana
9 Juana Xoco	19 Felipe de Santiago
10 unnamed	20 Juan Martín

property, he did so on the basis of inheritance rights defined in indigenous terms. It was ultimately a Spanish official, the *fiscal* Gasco de Velasco, who rephrased Felipe's argument in Hispanic terms, contending that Felipe's inheritance had originated as dowry property.

THE DRAMATIC STAGE: THE REAL AUDIENCIA

The case records of the Real Audiencia are highly significant because they include judicial records pertaining to Mexico City's indigenous population prior to the founding of the Juzgado General de Indios in 1591. The audiencia's legal records often go beyond simple administrative and judicial decrees to include sometimes near-ly complete, sometimes partial records of cases as they made their way through the labyrinthine legal system. Like Spanish royal councils and other administrative bodies, the New World audiencias performed multiple functions: they formulated colonial policies, advised viceroys, and served as courts of law. In Mexico City in the mid-sixteenth century, the audiencia consisted of four judges, called *oidores,* who heard both criminal and civil suits. By the seventeenth century, it numbered twelve judges: eight oidores who heard civil suits and four *alcaldes del crimen* who tried criminal cases (Haring 1963: 120; Carter 1971: 10–19; Burkholder and Chandler 1977: 3–10).[7]

By the early 1530s, a systematic structure for colonial governance had been established in New Spain and the audiencia began to hear lawsuits between Indians and between Indians and Spaniards (Borah 1983: 40). By the 1550s, it was clear to ruling Spaniards that a verita-ble flood of litigation had been unleashed.[8] By the late 1550s, the audiencia was regularly ruling on the civil legal affairs of the native population of Mexico City that lay within a five-league zone over which the viceroy and audiencia had direct supervision (ibid., 221; also see Markov 1983: 32, 43–44).

In 1553, a professor of Latin at the University of Mexico composed a series of dialogues in Latin in which two characters, Alfaro and Zuazo, recounted how the audiencia operated. Zuazo stated that the corridors of the palace were filled with "litigants, pleaders of cases, attorneys, notaries, and others who [were] appealing from the magistrates of the city to the royal counselors, who are the highest judges" (Cervantes de Salazar 1953: 43). Alfaro described the four oidores sitting around the

---

[7]For discussion of audiencias in other parts of Spanish America, see Parry (1948), Phelan (1967), and Cunningham (1919).

[8]This is clear from case records, but also see Borah (1983: 45).

viceroy on a platform, saying that "no one speaks except the judge whose duty it is this week to issue decrees and render justice" (44). Around the platform, but lower, sat the fiscal and alcalde of the court, the protector of the Indians, other lawyers pleading cases, councillors, and members of the nobility. Zuazo then stated,

> The two lower sides, to which one descends by steps, are occupied by attorneys and notaries, and in front of the judges, the prefect of the notaries and the reporter of the cases work at a table; one writes the decrees, the other announces the decisions reached. At the rear is a wooden grating dividing the courtroom, so that the general public and the common people may not sit together with the rest. Behind the grating stand those who have the right but nevertheless do not wish to sit, and others who, even though they may wish it, are not permitted to do so because they are entirely unworthy of that honor. (Ibid., 43–45)

Although lawyers (*abogados*) presented oral arguments before the judges, most of the formal legal decision-making process took place in writing. Witnesses responded to a written list of questions known as an *interrogatorio*. Scribes then wrote down their testimony. Supporting documents, including wills and documents of sale, were submitted to the court as well, along with translations from Nahuatl when necessary. The oidores probably read through summaries of cases prepared by trained lawyers (known as *relatores*) who organized documents and prepared case summaries for the judges (Borah 1983: 236) and then issued written rulings. Lawyers, scribes, and translators each had some ability to shape the written texts of a case and thereby influence what oidores or their secretaries read.

Like other contemporary Spanish courts, the audiencia could base its decisions either on royal law or on local law and custom (ibid., 7–8, 33–35). Thus Indians were able—at least theoretically—to appeal to pre-Hispanic norms and customs in court to buttress their cases. In actually rendering decisions, the oidores relied on summaries of the documents submitted, including Spanish translations of Nahuatl documents. But frequently, the Spanish translations distorted the meaning of the original testimony. In consequence, judges often remained unaware of the full intricacies and/or defects of the litigants' arguments. Nonetheless, regardless of the rigid formality of courtroom procedure and the bureaucratic procedures by which judges made decisions, Indians were able, as we will see in chapter 2, to shape the presentation of "facts" and thereby to shape sentiments and perceptions even though they could not create the Mexica equivalent of "customary" law.

THE CAST OF PLAYERS

We now turn to the social identities of the participants in lawsuits: the status position, the ethnic identification, and the gender of judges, lawyers, litigants, and witnesses.

Oidores

Although this book focuses most intensively on Indian litigants and witnesses, many Spanish and Indian officials played significant roles in lawsuits. Oidores—civil judges in the Real Audiencia—played a particularly important role. If an Indian failed to win in a dispute at a lower level, then the person would typically plead his or her case before an individual oidor.

Oidores occupied a highly respected position in colonial Mexico. Indeed, apart from the viceroys, they were among the highest-status officials in Spain's colonies. During the colonial period, most came from Spain (Haring 1963: 126; Phelan 1967: 139), though the percentage of Creoles increased over time (Burkholder and Chandler 1977: 11, 79–80, 103, 119–21). In contrast to judges in

Britain's seventeenth-century North American colonies, who consisted largely of members of leading families and lacked formal legal training (Mann 1987: 89–93), these men were *letrados*, individuals who held the highest university degree in law (Burkholder and Chandler 1977: 3) and generally had years of legal experience before their appointments to this position (ibid.; Carter 1971: 60).[9]

In theory, Castilian law required oidores to be honest and impartial in their rulings (*Siete Partidas*, P3, T4).[10] In his *Política indiana* (1776), for example, Juan de Solórzano y Pereyra declared that they were to be just, fair, and unbiased in rendering decisions.

> The *Principales* and Magistrates must be like the Sun, which communicates equally with the poor and rich, and they should not look at people, only causes, administering justice and grace equally. . . . [T]hey should examine [them] well before going so far as to judge them, withdrawing themselves totally from attention to persons, friendships, and enmities and consider only the substance and nature of their decision. (II:8:319)

In reality, however, many judges involved themselves in the important economic activities and political decisions of the period. A detailed study of four oidores of an early audiencia in Mexico City from 1543 to 1547 concluded that "personal interest was a factor in . . . decision-making" (Carter 1971: 133; also see Ruiz Medrano 1991). Nevertheless, these judges, particularly Francisco Ceynos, the oidor who heard most Indian cases during that early period, believed that the courts had a special responsibility to protect the powerless and sought to reach unbiased and equitable decisions in Indian law-

---

[9]On the training and career paths of letrados, see Kagan (1974: chaps. 3, 5).
[10]The *Siete Partidas* and other relevant law codes may be consulted in Martínez Alcubilla (1885).

suits.[11] Ceynos was recognized as an honorable, conscientious judge who did not use his office for profit. A lawyer who was also a close neighbor of Ceynos described how Ceynos labored "at all hours of the day and night with Indians in a room with air so close that no other Spaniards could tolerate it" (Carter 1971: 84). In practice, however, neither Ceynos nor other judges betrayed much knowledge of indigenous culture or languages and normally favored elite Indian litigants in their decisions.[12]

Lawyers and Their Strategies

In the earliest stages of a lawsuit (especially in litigation occurring during the mid-sixteenth century), Indian litigants did not rely on lawyers. Instead, participants simply made statements before scribes and submitted their pleas to individual Spanish or Indian officials. If their arguments failed, Indian litigants then turned to lawyers, sometimes peninsulars but increasingly Creoles, to guide the case before the audiencia. The lawyer, in turn, revised a litigant's plea to conform to Castilian legal norms. Indeed, one of the most striking features of sixteenth-century Indian lawsuits is the degree of difference between the "raw materials" supplied by the parties themselves and the legalistic arguments presented by their lawyers. But by the end of the seventeenth century, the cultural gap between the stories told by litigants and witnesses and the legal strategies devised by their lawyers had narrowed considerably (see chap. 2).

In taking their cases before the audiencia, Indians usually retained lawyers of a middle status, known as

[11]On the development of a protective strain of thinking toward Indians, see Hanke (1949), Phelan (1956), Pagden (1982), and Borah (1983).

[12]The outstanding exception to this general pattern was Alonso de Zorita, who served as an oidor in Mexico City from 1556 to 1566 and who became knowledgeable about indigenous cultures, especially those in the central regions of New Spain (Vigil 1987: 277–94).

SOURCES AND LEGAL TEXTS

procuradores, who had less formal legal training and experience than abogados[13] and who were only allowed to prepare substantive legal documents under the supervision and signature of an abogado (Borah 1983: 235; also see Kagan 1981: 60–65).[14] Certain procuradores appeared frequently in Indian lawsuits: Cristobal Pérez, who was himself later a defendant in a suit (AGNT 58–7, 1595), and Toribio González were especially active in Indian litigation in the 1560s and 1570s. González was a particularly energetic solicitor of business. Apparently, procuradores like Pérez and González sometimes had close ties to the Indian litigants. In 1576, the governor, alcaldes, and high nobles of Mexico City sued the wife, daughters and other heirs of Hernando de Tapia over the *tecpan* (palace, or houses of the community, as they were also referred to) of San Pablo Tozanitlán (AGNT 37–2, 1576: fol.1r).[15] Toribio González was the lawyer for de Tapia's Spanish wife and the others, and he also happened to live on a property adjoining this palace site. An innovation of the 1590s was that Indian plaintiffs in the audiencia were generally represented by the procurador general de los indios (General Attorney for Indians). Let us now look closely at the legal strategies devised by three lawyers whose names often appeared in early colonial Indian litigation: the procurador Toribio González, the procurador general de los indios, Pero Díaz Agüero, and the procurador Juan López de Parella.

Toribio González was active in the legal affairs of Mexico City's native population from the early 1570s until the early seventeenth century. While abogados

[13]Abogados were trained as letrados and had "studied the full course of law in a university and had been examined and admitted formally to practice before the *audiencia*" (Borah 1983: 234).

[14]On lawyers in Mexico City during the late colonial period, see Kicza (1984).

[15]Hernando de Tapia had been an interpreter for the audiencia before he died in 1555, and his father, don Andrés de Tapia Motelchiutzin, was a governor of Tenochtitlán from 1525 to 1530. Note also that González was the lawyer in a later case, over rural land, for a niece of Hernando de Tapia's (AGNT 46–4, 1581).

were responsible for the formal presentations of documents to the audiencia (Borah 1983: 234–35), procuradores, like González, in conjunction with translators and scribes, played a much more important intermediary role between court institutions and Spanish law and legal procedures, on the one hand, and Indian litigants, on the other. Among the duties of the procurador were the preparation and filing of procedural documents such as extensions of deadlines, preparation of accusations of *rebeldía* (failure to comply with legal deadlines), and petitions for provisional or final decisions (ibid., 235).

González served as a procurador in numerous cases before the Real Audiencia, representing at least seven plaintiffs and five defendants. In eight cases that resulted in decisions, he won two and lost six.[16] Fully half of his cases involved the rights of a wife to inherit from her husband. In these cases, in particular, he exhibited a striking ability to fashion arguments based on the special circumstances of Indian litigants tailored to the demands of Spanish law. González does not appear to have been particularly interested in Mexica culture; his cases included relatively little Nahuatl documentation, and he clearly emphasized Spanish law over native custom or practice.

In his earliest cases before the Real Audiencia, his pleas were simple and straightforward, arguing, for

---

[16]See AGNT 37–2, 1576, in which González apparently won two earlier cases connected to this suit. González's success rate also appears low because during the cases heard up until around 1585, plaintiffs had an especially strong chance of winning. For cases with decisions, the numbers are the following (measured approximately by decade during the sixteenth century, with the seventeenth century split only into two fifty-year periods): from 1557 to 1569, nine of thirteen cases were won by plaintiffs and four by defendants; those numbers are the same for the 1570s; during the 1580s, seven of nine cases were won by plaintiffs and two by defendants; during the 1590s, three cases were won by the plaintiffs and three by defendants. In the seventeenth century, during the period from 1600 to 1649, two cases were won by plaintiffs and two by defendants, and from 1650 to 1700, two cases were won by plaintiffs and three by defendants.

example, that the court should uphold the validity of a husband's will (see AGNT 20–1–3, 1573). In two later cases, one a victory, the other a defeat, he advanced more complex arguments. In 1577, he represented Francisca Ana, a "poor old widow" (AGNT 39–2–1, 1577: fol.1r), who brought a claim to a house site before the audiencia. Both sides in this dispute traced the ownership of the site back to Cahualixtla and his four sons, Tenoch, Quauhtli, Tetzauh, and Xocotzin, during the later pre-Hispanic period (see fig. 2). Descendants and affines of two of these brothers, Tenoch and Quauhtli, still lived on the site in the late 1570s, but conflict had broken out among them. Francisca Ana was the widow of one of Tenoch's sons (Martín Coatl), and she was probably the oldest member of the group living there and the last survivor of her husband's generation. The conflict erupted when Francisca Ana attempted to sell some of the land belonging to the site. Other residents of the house site, including the grandchildren of Tenoch and Quauhtli, challenged Francisca Ana's right to sell the land.

In his arguments before the Real Audiencia, González grounded Francisca Ana's rights to the site in a complex chain of inheritance. The lawyer maintained that Francisca Ana's husband, Martín Coatl, had inherited the property from his father, Tenoch, who had died prior to the conquest. The property then passed into the possession of Martín Coatl's daughter, Angelina, on his death in 1543. This child died in 1548. The lawyer argued that on the daughter's death, Francisca Ana inherited the property.[17] In ruling against Francisca Ana, the audiencia dismissed the lawyer's argument, assigning greater weight to the rights of the surviving descendants of Cahualixtla.

In 1578, González advanced a similar argument before the Real Audiencia. This time, he successfully persuaded

[17]See the *Siete Partidas*, P6.T13.L4, on parental inheritance from children.

16

Fig. 2
Source: AGNT 39-2-1, 1577

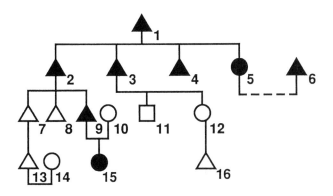

1 Cahualixtla	9 Martín Coatl (*d. ca.* 1543)
2 Tenoch	10 Francisca Ana
3 Quauhtli	11 unnamed
4 Tetzauh	12 Mocel
5 Xocotzin	13 Martín Jacobo
6 Ahuitzotl	14 Isabel Juana
7 Yaotl	15 Angelina (*d. ca.* 1548)
8 Yehuatl	16 Baltasar Tlacenen

the court to recognize property rights rooted in another complex chain of inheritance (see AGNT 39–1–2, 1578; fig. 3). In this case, González represented Magdalena Ramírez, who was acting as guardian for her daughter, Juana Xoco, in a dispute over the sale of a house site.

Both Magdalena's claim to residence and her ownership rights appeared weak. Magdalena dwelled on the site because she relocated there when she married her husband, Pedro Luis. He himself had moved onto the site to reside with his first wife, Mariana, and Mariana lived there because her mother, Ana Tlaco, had been invited to settle there by one of her aunts.[18] To strengthen Magdalena's claim, González argued that Pedro Luis and his first wife had a child, Esteban, who had inherited the property on his mother's death. González then insisted that when Esteban died, his father, Pedro Luis, inherited the property. On Pedro Luis's death, González insisted, his second wife, Magdalena Ramírez, had gained residence rights. In this case, the Real Audiencia accepted González's argument that parents had a right to inherit property from their children and awarded Magdalena and her daughter control over a portion of the house site.

In a 1583 case (AGNT 48–4, 1583), González unsuccessfully argued that a minor should be denied rights to a house site on the grounds that she was the illegitimate child of an incestuous marriage. The lawyer maintained before the audencia that the minor's mother had cohabited with the brother of her deceased first husband. The court rejected this argument on the grounds that the minor descended from a sibling group that owned and controlled the site.

As these cases suggest, a lawyer's success in property disputes, especially those heard during the sixteenth century, often depended on his ability to persuade the audiencia that a litigant had a legitimate "prior right" to the property, a right that might be rooted in pre-Hispanic custom, particularly inheritance, or purchase. The court's procedures stressed the individuality of disputes rather than general principles of law, and cases' outcomes hinged on the facts of particular disputes rather than on technicalities of Spanish law. These procedures encouraged litigation because people could reasonably believe they had some chance of prevailing.

[18]This was a somewhat distant relationship as Ana Tlaco was referred to as a "distant niece" of María Xoco, the aunt who had invited her to live on the site ("in ipilo ytoca catca ana tlaco huecapa" [her distant niece was named Ana Tlaco]; fol.8r).

Fig. 3
Source: AGNT 39-1-2, 1578

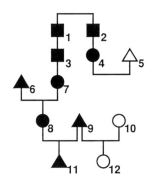

1 unnamed	7 Ana Tlaco
2 unnamed	8 Mariana
3 unnamed	9 Pedro Luis (*d.* after 1575)
4 María Xoco (*d.* 1575)	10 Magdalena Ramírez
5 unnamed	11 Esteban
6 Miguel Ocelotl	12 Juana Xoco

Pero Díaz Agüero, who served as procurador general de indios[19] in the last decade of the sixteenth century, also figured prominently in Indian litigation. He participated in nine cases whose records survive; six resulted in decisions, and of these, he won four. Less crafty as a strategist than González, Díaz Agüero constructed arguments that stayed relatively close to the relevant "facts." If these called for emphasizing the exclusive inheritance of half-siblings, he did just that (e.g., BNP 112, 1593; AGNT 49–3, 1595); if the facts warranted a reliance on a generalized concept of Indian ownership, whether individual or communal, he addressed that (e.g., AGNT 58–

[19]This functionary was a "general salaried defender who would bring and defend Indian lawsuits before the *audiencia*" (Borah 1983: 63). The title does not occur in cases of Indians heard by the audiencia after 1600, but Indians did have access to procuradores licensed to the audiencia. (This official did continue to function in the Juzgado General de Indios, however) (ibid., 259).

7, 1595; AGNT 70–4, 1601). Toribio González had been practicing at a time when he often had to graft alien legal concepts onto sets of facts that did not fit that system very well. Díaz Agüero, in contrast, was practicing at a point when more developed notions of colonial law were coming into being (even if these were only partly consciously recognized [see chap. 2]).

Díaz Agüero's cases demonstrate that the colonial legal system recognized certain Indian rights, even in disputes in which Indian litigants were opposed by Spaniards. Consider a lawsuit from 1601. This case involved a claim that a Spaniard, Diego Arias, had illegally built a store and a house on a plot of land adjacent to the market of San Juan (see AGNT 70–4, 1601). Diego Arias argued that he had purchased the site from an Indian woman who had left instructions in her will to sell the property on her death.

To substantiate a claim that the Spaniard had acted illegally, Díaz Agüero drew on the interrogatorio of the Indian officials, who indicated that the land surrounding the market was also property of the Indian community, whose members customarily held use rights (*útil dominio* [fol.19r]) to it. Spaniards and others might use the land but only if they made an annual payment (*censo* [fol.19r]) to the community. Díaz Agüero contended that no member of the Indian community had a right to permanently alienate the land. No final decision was ever issued in this case, apparently because Arias departed Mexico (*es ydo a la China* [fol.34r]) and the case was rendered moot.[20]

Juan López de Parella, who served as a procurador from about 1682 to 1695, participated in four cases; he won two and lost one (there was no decision in the remaining case). The case records testify to his legal skills. The arguments he made on behalf of his clients

---

[20] Note also that the opposing side's argument was *not* that Indians did not hold rights in this area or customarily use the property in the ways described but that they were commonly selling the plots.

show that he shared the pragmatic approach of Díaz Agüero but that the nature of the conflicts themselves and the ways they were argued had changed. Like most lawyers during the latter part of the seventeenth century, he focused on issues of documentation (see chap. 2). When his clients managed to produce documents that supported their cases, he rested his arguments on the strength of these records (e.g., AGNT 128–2, 1682). Conversely, when the other side produced stronger documentation, he attacked the records as fraudulent (e.g., AGNT 157–7, 1694).

During the seventeenth century, Indians drew on a wider range of Spanish officials than they had in the previous century.[21] This shift reflected both the greater bureaucratization of the colonial legal system and the relative ease of access that Indians in Mexico City had to an array of colonial officials. Among those lower-level Spanish officials whose titles appeared in these documents were alcaldes, alguaciles, and scribes (also see Borah 1983: 234–36; Haskett 1991: chap. 4).

Indigenous Officials

During the sixteenth century, many Mexica pleaded before local Indian officials prior to taking their cases to the Real Audiencia. Court records indicate that litigants often had previously appeared before such officials as the *gobernadores,* or *jueces gobernadores,* of the Indian barrios.[22] Indian alcaldes, *regidores,* alguaciles, scribes, and interpreters were also frequently mentioned. We

---

[21]Titles such as *receptor,* a notary with special training who could hear and record testimony, and fiscal, crown attorney, become common in the records (also see Borah 1983: 236). New titles for judges also began to appear, such as the *juez de la cuenta personal* (AGNT 1720–7, 1633) or the *juez de visita personal de los naturales* (AGNT 101–2, 1642). These may have been judges appointed for specific, temporary undertakings.

[22]On the distinction between gobernadores and jueces gobernadores, indigenous governors who came from outside the community they were appointed to oversee, see Lockhart (1992: 34–35).

may assume that during the years immediately following the conquest, indigenous officials continued to make judicial decisions based on local and customary practices. But such officials also had access to texts that detailed, in Nahuatl, Spanish expectations about their duties, the rules they were to enforce, and how they were to conduct investigations and court proceedings (Bancroft/MM 460, 16th century; 467, 1629).[23]

Surviving records indicate that during the sixteenth century high-level indigenous officials sometimes used threats of jail, physical punishment, or forcible removal and exile of individuals from a barrio to enforce their decisions. In 1563, don Luis de Santa María Cipactzin,[24] gobernador of México Tenochtitlán, threatened litigants in a long-running conflict (dating back to 1552) over access to a small plot of land and water rights with being punished "with all judicial rigor and they should be thrown out of the barrio and they may not have nor should they have their canoe where at present they have it; we compel it on pain of ten pesos in *tomines* for the treasury of his majesty" (AGNT 29–5, 1570: fol.4v).[25] In

[23]These two fascinating texts allow us a glimpse into the ways indigenous officials might have learned (either through reading or by listening) about Spanish expectations about rules to be enforced for daily living and community governance and basic Castilian legal procedures. The sixteenth-century document, entitled "Ordenanças de su magestad," gives general rules for conduct to be encouraged and is directed to gobernadores, alcaldes, and *topileques* (lower-level, constablelike officials) (Haskett 1991: 99). The other document, from 1629 and entitled "Ordenación," consists of specific judicial instructions for alguaciles on how to conduct investigations and orderly court proceedings. These documents are similar in form to the "Ordenanzas para el gobierno de Cuauhtinchán" [1978]. Other known Nahuatl legal texts come from Tlaxcala and include the *cabildo* records translated by Lockhart, Berdan, and Anderson (1986) and Nahuatl texts of lawsuits heard by local courts in Tlaxcala translated by Sullivan (1987). Note also that Chimalpahin's writings suggest that lawsuits were known about by a wider group than merely the participants. A broader network of Indians, some of whom were governing officials and some of whom were literate and perhaps constituted an indigenous intelligentsia, also had knowledge of some of the cases (e.g., Chimalpahin 1963–65: II:125–26).

[24]See Lockhart (1992: 34) for a list of indigenous gobernadores of Tenochtitlán for the sixteenth and early seventeenth century.

[25]"seran castigados por todo rrigor de justicia e serian echados del dho

1576, the alcaldes Gaspar de Aquino and Pablo Xuárez presided over the sale of a house site in San Pablo Tozanitlan to Magdalena de San Miguel. She was involved in a conflict over rights to part of the site, and the Indian alcaldes threatened anyone who tried to impede her possession with imprisonment and "forty lashes" (AGNT 42–5, 1579: fol.22v).

Native scribes, or notaries, and interpreters played an important mediating role between indigenous litigants and Spanish officials. The role of scribe predated the Spanish Conquest (Gibson 1964: 181; Molina 1977: I: fol.58r; Haskett 1991: 110–11; Lockhart 1992: 40–41). During the late pre-Hispanic era, scribes (known either as *tlacuilo* or *amatlacuilo*) kept a variety of religious, historical, and legal records "in a form as much pictorial as glyphic" (Lockhart 1992: 40). But in the sixteenth century, scribes acquired an enhanced legal and cultural significance. They played an important role in shaping legal cases and documents in Nahuatl or Spanish both for litigants and lawyers. In addition, scribes were responsible for record keeping and the production of legal documents such as wills or bills of sale.

The interpreters, or *nahuatlatos*, who translated for the audiencia also emerged as prominent intermediaries. The highest Spanish authorities expressed their concern about the intercultural role these men played. In Viceroy Antonio de Mendoza's 1548 compilation of ordinances, a number deal with the nahuatlatos, prohibiting them from receiving gifts or bribes from Spaniards or Indians, hearing cases in their houses, or acting as procuradores, or soliciters (1945: fols.30r–31v). In the early 1560s, these ordinances were repeated and further prohibitions, such as receiving food or jewelry, were added (*CeI* 1596: II:fol.369). In 1579, the nahuatlatos were forbidden to build houses or sell either building

---

barrio yq̄ no puedan tener ni tengan la dha su canoa en donde al prest⁀e la tienen e le ponemos de pena diez p⁀os en tomines pa la camara de su mg⁀t"

materials or basic foods including eggs or maize (Montemayor y Córdova de Cuenca 1787: 26). Thus, Spanish officials regarded the interpreters as especially likely to try to function as quasi-lawyers or to attempt to profit from their position.

Litigants

Who were the litigants in Indian legal disputes? I shall answer this question by analyzing three features of their "social identities"—their status position, their racial and ethnic identification, and their gender—that influenced the outcome of litigation.

Status Position: Gibson has argued that one effect of colonization was to compress the indigenous class structure, "to move all classes towards a single level and condition" (1964: 153). While this statement is accurate in an economic sense, it does not fully describe the social and cultural stratification that continued to exist within Nahua communities (also see Cline 1986: 107–12; Haskett 1991: 132–37; Lockhart 1992: chap. 4).

Throughout the colonial period, an indigenous elite existed, although its material base and social character changed over time. I classify litigants as members of the elite if they were, first, descendants of high-ranking nobles in the pre-Hispanic period; second, members of the families of wealthy merchants or members of families owning large amounts of landed and/or movable property; or third, members of the families of Indian officials who served in the colonial governing structure. Over time, the proportion of elites falling into the first two categories decreased dramatically. By 1600, elite status had become largely synonymous with membership in the families of indigenous officials (also see Haskett 1991: 131–37; 161–65).

In the period from 1550 to 1584, legal documents draw a sharp distinction between wealthier, more socially privileged litigants and poorer, nonelite litigants. Litigants themselves employed a variety of terms that recognized these differences: *principales* and *dons,* and *pobres, macehuales,* or *terrazgueros.* Frequently, nonelite litigants were urbanites who had left their house compounds during or soon after the conquest and had returned to them later to reclaim them, only to find occupants who had bought or held grants to the property or squatters.

Two early lawsuits from the 1560s contrast the hereditary rights of rural macehuales with urban, nonresident owners, Spanish or elite Indian, who bought or were granted property and rented out the land to terrazgueros to work it (see AGNT 17–2–1, 1557; 24–3, 1569). Elites descended from noble families were trying to strengthen their own rights to rural lands (at the same time that their fragmented holdings were being consolidated and were decreasing in size [see Hicks 1986]) by circumventing customary labor and exchange practices. Thus, some cases suggest heated conflict between elites— especially the descendants of ruling families who were struggling to maintain their landholdings—and nonelites.[26] But the relationship between elites and nonelites was sometimes more complex, as will be shown in a case discussed below.

Contrary to what one might suppose, many litigants during the sixteenth and seventeenth centuries did not belong to elite families. In the earliest surviving court cases, from the period stretching from 1536 to 1584, three-fourths of the lawsuits involved nonelite litigants (i.e., nonelites made up at least one side in thirty of forty cases). During the seventeenth century, two-thirds (or

[26]Both Spalding (1970) and Stern (1982: 92–95, 132–35, 158–83 [chap. 7]) find a stark relationship between colonial Indian elites, allied with the Spanish state, and the indigenous peasantry. On the relationship between Indian elite women and commoner women in the Andes, see Silverblatt (1987: chaps. 6, 7). For a perceptive discussion of widening degrees of economic differentiation within Indian villages in the late colonial Guadalajara region of New Spain, see Van Young (1984).

twelve of eighteen) of the lawsuits include nonelite litigants on at least one side of a dispute.

In sixteenth-century lawsuits, nonelites tended to portray themselves as poor and needy, while elite litigants preferred to emphasize their connections to pre-Hispanic noble families, especially to previous tlatoani. By the seventeenth century, a new, distinctively colonial Indian elite had emerged (Haskett 1988). Often lacking traceable, hereditary ties to the preconquest nobility, their status and power rested on ties to Spanish authorities. But many members of the new elite were not particularly affluent. During the seventeenth century, many witnesses who were identified by the term *don* and who held or had held governing positions such as that of alcalde within the Indian governance system also designated themselves as craftsmen, such as carpenters or tailors (see, e.g., AGNT 103–2–6, 1653: fols.58v–59v).

Two lawsuits, one from 1567 and one from 1693, may serve to illustrate changes that took place in elite–nonelite relationships between the sixteenth and the late seventeenth century. In the early colonial period, the social and economic distinctions between nobles and commoners remained quite clear; nevertheless, nonelites sometimes traced ownership of property back into the pre-Hispanic period through quasi-patron–client relationships.

In 1567, Juana Tiacapan sued Juan Quauhtli, claiming he illegally purchased a house site that actually belonged to her (AGNT 22–1–5). Quauhtli defended his ownership by saying he bought the property from two high-ranking nobles, don Pedro Xicomic and his mother, doña María, the widow of don Diego de San Francisco Tehuetzquititzin, Indian governor of the city during the years 1541 to 1554. Don Pedro and doña María testified to this effect during the sale of the site. They later became parties to the suit before the Real Audiencia and argued that the property was theirs on the basis of inheritance from their grandfather, a son of Tizoc, a former tlatoani who ruled from 1481 to 1486 (see fig. 4). Juana then introduced evidence arguing that the *solar* (plot of land that was part of the house site), which she had claimed to inherit from her mother, had been donated to her mother. Both don Francisco Velásquez and don Diego Ahuitzotzin, governor of Ecatepec, both also sons of don Diego de San Francisco, testified that their family had given the property to Juana's mother for her "good works" (fol.163r). The audiencia found this story compelling and ruled in Juana's favor. In short, both parties to the suit emphasized patron-client ties between nobles and commoners.

The 1693 lawsuit offers a sharply contrasting picture of the relationship between elites and nonelites (see AGNT 186–9). This case pitted a principal, don Pedro Juan (a former alcalde), along with his wife, Luisa de la Cruz, from the pueblo of Santa María Magdalena Coatlayauca, a subject community *(sujeto)* of San Juan, against Juan Bautista, Juan Pedro, and Nicolás Diego, *merinos* (minor officials) from the same pueblo. Don Pedro Juan claimed that his wife had inherited from her parents a piece of land, a house with three rooms, and a quince orchard with a spring. Juan Bautista and his cohort argued that don Pedro was seeking to extend his ownership into fields that were not his and that the merinos had already sown.

Especially striking is the detailed description of the harassment of don Pedro Juan by the merinos. Don Pedro accused his adversaries of marshaling a crowd of Indians who threatened to stone him and his wife to death if they returned to the barrio. Several witnesses for don Pedro also described an incident in which he was thrown out of the church on a Sunday morning, his shirt was ripped, and he was beaten and called a cuckold. Tellingly, the merinos never refer to their adversary as a noble or don.[27] The bitterly adversarial relationship

---

[27]Don Pedro Juan's procurador was Juan López Parella. The one great burst

Fig. 4
Source: AGNT 22-1-5, 1567

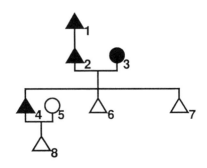

1 Tizoc
2 Tezcatlpopoca
3 Cihuatzitzin
4 Don Diego de San Francisco Tehuetzquititzin
5 Doña María
6 Don Francisco Velásquez
7 Don Diego Ahuitzotzin
8 Don Pedro Xicomic

between an elite family and its neighbors contrasts strongly with earlier cases in which litigants tended to agree on the status position of those involved and a wider array of relationships between elites and nonelites was depicted.

In its decision, as in others involving elite Indians, the audiencia underscored the connections between the new elite and the colonial state. Not only did it find on don Pedro Juan's behalf but the oidores threatened Juan

of legal creativity that López Parella had was evident in this case. He helped to construct a narrative that went way beyond the dramas and conflicts generally depicted even in the late cases, which were so textually rich (see chap. 2), to play on a racial fear of violent Indians so as to help a greedy native principal, rejected even by other important Indian officials. It is probably no coincidence that this case occurred in the year after Mexico City's uprising of 1692.

28

Bautista, Juan Pedro, and Nicolás Diego with confinement in an obraje for two years if they did not cease their harassment. During the sixteenth and seventeenth centuries, elite status was a strong predictor of success in lawsuits. When pitted against nonelites, elite Indians won seven of ten suits with decisions.

Ethnicity: Spaniards were parties to one third of all Indian litigation heard by the Real Audiencia in the sixteenth and seventeenth centuries. Most of these lawsuits were concentrated in the sixteenth century; there is only a single surviving property case heard by the audiencia involving both Spaniards and Indians after 1620. Indians initiated and won most of these lawsuits; during the sixteenth century, Indians prevailed in ten of thirteen interethnic cases that resulted in a decision. This tendency led Gerónimo López to make the claim that the colonial legal system was biased against Spaniards: "I notice that when a Spaniard is accused, justice is on the side of the Indians, but when the accusation is against the Indians, there is no justice" (1984: III:449).

In a number of lawsuits from the very early colonial era, Spaniards sought to prove that they had acquired legal title to indigenous land by calling on Indians to testify on their behalf as to how they had gained title. Sometimes Indians even became parties to lawsuits as if Spaniards felt that an indigenous claim of ownership would have greater legitimacy in the eyes of the oidores. A lawsuit involving precisely this issue (AGNT 22–1–3 [continued as AGNT 22–1–4]) took place in 1576. Two Spaniards, Francisco de Velásquez and Alonso de Peralta, each claimed ownership of a solar in the *traza,* the central part of Mexico City where Spaniards lived. Velásquez stated that he had bought a large piece of urban property (1350 square *brazas* [1 br. = 1.67m]) from another Spaniard who held it through a *merced* (a legal grant of property). Peralta also claimed ownership on the basis of a merced; however, his came, not from the *cabildo* (city council) as Velásquez had claimed, but from the then native governor of México Tenochtitlán, don Luis de Santa María, and his brother, don Martín Momauhtin. The native governor and his brother provided the court with documentation in Nahuatl that traced ownership of the property to their father, Acamapichtzin, and his father, Ahuitzotl, a tlatoani (who had ruled from approximately 1486 to 1502). In 1576, before the Nahuatl testimony had been received, the audiencia ruled for Velásquez; two years later, the oidores reversed their decision. The audiencia apparently based the reversal on its belief that legitimate ownership of the land originally resided with this indigenous noble family.

At the end of the sixteenth century, the audiencia remained receptive to claims of ownership rooted in indigenous ownership, custom, or tradition. In 1595, Bartolomé Sánchez, an Indian native of Mexico City, sued Cristobal Pérez, a Spanish procurador, alleging that Pérez was illegally removing earth and stone from property that he had inherited from his parents and grandparents and had used for many years "without contradiction" (AGNT 58–7, 1595: fol.7r). To buttress his case, Sánchez presented testimony from three witnesses. The procurador Pérez responded by asserting that he had purchased the property "many years ago" and received a merced from the cabildo in 1592 to further substantiate his claim (fols.17r–18r). He then attacked the credibility of Sánchez's witnesses, calling them "vile drunks" and charging that Sánchez had paid for their testimony (fol.30r). Finally, he presented testimony from seven witnesses (none from the barrio) who challenged the credibility of the plaintiff's witnesses. Three times the audiencia ruled in Sánchez's favor, ordering Pérez to make restitution for the earth and stones that he had removed.

By the mid-seventeenth century, establishing legal title based on claims of pre-Hispanic ownership was becoming more difficult. In 1653, a complex conflict flared up between the convent of San Francisco and the chapel of San Joséph of the *parcialidad* of San Juan and Captain Francisco de Córdova Villafranca, *contador de cuentas* (chief accountant) for the audiencia, in which the convent and chapel alleged that he had improperly deprived them of a small plot of land and adjoining passageway (AGNT 103–2–6, 1653). The religious institutions claimed that they had traditionally owned one portion of the property and that the other part had been donated to the chapel.

The Indian alcaldes and principales of San Juan, referring to themselves as officials of the *"República de los naturales"* (fol.43v), intervened in the suit on behalf of the convent and chapel, which many local Indians attended. These officials made three points in their testimony: that the property had originally belonged to their ancestors (but they made this argument only in a very general way); that Córdova Villafranca was obstructing both access to and light for the chapel; and that in the past they had successfully sued his mother to prevent her from acquiring the property.

Córdova Villafranca responded by asserting that he had legally inherited the property from his mother. He then sought to impeach the testimony of the Indian officials by claiming that they were untrustworthy and of "vile and low condition" (fol.85r). In their decision, the oidores—basing their information on descriptions and surveys of the disputed area—found in Córdova Villafranca's favor, recognizing his property rights in the solar and *callejon*. But they also made a gesture toward the convent and the chapel by forbidding him from taking any further action that would injure the chapel (fol.115r). While the racial identity "Indian" was a significant and positive factor in the early decisions of the audiencia, it became less so during the more racially charged atmosphere of the seventeenth century.

Gender: During the sixteenth and seventeenth centuries, indigenous women, whether widowed or married, actively participated in litigation: well over half of all property litigation involving Indians included them as plaintiffs or defendants. Between the 1530s and 1584, women were parties to 65 percent of all lawsuits (twenty-six of forty); between 1585 and 1649, women were parties to more than 59 percent of the cases (thirteen of twenty-two); and between 1650 and 1700, 82 percent of the lawsuits included female litigants (nine of eleven).

Widows and unattached women over age twenty-five were free to initiate lawsuits independently, without male guardians (Arrom 1985a: 58–61). Those who were married, in contrast, had to receive permission from their husbands to participate in suits; but once such permission was granted, they often acted quite independently of their spouses (Kellogg 1984:26; Arrom 1985a: 86; Lavrin and Couturier 1979).

Over time, women's participation in lawsuits underwent a marked change (also see chap. 3). During the sixteenth century, women who were the inheritors of property subject to a lawsuit tended to occupy a predominant role in the legal documentation. Frequently, they were identified as the primary party in the case and interrogatorios or *probanzas* (collations of documents that included interrogatorios and the testimony of witnesses) were submitted in their names. After 1600, however, the number of women initiating lawsuits independently dropped sharply. By the seventeenth century, Indian households were increasingly adopting a more nuclear structure (see chap. 5) and husbands were becoming more active participants in lawsuits involving their wives' property. Clearly, the meaning of women's legal participation had undergone a profound transformation, even as women continued to figure prominently in lawsuits and legal procedures.

There was a pronounced gender difference in the kinds of property over which men and women litigated. Cases with male litigants only tended to fall into one of two categories: disputes that were communal in nature, involving the boundaries or political standing of communities (e.g., see AGNT 1–1 and its continuation, 1–2, 1561); and disputes over rural land, which was usually held by men (e.g., see AGNT 55–2, 1589). Women, in contrast, were typically involved in lawsuits over either urban house sites or chinampas, and only occasionally were involved in disputes over rural land.

There is strong reason to believe that the legal status of women declined in the seventeenth century. One piece of evidence suggesting such a decline is the fact that fewer women initiated lawsuits. Before 1650, men and women were equally likely to be plaintiffs in lawsuits. After 1650, women were less likely to be plaintiffs, even when one counts joint suits undertaken by a wife and her husband. Moreover, during the seventeenth century, an increasing number of women were represented before the Real Audiencia by their husbands. In virtually every seventeenth-century case in which a husband and a wife litigated together, the woman had actually inherited the property in dispute; nevertheless, the husband was the primary legal actor. He was identified as the primary party in the suit; and his name appeared on all legal documentation. Women had been reduced to the status of legal minors.[28]

Witnesses

Each side in a case presented testimony from witnesses to support their arguments, and each witness, in turn, answered a written list of questions, an interrogatorio, before a scribe. Under Spanish law, litigants were "entitled to as many as thirty witnesses, and in addition there might be witnesses summoned by the judge" (Borah 1983: 54). No litigant, however, presented as many as thirty witnesses; in fact, the largest number of witnesses

---

[28]For further discussion of gender differences in patterns of property ownership and political and legal processes, see chaps. 3 and 4.

presented in early cases was twelve, and the average was six or seven.

In the early 1570s, to streamline litigation, the audiencia decreed that each party could only present five witnesses and submit a single probanza (ibid., 58). These regulations had only a limited effect: in the later sixteenth century, the number of witnesses declined slightly. Litigants commonly presented five or six witnesses along with a probanza as part of each stage of a lawsuit (i.e., the first instance and subsequent appeals). While the seventeenth century saw no further decline in the numbers of witnesses, there was a trend toward the presentation of fewer probanzas, probably because there were fewer appeals.

Before questioning witnesses, scribes wrote down their names, their races, their barrios of residence, their approximate ages, and occasionally their occupations.[29] In the seventeenth century, the scribe also identified the language in which the testimony was given. Some 700 Indian witnesses offered testimony to the Real Audiencia in the sixteenth-century cases, and about 225 presented testimony in the seventeenth century. For an ethnohistorian, these records provide a significant source of information.

In lawsuits from the 1550s and 1560s, certain Nahuatl second names suggest higher-status witnesses. Some of these relate to terms used for various officials (such as the *tlacochcalcatl,* a pre-Hispanic high office title) and functionaries during the pre-Hispanic period; others may suggest ties to palaces or elites (also see Lockhart 1992: 119–21). After 1560, elites were also identified by the use of the terms *don* or *principal.* After 1570, members of the elite were also identified by specific titles, such as alcalde, regidor, or alguacil, or the titles of guild

---

[29]These occupational identifications are interesting and include (in approximate numerical order): laborer, carpenter, silversmith, tailor, embroiderer, merchant, weaver, adobe layer, mat maker, jar maker, candle maker, lathe maker, painter, scribe, interpreter, hosier, hatmaker, blacksmith, and salt maker.

officials, and less often with Nahuatl second names. In fact, however, titles and terms that denote elite status appear infrequently in the scribes' records of witnesses during the sixteenth century.

Nobles and barrio officials accounted for only one in eight of the witnesses heard during the period from 1536 to 1585. But after 1600 and especially after 1650, a growing number of witnesses used the title "don"—the proportion increasing from one in ten prior to 1650 to one in three between 1650 and 1700. The terms used to denote high status in the second half of the seventeenth century continued to be don, principal, or particular office titles.

During the sixteenth century, native litigants rarely presented testimony from Spanish or *mestizo* witnesses. Spanish litigants, however, called on Indians to describe property transfers, whether by sale, grant, or donation. During the seventeenth century, in contrast, one-third of the witnesses presented by Indian litigants were non-Indians, either Spaniards or castas.

Female witnesses were relatively uncommon during the early colonial period. They made up one in twenty of the total between 1536 and 1584, climbing to one in ten between 1585 and 1700. This modest increase seems to reflect a decline in the number of lawsuits pursued by urban nobles over land and by the Indian barrios over communitywide issues—disputes in which, in their legal form, only men had participated. Female litigants had no particular tendency to present testimony from female witnesses. But neither were male or female litigants disadvantaged by using female witnesses.

CONCLUSION

Certain historical documents permit normally voiceless people to speak. Such are the records of property litigation heard in the Real Audiencia in Mexico City during the early colonial period. These records include not only court decisions but also the complaints and pleadings of indigenous litigants, drawings of domestic compounds, genealogies, wills, and the testimony of hundreds of sixteenth- and seventeenth-century Indians. Out of these records I have sought to reconstruct the nature of colonial Mexica life—kinship and family structures, gender roles, inheritance practices, and conceptions of property and community—and the ways in which it changed over time.

The records are surprisingly inclusive. Virtually all significant Indian occupational categories, skilled and unskilled, are represented in the records of the Real Audiencia. So are all levels of social status, from elite to nonelite. Women, too, appear frequently in the case records. This is not to say, however, that the records are completely representative of colonial Mexico City's Indian population.

The wealthier sector of the indigenous populace is well represented (though, I would argue, not overrepresented) both in number and in social and material power. The seventy-three surviving litigations contain testimony from over nine hundred sixteenth- and seventeenth-century Indians, not a negligible number, to be sure, but only a minuscule proportion of the total indigenous population. In other words, the case records, like any historical source, must be used with caution and discrimination. Nevertheless, these records provide rich insights into the social and cultural history of the colonial Mexica and the processes through which Spain established cultural hegemony.

CHAPTER 2

Social Dramas as Narratives: Texts, Representations, and Symbols

This chapter and those that follow turn to the case records themselves, to the suits through which the native people of Mexico City defended their property rights in disputes with other Indians, Spaniards, and Spanish institutions such as the cabildo between approximately 1530 and 1700 and the evidence and testimony they provided to buttress their legal claims. Succeeding chapters treat the court records as a valuable source of information about Tenochcan Mexica cultural and social history which can be used to reconstruct indigenous inheritance practices, kinship and family structures, and gender roles and how these changed over time.

Here, however, we will examine these records as a source of ethnographic information about the cultural history of Mexico City's indigenous population: the rhetoric and forms of argumentation that Indians employed to demonstrate and legitimate property ownership, the symbols they used, and their representation of such key concepts as time, history, property, and community. The primary argument made in this chapter is that while the indigenous participants exerted a strong influence on the results of particular lawsuits, the very process of enacting social dramas through the written legal procedures described below (at first done self-consciously but later done in more "natural," less purposeful ways) exerted a strong acculturative influence.

In analyzing the legal documents presented to the

Real Audiencia, I approach them as texts,[1] susceptible to close critical analysis. Legal pleadings and petitions, like other texts, require careful interpretation. One cannot assume that they offer accurate statements of fact or transparent descriptions of social realities. Even though these documents had real and lasting economic, political, and social implications for the individuals, families, and communities involved, they are treated here as a form of narrative, as a compendium of dramatic stories and carefully crafted fictions rooted in real conflicts and struggles. In many instances, statements presented to the audiencia are contradictory; some documents are clearly fraudulent. But even when litigants or witnesses sought to be as accurate as possible, their statements must be regarded as constructs, selective in the points they emphasize and the sequence of events.

Rather than using legal records simply to uncover the "true" realities of early colonial indigenous life, this chapter employs close textual analysis to recover underlying cultural assumptions, attitudes, and perceptions. In short, the court records offer a window on a changing and developing colonial culture, but one that is clouded by the very disputes and rhetoric described.

THE FORMS OF DOCUMENTATION

Anyone interested in recovering the voices of sixteenth- and seventeeth-century Indians will find a wide range of archival documentation, for example, civil lawsuits over property (houses, land, or chinampas); wills; property sales or other transfers; and letters and petitions (also

[1]In addition to sources on legal texts and narrative mentioned in fn. 3, chap. 1, I have found many other sources on narrative analysis helpful: Adorno (1982, 1986), Clifford and Marcus (1986), Davis (1987), Derrida (1976), Dollimore and Sinfield (1985), Foucault (1970), Genette (1980), González Echevarría (1990), Greenblatt (1988, 1991), Hulme (1986), Jameson (1972), Marcus and Cushman (1982), Pastor Bodmer (1992), Rabasa (1993), Said (1983), Scholes and Kellogg (1966), Seed (1991), Smith (1981), Todorov (1977, 1984), Turner (1971), White (1978), and Williams (1977).

see Anderson, Berdan, and Lockhart 1976: 23–30; Lockhart 1992: chaps. 8–9). Particularly rich sources for such documentation are the property lawsuits from the Real Audiencia.

Tenochcan Mexica colonial property suits consist of various kinds of written texts: pleadings of *demandantes* (plaintiffs); statements by *defendientes* (defendants); interrogatorios (lists of questions answered by each party's witnesses); probanzas (the witnesses' answers together with the interrogatorios); and the testimony by experts summoned by the judges to investigate specific issues. Also incorporated may be documentary evidence (generally referred to as *recaudos*, including wills, bills of sale, and drawings and maps presented to substantiate claims);[2] summaries and petitions presented by lawyers; and the judges' decisions.

One of the most striking features of Indian petitions and pleadings from the very early colonial period is the clarity of the voices of the indigenous litigants and witnesses. The legal procedures of the late pre-Hispanic period were primarily oral (Offner 1983: 246–47); but even though the colonial legal system placed a greater emphasis on writing and Spanish lawyers played an increasing role in shaping the legal presentation of cases before the Real Audiencia, the statements of litigants and witnesses are permeated by a strongly oral character. The accounts given by litigants before scribes were worded as if they were addressed directly to the judges

[2]Documents such as those that make up the recaudos may be found as part of litigation, but they may also be found in collations of colonial documentation not rooted in lawsuits. Sale documents may be found in the Archivo de Notarías and the Biblioteca Nacional de México; letters and petitions by Indians in Nahuatl or Spanish may be found in the *ramos Bienes Nacionales, Civil,* or *Hospital de Jesús* of the AGN, and there are also scattered documents in a broad range of collections including the Bibliothèque nationale de Paris, the Gates Collection at Tulane's Latin American Library, and the Ayer Collection at the Newberry Library. Much surviving documentation exists, however, precisely because it was submitted as evidence in lawsuits. Helpful guides to native language materials include Reyes García et al. (1982), Schwaller (1986), and León-Portilla (1988).

of the audiencia. Some were flowery and deferential ("I kiss [the] feet and hands of Your Majesty," María Tlaco stated in 1561 [AGNT 19–2–3, 1561: fol.1r]); others were unembellished with rhetorical devices (Pablo Maquex began his appeal to the court, "Pablo, Indian of the barrio of San Pablo, I appear before Your Majesty" [AGNT 55–5, 1564: fol.1r]). But whether elegant or unadorned, the discourse was in the first person; the verb forms, pronouns, and inflectional affixes referred directly to the speaker (also see Sullivan 1987).

Throughout the 1560s and 1570s, plaintiffs invariably presented their opening statements to the oidor or the audiencia in the first person. Toward the end of the sixteenth century, however, another voice began to appear regularly, the lawyer's. Around 1585, Spanish colonial authorities instituted a procedure by which an appointed procurador presented the Indians' arguments. From 1585 until 1610, cases opened with a statement from this official. Under Pero Díaz Agüero, opening remarks began, "Pero Díaz Agüero, General Attorney for Indians, I say that . . ." (e.g., AGNT 56–8, 1592: fol.2r). These opening declarations were then followed by a brief statement of the plaintiff's complaint. But the details of the complaint appear to have come directly from the plaintiff's mouth.

In the earliest suits, the written record almost always begins with the plaintiff's complaint, which frequently involved an allegation that an indigenous official had improperly awarded a piece of property to the defendants in the case. Following the complaint was the plaintiff's supporting evidence: the interrogatorio, the testimony of witnesses, and then the documentary evidence. Next, the defendant responded, providing documentary evidence and witnesses' testimony. Only then do statements by the parties' procuradores appear, summarizing each client's case and disputing the other side's arguments. The case records conclude with any further petitions and the judges' decision.

40

Sometimes, one of the parties appealed the judges' decision. The appeals generally consisted of new interrogatorios and testimony accompanied by new statements from lawyers. While this testimony usually repeated the themes of the case as already stated, it often also dealt with a narrower set of issues, such as the credibility of witnesses or the costs of repairs to a house site,[3] indicating the audiencia might return a site to its previous owners but that its current residents should be reimbursed for repairs or improvements. The appeal might or might not be followed by another decision, a *sentencia definitiva*.[4]

The order in which various types of documents were presented to the audiencia changed over time. After 1585, the cases generally began with a statement by the procurador describing the plaintiff's complaint and requesting relief. After 1650, a third of the case records opened with documentary evidence, usually wills, around which the plaintiffs built their cases.

The language in which Indians submitted documentation also changed over time. During the 1560s and 1570s, Indians submitted to the Real Audiencia a broad range of documents in Nahuatl: witnesses' testimony; wills; documents concerning the sale, transfer, and/or possession of property; orders issued by indigenous

[3]It was rare, but not unheard of, for documentary evidence like wills to be submitted during the appeals process.

[4]The rates of appeal by decade are revealing. They indicate that Indians pursued their cases with great commitment but that the audiencia and the procedures instituted with the founding of the Juzgado General de Indios, especially in the years soon after its founding, were somewhat successful in decreasing the numbers of appeals. The figures by approximate decade (until the seventeenth century [note that the figures begin in 1560 due to the small number of cases before that year]) are:

    1560–69: 10 of 18 cases were appealed
    1570–79: 13 of 16 cases were appealed
    1580–89: 6 of 10 cases were appealed
    1590–99: 4 of 8 cases were appealed
    1600–49: 2 of 7 cases were appealed
    1650–1700: 6 of 11 cases were appealed

41

officials; and litigants' statements to such officials and/ or the judges of the audiencia. Over time some kinds of Nahuatl documentation presented in lawsuits diminished in frequency: litigants' statements, indigenous officials' orders, and house plans accompanied by descriptive text. Sale and property transfer documents, in contrast, did not decline in frequency, and the number of wills written in Nahuatl actually increased.

The cultural significance attached to Nahuatl documentation underwent change. By the late seventeenth century, Nahuatl was no longer simply a vehicle for presenting information; it had also become a textual signal of Indian identity. That is, litigants who sought to ground the legitimacy of ownership claims in special legal rights tended to rely heavily on Nahuatl documents. During the seventeenth century, the use of Nahuatl texts—in particular the introduction of Nahuatl wills as evidence—became an increasing point of legal contention.

ARGUMENTATION AND RHETORIC

The arguments set forth in indigenous property litigation have two distinct levels. One level, which we might call the "explicit" argument, refers to the modes of argumentation, the rhetorical devices, and the legal strategies that lawyers and litigants employed to persuade the judges to rule in their favor. The other level, which might be termed the "implicit" argument, refers instead to contested, but only partially articulated, assumptions about the nature of property rights and the foundations of legitimate ownership.[5] Particularly in the

[5] I referred to this level of argument (or "dialogue," noting that inherent in the dialogue are multiple layers of conflict embedded in a complex system of power; i.e., these are not simply discussions between equals) as the "hidden transcripts" laying behind much of the litigation unleashed by the Spanish Conquest (Kellogg 1992: 33). See Scott (1990) on the concept of "hidden transcripts."

earliest surviving court cases, those dating from 1536 to 1584, these implicit disputes over the nature of property rights and ownership were of enormous significance, reflecting the diverse responses within Indian society to the developing colonial system.

Explicit Arguments: Plots and Narratives

Efforts to reconstruct the history of property ownership form the bulk of documentation within these lawsuits. The "plot"[6] of such "narratives" was made up of descriptions of the transmission of ownership along a chain of owners culminating in the "current" owner. The plot of the earliest suits detailed the inheritance of property across three to five generations of people, usually one or two generations back into the pre-Hispanic period. The emphasis in these stories was on people and their inter-relationships with each other; less stress was placed on the nature of the property itself. In 72 percent of cases heard prior to 1585 (twenty-eight of thirty-nine), ownership was traced back to the pre-Hispanic era—usually through a version of this plot. A 1561 lawsuit offers an

[6]How can legal cases, consisting of a multiplicity of different types of documents, be said to have a plot? A useful definition of plot is to view it as the "dynamic, sequential element in narrative literature" (Scholes and Kellogg 1966: 207). While there often was not a single plot in each side's documents, the various stories told were shaped into a dominant story through an interplay of the raw story materials and lawyers' strategies and written summaries. A related issue is that of authorship; i.e., who was the primary author of these legal narratives? It is my contention that indigenous litigants were the primary authors, although Indian scribes and interpreters along with Spanish lawyers played a role in shaping the arguments made. On indigenous authorship in a very different context, see Burkhart (1992: 339–41).

There is a brief but incisive discussion of the issues raised by converting legal cases into case studies in Stone (1993: 7–9). Case studies smooth out masses of material that are often more contradictory in the record than they are in the storylike way they are conveyed by historians. When working with legal cases, one also has to remember that neither litigants nor witnesses offered the "full and unvarnished truth" (ibid., 7). One is comforted by the thought that the richness of insight into behavior, speech, and perhaps even psychology that is possible through these sources outweighs the lapses of truth that are present (ibid., 7–8).

43

example of a case in which both parties based their claim to a piece of property in a chain of inheritances rooted in the pre-Hispanic period (AGNT 19–2–3) and also shows how litigations might manipulate and evade "the facts." The case involved a dispute over a chinampa.

María Tlaco, who described herself as a woman reduced to poverty, complained to the audiencia that while she was away from Mexico City, don Luis de Paz, an Indian alcalde, had usurped a chinampa (or chinampas [the property was described differently at various points in the suit]) that was rightfully hers; she had inherited it from her grandfather, Yaotl, and it had been in the possession of her family for more than fifty years. She claimed that several years earlier (ca. 1554), the alcalde had filed a complaint with the native juez gobernador, Esteban de Guzmán, in an attempt to acquire the chinampa but that he had failed to present any supporting documentation and Guzmán thus had ruled on her behalf. She stated that she had continued to use the chinampa until 1559. Initially, in May 1561, the oidor, Gonzalo de Villalobos, found in her favor. Don Luis appealed, however, and at the end of November the audiencia ruled for him.

Further angered by this loss, María Tlaco appealed the case anew. She sought to discredit don Luis by asserting that he had "tyrannically taken" several pieces of property from their rightful owners in order to sell them (fol.123r). She also submitted a drawing that identified several plots of land that she alleged don Luis had improperly sold and provided the court with a picture of don Luis's father accompanied by the following inscription: "This was the father of don Luis and they killed him for being an adulterer" (unnumbered folio). And finally, she claimed don Luis was a "foreigner," that is, he was not a native of México Tenochtitlán.

Don Luis and his procurador, Juan de Salazar, indignantly protested María's charges. Don Luis denied usurping the property and claimed that his father's death as an adulterer was irrelevant to the matter at hand. He stated that he had temporarily exchanged the land with a native governor but that it had been returned to his possession in 1550. The alcalde further defended his claim to the land on the grounds that it was his rightful inheritance. He stated that he had inherited the chinampa from his "parents, grandparents and ancestors" (fol.124r). Fifty years before, he said, his grandfather, Cacamatzin, a descendant of past tlatoani, including Acamapichtli and Huitzilihuitl, had inherited a share of the property. What both María Tlaco and don Luis left out of their stories was that they themselves were cousins because Yaotl and Cacamatzin were brothers (see fig. 5). That the ownership of the chinampa resided in the multiple descendants of the two brothers (along with a third brother named Tilpotoncaz) and that the litigants were battling over use rights was similarly omitted.

In many legal disputes of the years following the conquest into the 1580s, Tenochcan Mexica used the "moral authority" of the preconquest past to lend legitimacy to their property rights. In most suits of this time, at least one party traced ownership back to the pre-Hispanic period, as shown above. Rightful ownership was defined both by ownership during the pre-Hispanic period and by the assertion of an unbroken chain of inheritance. But as the dispute between María Tlaco and don Luis reveals, it was often possible for both parties to construct equally compelling versions of the past. The audiencia reinforced the tendency, based in pre-Hispanic culture and practice, to view property rights as rooted in people and chains of inheritance by responding positively to these arguments.

A variant of this pattern involved cases in which indigenous litigants sought to reactivate claims to lands on which they had not recently resided. During the 1560s and 1570s, the issue of reasserting property rights appears frequently in the court records. Why in the 1560s and 1570s—forty to fifty years after the con-

Fig. 5
Source: AGNT 19-2-3, 1561

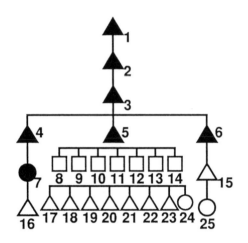

1 Acamapichtli	14 unnamed
2 Huitzilihuitl	15 Mazohuatzin
3 Eleltzin	16 Don Luis de Paz
4 Cacamatzin	17 Miguel Yacaxiuchcatl
5 Tilpotoncaz	18 Pedro Yecatlacatl
6 Yaotl	19 Antonio Tecicua
7 unnamed	20 Martín Tlacochcalcatl
8 unnamed	21 Diego Tomi
9 unnamed	22 Miguel Miccacatl
10 unnamed	23 Martín Huitzopolcatl
11 unnamed	24 Ana Tecalco
12 unnamed	25 María Tlaco
13 unnamed	

quest—did many Indians seek to reclaim sites that they, their parents, or their grandparents had abandoned? The explanation appears to involve the imposition of tribute obligations on Mexico City's Indians in 1564 (see chap. 5).

The sources of the actual conflicts varied. In some instances, property had been transferred informally; in others, it had temporarily lain unoccupied and barrio officials allowed newcomers to use it. Previous owners or their descendants responded by seeking to reclaim their ownership rights. In their legal narratives, these litigants also traced ownership back in time along a chain of inheritance. But their accounts dealt with the issue of why the legitimate owners had lost control of the property and the pre-Hispanic roots of ownership (see, e.g., AGNT 20–1–2, 1572). In a number of cases, those involved charged that colonial authorities had improperly given away a particular house site or plot of land (see, e.g., AGNT 55–5, 1564). In several other cases, a member of a family or kin group, usually an older woman who resided in a section of a house compound alone, had invited distant relatives or others to live with her (see, e.g., AGNT 30–1, 1570). When the actual residents of the site sought to pass the house compound to their children, conflict often arose. The nonresidents would try to reclaim their rights by emphasizing genealogy and chains of inheritance.

While it was common to pit legitimate rights rooted in the pre-Hispanic past against the dubious procedures of the colonial present, sometimes both parties were more concerned with the latter, basing their arguments in Spanish forms of property transmission and procedure, especially wills and dowries. An illustration of this line of response can be found in a 1573 dispute between Antón Ximénez and his stepmother, Ana Tepi (AGNT 20–1–3; also see Markov 1983). Following the death of her husband, Martín Lázaro Pantecatl, Ana took possession of a house site in San Juan Tecpancalti- tlan and a plot of land near Tula. Antón then brought suit, claiming that he was the legitimate heir of his father's property and that his stepmother had improperly asserted control over the properties while he was away. Ana, and her procurador Toribio González (see chap. 1), argued that the properties had been left to her in her husband's will. Antón countered by claiming that the property had been the dowry of his mother, Martín Lázaro Pantecatl's first wife, Beatriz Xoco (see fig. 6). He further argued that under Spanish law, his step-mother was entitled at most to a fifth of his father's total property (the *quinto*) and that in fact she had received over half of his father's estate. The alcalde was per-suaded by Antón's arguments and awarded him posses-sion of the properties. Ana appealed, arguing that un-der her husband's will she was entitled to a portion of the house compound. The audiencia ultimately decided that Ana and an illegimate son of her deceased husband should divide one-fifth of Martín Lázaro Pantecatl's property.

Another common form of argumentation found in the early lawsuits rested not on chains of inheritance but on a pre-Hispanic notion of customary land use. In disputes against nobles, a number of nonelite Indians (and in a few cases, entire communities) claimed the right, rooted in the preconquest period, to use certain plots of land. On the basis of this notion of customary land rights, litigants challenged the right of nobles to charge rents or to alienate the land through sale or donation. In responding to this argument, nobles asserted their ownership of the plots of land. Generally, the nobles traced *their* claims of ownership not to the pre-Hispanic period but to the postconquest period, and they based their claims not on inheritance but on distri-butions of lands by Hernán Cortés and other Spanish officials or on the actual purchase of the plots. These latter lines of argument suggest that some Indians (a minority—but a growing group over time) viewed Span-ish forms of property ownership and alienation as offer-ing firmer rights over and control of property than had indigenous customs; yet the audiencia did not consistently favor arguments rooted in colonial events or Spanish processes of property transmission. In the six cases in

Fig. 6
Source: AGNT 20-1-3, 1573

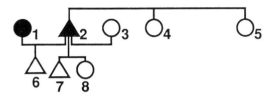

1 Beatriz Xoco (*d. ca.* 1543)
2 Martín Lázaro Pantecatl (*d. ca.* 1550)
3 Ana Tepi
4 unnamed
5 Ana Tlaco
6 Antón Ximénez
7 Hernando Icnoxochitl
8 Beatriz

which these two lines of argumentation competed (and for which decisions exist), five of them were decided in favor of the side drawing on a discourse that emphasized pre-Hispanic events and practices.

After 1585, the style of argumentation shifted. As lawyers assumed a more active role in litigation, Indians made fewer direct statements to judges. Likewise, less testimony was presented in Nahuatl; indeed, after 1610, no testimony in Nahuatl became part of the body of documentation presented to the audiencia. The use of Nahuatl was confined to documentary evidence: wills, sale and transfer documents, orders from native officials, and the texts accompanying house plans.

Coincidentally, far fewer litigants traced ownership back to the pre-Hispanic period. In only three instances

(out of twenty-two) did a party to a lawsuit root ownership in individuals alive before the conquest. And in no
instances at all did both sides in a suit trace ownership
back to the pre-Hispanic period. In another three cases,
litigants based ownership on the customary rights and
long-standing traditions of Indians. Significantly, litigants declared that these were the customary rights of
the colonial "*communidad de México.*"

During this period, litigants' narratives became less
thorough and more superficial. Litigants offered fewer
genealogical details to substantiate their claims and less
elaborate explanations of how disputes had arisen. Most
litigants claimed ownership on the basis of purchase or
on inheritance from parents who had bought the property; some, however, referred to other modes of acquisi-
tion, such as grants or rentals. While the narratives grew
more perfunctory and mechanical in style, the legal
issues raised grew increasingly complex. Among them
were the property rights of renters, the fairness of sale
prices, and the rights conferred by colonial grants of
property.

After 1650, certain trends evident in the earlier period persist: fewer people based ownership claims on
chains of inheritance, genealogy, or indigenous tradition. None at all traced ownership back to the precolonial
period though general notions of customary ownership
persisted. Nevertheless, the style of argumentation did
shift in significant ways. For one thing, narratives dating
from the second half of the seventeenth century contain
a wealth of detail and a textual richness that were not
evident in the cases between 1585 and 1650.

A 1699 lawsuit provides an example of the kinds of
detail that can be found in the late seventeenth-century
case records (AGNT 163–5, 1699). The dispute turned
on the issue of whether Felipe de Santiago had bequeathed a plot of land to his wife (via a will) or whether
he had sold it to his neighbors. The neighbors and their
witnesses claimed that the will, presented by Felipe de

Santiago's widow and nephew, was fraudulent. They insisted that he was incapable of writing a will and furthermore that the will presented to the audiencia was dated after the man's death. To substantiate their claim, the neighbors and their witnesses presented vivid testimony of Felipe's death scene. Several people insisted that he had been wounded by a bull during a fiesta in the plaza of San Joséph de Gracia. Subsequently he was carried to the "royal Indian hospital wounded by a bull with his intestines hanging" (fol.42r).[7] Too gravely wounded to receive the sacraments or to make a will, he died during the night.

The most important shift in the line of argumentation during the second half of the seventeenth century is a new emphasis on legal procedure. While litigants continued to describe property transfers at length — transfers of ownership through inheritance, sale, donation, grant, and the renting and even pawning of property — procedural arguments assumed a heightened importance. Occasionally during the sixteenth century, lawyers had raised procedural issues on appeal; by the late seventeenth century, in contrast, such matters occupied a significant role in the initial presentation of cases before the audiencia.

These procedural arguments took one of two forms: rebeldía (failure to meet legal deadlines) or fraud, including the presentation of false testimony and forged wills and letters of sale. While these changes to some degree reflect the decreased likelihood of the audiencia serving as a court of first instance, they also illustrate a significant change in Indian legal strategies: instead of emphasizing the legitimacy of their own property claims (which might be rooted in inheritance, purchase, or custom), litigants shifted the focus of attention onto

---

[7]"Lunes que hubo fiesta de toros en la Plasuela de san Joseph de Grasia lleuaron a el dho felipe de santiago a el ôspital R¹ de los yndios herido de vn toro con las tripas colgando . . ."

issues of documentation, procedure, and their adversaries' character.

Implicit Arguments

Also at stake in property litigation—apart from the particulars of any individual case—were such fundamental issues as the nature of property rights and the foundations of legitimate ownership. Especially during the sixteenth century, Indian legal cases implicitly raised a series of essential questions dealing with property rights rooted in the pre-Hispanic past. For example, would colonial law recognize indigenous kinship groups as a source of property rights? How would colonial law address issues of multiple ownership of property rooted in pre-Hispanic custom? Would the new legal system accept property rights based on marriages contrary to the tenets of Catholicism, such as polygynous unions or marriages between close kin? Would it acknowledge customary land use rights dating back to the preconquest period? Would precolonial conceptions of women's property rights be viewed as valid? Other sources of contention involved the nature of property rights on land or house compounds acquired through purchase. How broad were the property owner's rights? Could a buyer, for example, enclose the property in such a way as to block the access of other households to water or passageways?

Certain issues were actually outside the boundaries of discussion. For example, early litigants chose not to bring the issue of property rights based on polygamous or incestuous unions before the Real Audiencia. In several cases, Indians actually constructed genealogies that were designed to disguise certain kinds of consanguineal or affinal relationships (see, e.g., AGNT 35–1, 1573). In other cases, they offered only those portions of genealogies that they deemed relevant to the case at hand and failed to disclose the full range of people living at a house site or all the genealogical links through which the residents had established their rights (see, e.g., AGNT 20–1–2, 1572).

One issue that the Real Audiencia did feel compelled to address during the 1550s and 1560s involved land rights dating from the pre-Hispanic period. During this period, more than half of the surviving cases—twelve out of twenty-one—involved disputes over land. Frequently at issue was a conflict between the rights of indigenous nobles, who claimed ownership of particular plots of land, and the rights of the actual residents to collect crops raised on the disputed properties (see, e.g., AGNV 255–1 and 255–2, 1562). While elites often won these cases, in the following instance the result was different.

In 1569, the community of Santa María Tepetlalcingo sued Luis de Avila, a Spaniard, after he pressed a claim that the community owed him twenty loaves (*panes* [AGNT 24–3, 1569: fol.111r]) of salt, part of their obligation as macehual renters of land he owned. Avila based his rights of ownership on the fact that he had received the land as part of an arrangement in which he and don Gerónimo Velásquez, the son of Juan Velásquez Tlacotzin, the *cihuacoatl* (second-in-command and close advisor) under Cuauhtemoc and an early governor, had exchanged (*trocaron* [fol.112r]) houses in Mexico City, with the land included in the deal. Avila claimed that Velásquez's right to the land lay in a chain of inheritance going back to the pre-Hispanic era and that these rights had been recognized by Spanish authorities in their early postconquest distributions of land and had been reaffirmed by the native juez gobernador don Esteban de Guzmán in 1561.

The Indians contended that Velásquez's property had actually consisted of lands near theirs but separated by a fence (*tlaltenamitl* [fol.200r]). They also claimed that their lands were part of a category of lands known as *mexicatlalli* (fol.200r) (lands of the Mexica [also see Cline 1986: 150]) and implied that these were not subject to any tribute obligations. While Avila's documentation strongly supported his argument, the Real Audiencia ruled on behalf of the Indian plaintiffs, who thus managed to end an unwanted obligation.[8]

Another fundamental issue raised in litigation in the 1550s and 1560s involved disputes over who could reside in house compounds and transmit residence rights. It appears that the precolonial practice of polygyny was at the root of some of these disputes; polygyny produced multiple groups of families claiming residence and ownership rights over house sites. But as we have already noted, litigants did not directly address the issue of polygyny.

A 1563 case illustrates the complexity of cases involving possible polygyny and multiple claims of ownership (AGNT 20–2–2). Magdalena Teguycho and her niece Ana Mocel sued María Xoco over ownership of a house compound containing six rooms and six chinampas. Magdalena and her niece traced ownership of the property to Magdalena's mother (and Ana's grandmother), Matlalcihuatl Tiacapan, and to her parents, Chichimecacihuatl and Nohuehuetzin (see fig. 7). Magdalena and Ana claimed that they had allowed María to live on the site out of friendship; they denied that she had any legitimate right to the property. In response, María maintained that she was the only child of an Indian noble named Xochipanitzin, who had bequeathed her the property.

Much of the legal testimony centered on issues of kinship. Magdalena and Ana denied that María was a legitimate daughter of Nohuehuetzin and insisted that they did not know the identity of her father. Several witnesses on their behalf said that Magdalena and her sister Mocel (Ana's mother) were Nohuehuetzin's only *legitimate* children. One witness stated that "the said

<hr />

[8]On pre-Hispanic forms of land tenure, see Caso (1963); Cline (1986: 125–59); Gibson (1964: 257–64); and Kirchhoff (1954–55).

Fig. 7
Source: AGNT 20-2-2, 1563

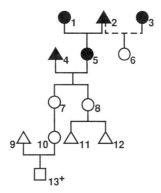

1 Chichimecacihuatl (*d. ca.* 1505)
2 Nohuehuetzin (*d. ca.* 1503)
3 Tlacocihuatl
4 Conatzin (*d. ca.* 1540s)
5 Matlalcihuatl Tiacapan
   (*d. ca.* 1540s)
6 María Xoco

7 Mocel
8 Magdalena Teguycho
9 Bartolomé
10 Ana Mocel (*b.* 1539)
11 Martín Cocoliloc
12 Juan Tentli
13 unnamed children

María is not the legitimate daughter of Tlacocihuatl but illegitimate" (fol.84r).[9] María, in turn, denied that she was related to Magdalena or Ana. But the case records raise doubts. In her interrogatorio, María very carefully avoided identifying her mother.

An oidor decided the case in María's favor. Magdalena and Ana appealed the decision. They again denied that they were in any way related to María and claimed that she was the illegitimate daughter of a slave. For her part, María repeatedly stated that her father was Xochipanitzin and evaded the issue of her mother's identity. Yet despite these repeated denials of kinship, there are some indications within the case records that the women were re-

[9]"la dha maria xoco no es hija legitima de tlacoguata sino bastarda . . ."

55

lated. Several of Magdalena and Ana's witnesses testified that María was the daughter of Tlacocihuatl, one of Nohuehuetzin's female slaves. Several of María's witnesses also stated that Tlacocihuatl was her mother. Rather than explicitly stating that María was not related to Magdalena or Ana, they said that they did not know if she was related to them. It seems clear that neither side in this case was interested in accurately describing the relationship between María, Magdalena, and Ana. It appears that this reference to a "slave woman" was a euphemistic way of describing a polygynous marriage. The audiencia's ultimate decision in the case is unknown. However, a later case, dated 1578, makes it clear that María Xoco, indeed, remained resident on the house site (see AGNT 39–1–2).

Similar issues of multiple ownership arising out of polygyny were apparent in a 1565 case (AGNT 21–1–2). The plaintiff, Pedro de San Nicolás, sought to establish ownership rights over a house compound. San Nicolás testified that his mother, Papantzin, had invited a distant relative, Martín Oçuma, to live in the house compound following her husband's death. Oçuma subsequently died, but his widow and children continued to reside there. San Nicolás asked the court to evict the widow and her child, so that he could bequeath the house compound to his own wife and children.

It appears that Oçuma was actually San Nicolás's half-brother (see fig. 8). One of the latter's witnesses testified that "Martín Oçuma, husband of the said Indian woman, María, has resided in the said houses because he is the son of an Indian slave of Quauhquechol [who was] the father of Pedro de San Nicolás" (fol.52r).[10] Once again, a reference to a slave woman appears to be, in fact, a veiled description of a polygynous marriage.[11]

[10]"min oçuma marido de la dha maria yndia a residdio en las dhas casas porques hijo de una yndia esclaba q̃ fue del dho quoavquechol padre del dho pᵒ de san nicolas . . ."

[11]Both these cases raise the interesting question of why, if they do concern

Fig. 8
Source: AGNT 21-1-2, 1565

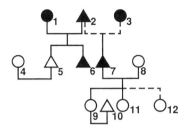

1 Juana Teucocho (*d. ca.* 1531)
2 Quauhquechol (*d. ca.* 1521)
3 unnamed
4 unnamed
5 Pedro de San Nicolás
6 Pablo Yopitli

7 Martín Oçuma (*d. ca.* 1551)
8 Marina Papan
9 unnamed
10 Gaspar (mestizo)
11 unnamed
12 unnamed

In retrospect, it appears that the underlying sources of Mexica property litigation in the sixteenth century lay in certain far-reaching demographic, economic, and social developments that had weakened earlier authority structures within indigenous society. To take one example, the high sixteenth-century Indian mortality rate, which took the lives of a disproportionate share of the male population, created an unusually large number of widows who were functioning as household heads. These women often turned to the audiencia to resolve disputes. Thus we find that the rights of widows (and their chil-

---

polygyny, did the litigants, having taken the offensive in suing kin born from secondary, polygynous unions, *not* openly raise this issue. Two explanations are possible (and these are not mutually exclusive): one is that Mexica litigants knew this practice was so abhorrent to Spaniards that they were afraid it would undermine their own ownership claims as well; a second explanation involves cultural resistance, i.e., polygyny, which probably still existed to some extent in the 1560s, was viewed as a matter that should remain internal to the Mexica community. While Indians would use Spanish law for their own material, social, or psychological good, there likely were cultural and communal limits on what they would say in pressing their claims.

dren) to inherit property—especially houses—became a major source of litigation during the mid-sixteenth century. In the 1570s, a number of lawsuits involved disputes between a deceased husband's kin group and his widow from a virilocal marriage. In the 1580s, a number of cases involved property disputes among the children of successive marriages.

Similarly, a weakening both of headship within households and of the Mexica kinship system made it increasingly difficult for extended kinship groups occupying a common house site to resolve disputes outside of the colonial legal system. The precolonial kinship system had created a complex pattern of multiple ownership of property with which demographic decline played havoc. Litigation frequently occurred when one group of residents of a house site, desperate to raise needed funds, attempted to sell their share of communal property (e.g., AGNT 42–5, 1579).

Another underlying source of litigation lay in the growing disputes between indigenous nobles and commoners over the extent of their obligations and rights. During the 1560s and 1570s, Nahua communities, even urban barrios, heavily burdened by the imposition of Spanish tribute obligations, turned to the audiencia in the hope of freeing themselves from their remaining obligations to Indian nobles. A lawsuit from the early 1560s described in the *Códice Osuna* (1947) offers an illustration of this theme. In this case, the Indian officials of a series of craft guilds sought to relieve the guilds of obligations to the alcaldes, regidores, and principales of San Juan.

A related source of litigation stemmed from claims that Indians holding high positions in the colonial governance system were abusing their positions. For example, in a 1576 case, the Indians of San Juan Tenochtitlán sued the Spanish widow and mestiza daughters of an Indian interpreter, Hernando de Tapia, over a tecpan, or palace, accusing the family of improperly seeking to privatize a piece of communal property (AGNT 37–2; also see chap. 1).

After 1590, certain issues that provoked extensive litigation during the early colonial period dwindled in frequency. Disputes over rural land became less frequent. So, too, did disputes over spousal inheritance and over the reactivation of claims to previously abandoned plots of land. Cross-status litigation between nobles and commoners also decreased.

In their place, new property issues arose. Many of the lawsuits involved disputes between descendants over the ownership of urban house sites following an owner's death. In a number of cases, nonresident children or others (many of whom were half- or stepsiblings, or more distant kin) who construed themselves as the original owner's heirs litigated to establish ownership claims (e.g., BNP 112; see chap. 1). In other cases, then-current residents of the house site argued that a then-deceased owner had sold or rented the property to them, but the owners' children or other kin claimed ownership rights (see, e.g., AGNT 163–5, 1699).

Property disputes between the indigenous population and Spaniards continued, for a time, to spawn litigation. But the terms of argumentation changed. Whereas in the earliest cases, Mexica based their claims in the pre-Hispanic past—in chains of inheritance dating back to the preconquest period or in membership in household or kin groups invested with customary rights—later litigants increasingly adopted a new line of argument: that Indian communities had a customary right to control certain distinct lands or properties, whether urban or rural (e.g., AGNT 55–2, 1589; 95–8, 1613).

This examination of the narrative structure and rhetoric embodied in property suits suggests that the Mexica were successful in manipulating the audiencia. It also suggests that the pre-Hispanic era and its "traditions" (however carefully these were constructed and crafted so as not to offend Spanish sensibilities and to meet, however vaguely, the requirements of Spanish law) had great symbolic value for a time. Yet the causes of conflict, narrative structure, and rhetoric used in legal cases underwent certain shifts. The self-conscious manipulation of Mexica and Spanish elements gave way to conflicts, narratives, and rhetoric more comfortably rooted in Hispanic legal concepts but still reflecting the special legal rights and specific social conditions of Mexico City's indigenous population.

THE REPRESENTATION OF KEY CONCEPTS

The early colonial era witnessed a critical transition in Tenochcan Mexica conceptions of property—a transition from a society in which ownership was shared and in which there were different levels of property rights to a new society in which property rights were unitary, more expansive, and much more precisely defined legally. Did Mexico City's early colonial indigenous population conceive of property as something that a person had an exclusive right to possess and dispose of in any way he or she wished? How did colonial Indians characterize and represent themselves and other individuals? Did they emphasize people's physical attributes, their social status, or their psychological character?[12] And in what terms did colonial Indians conceive of time—as a continuum, a series of historical stages?

The case records of the Real Audiencia offer cultural historians a range of voices from which to try to extract an answer. Below I examine certain underlying cultural assumptions—about property, individual character, and time—that are revealed in the court records and the way these cultural assumptions changed over two centuries.

[12]My discussion of the concept of character was influenced by Scholes and Kellogg (1966: chap. 5) and Davis (1987).

60

Property

Descriptions of property in the court records are imprecise. In the earliest cases, bills of sale and house plans sometimes provide detailed measurements of plots of land and house sites. But the litigants themselves rarely offered sharply defined descriptions of the disputed property. Indeed, at different points in a suit, litigants often presented contrasting or conflicting descriptions. For example, in the 1561 case in which María Tlaco and don Luis de Paz disputed ownership of one or more chinampas, the litigants mentioned varying numbers at various points in the litigation; in a 1579 case, both parties to the suit gave varying accounts of the number of rooms in a house that was subject to litigation (AGNT 42–5); and in a 1589 suit, both sides offered varying accounts of the size of the fields whose ownership was contested (AGNT 55–2).

There are a number of explanations for the variations in the descriptions of property. No doubt, inexact translations of testimony by Nahuatl-speaking witnesses was one problem. Another was that litigants sometimes altered their stories, especially on appeal. But probably a more important factor was that litigants had a material interest in exaggerating the size of a particular piece of property; in certain cases, their financial gain depended on the property's size, and in others, litigants may have been attempting to imply ownership of adjacent properties.

But there was yet another explanation for the imprecision in descriptions of property under litigation: the disputes were not simply over ownership of particular pieces of property; they were over social relationships. Litigants were seeking to control who could or could not live in a house compound or utilize a particular piece of land; they were seeking to determine what inheritance rights wives possessed and whether owners could sell or rent a property that they owned.

One of the most striking changes that took place in conceptions of property involved shifting notions of what constituted a house. During the sixteenth and seventeenth centuries, the usage of the Nahuatl and Spanish terms for house underwent change, reflecting a shift from earlier multiple-family residence patterns toward a greater emphasis on and occurrence of nuclear residence patterns (also see chap. 5).

Sixteenth-century Nahuatl legal texts generally referred to houses as *calli* (house or room), with the internal sections differentiated by function. In the seventeenth century, Nahuatl legal texts instead used the term *caltzintli* (calli + diminutive or reverential suffix) and rooms were rarely identified by function.[13] The term *aposento* even began to be used in Nahuatl—in place of calli—as in one will in which a house structure is referred to as simply *ome aposento* (two rooms; NL/Ayer 1481B [3d], 1679: fol.1v).

In the sixteenth century, when calli was translated into Spanish, it was often used in the plural, that is, *casas,* perhaps to indicate that each house compound was made up of separate rooms that could be owned and occupied by distinct nuclear families but also mirroring Spanish usage (Lockhart 1992: 64). Even when calli referred to a room within a structure, it might be translated variously as casa or as aposento. Over time, this usage shifted somewhat in Spanish-language documents. After 1585, it became more common to find the internal rooms of compounds referred to as aposentos. After 1600, descriptions of house structures varied more widely: casas still was used with some frequency, but other terms might be used as well, such as *aposento(s)* and *jacal(es).*[14]

Over time, however, a significant change occurred in the way that urban Indian litigants attached value to

---

[13]See Lockhart (1992: 490 [n. 16]) for a brief discussion of the somewhat ambiguous meaning of *caltzintli.*

[14]Because few seventeenth-century lawsuits dealt with land, I discuss changing land terminology in chap. 4 (which deals with wills).

property. Up to about 1585, in litigation over house sites, Indians tended to regard the house compounds themselves as the most valuable property. After that date, it was the ground on which they were built that was most highly valued. In the earlier cases, when the compound and its surrounding land was described, litigants referred to the site with the words *casas con solar* (i.e., houses with a plot of land);[15] and measurements of both the house and the house site were given. In later cases, sites were frequently described as solares[16] and less attention was paid to the house structures built on them or the measurements of the house structures. Measurements given were often confined to the solar exclusively.[17]

After 1650, litigants increasingly referred to the monetary value of house sites. By the seventeenth century, they were less interested in asserting residence rights; instead, they sought to affirm ownership rights so that they could sell or rent the property. Indeed, when seventeenth-century litigants stressed their "actual possession" of particular sites (see, e.g., AGNT 157–6, 1694), this did not necessarily mean that they were actually living on it; in many cases, this simply meant that they were receiving rents from the property.

People

How did litigants portray themselves and their adversaries in lawsuits? Throughout the early colonial period, both were portrayed in terms of a series of recognizable social types that changed over time. While such portraits

[15]This might be referred to in Nahuatl as *yn calli yn tlalli* (e.g., AGNT 48–4, 1583: fol.15r); in this case this phrase was translated into Spanish as *vnas casas y tierra* (fol.17r).

[16]See AGNT 157–7, 1694, for an example of a case focusing more on the plot of land and less on the structures. Solares were referred to in Nahuatl either as *tlalmantli* (see, e.g., the will of Juan de la Cruz, 1679, NL/Ayer 1481B [3d]: fol.1r) or simply as *tlalli* (e.g., will of Martin Xochitl, 1604, AGNBN 1455–5: fol.29r).

[17]Here I am referring to how litigants described property within the actual texts of litigations, not bills of sale. On bills of sale, see Horn (1989a: chap. 4).

of distinct character types were certainly stereotypical, they remain valuable because they point to the emergence of new social roles and identities across the colonial period.

One social type that appears frequently in the earliest legal texts is the lone woman or widow defending her rights. Another is the noble, descended from kings, surrounded by supporters, and tied politically to Spaniards. Yet another character type is the "common" man who claimed ownership of modest holdings. Sometimes he appeared before the audiencia to make a claim for his own holdings; sometimes he went to defend his wife's ownership of property.

A minor character type found in the court records is the Spanish litigant. This character was virtually always male; during the sixteenth century, he tended to attach himself to Indians who actually pursued the suits as the prior owners. He was portrayed as a bystander who allowed Indians to defend his property rights.

Alongside these social types stood a number of collective actors, such as the kinship group, centered around a core of siblings and cousins. It also could consist of more distant kin and sometimes friends and political supporters of the nobles and/or colonial officials who might be members of these groups. Frequently, but not invariably, these kin groups claimed to be able to trace their genealogies back to a high noble or tlatoani in the pre-Hispanic period.

Another group of collective actors one frequently encounters in the court records was the Indian community—the barrio, *estancia* (small, subordinate indigenous community), or pueblo. This group, which was always represented by its governing officials, appears in disputes in which the collectivity was asserting its customary communal rights against claims of individual ownership. Communities based their rights on some form of tradition, which could usually be traced back to the precolonial period. This is precisely what the pueblo

of Cuitlatenamic did in 1573, when it sued Juana Her-
nández and her sister Magdalena Xoco over a house site
in San Juan Necaltitlan. The gobernador, alcaldes, regidores, principales, and *tequitlatos* (officials who were
charged with assessing tribute) of Cuitlatenamic argued
that they had owned and occupied this site for a lengthy
period prior to the conquest, residing there whenever
they came to the city of Mexico to conduct business and
pay tribute to Moctezuma II. We earlier saw the parcialidad of San Juan appeal to both pre-Hispanic practices and an emerging colonial tradition in their suit
against the wife and daughters of Hernando de Tapia.

In case records of the earliest colonial period, litigants tended to present themselves in certain stereotypical ways: female litigants constantly referred to themselves as poor; male commoners identified themselves as
hardworking and responsible craftsmen or agricultural
laborers; communities portrayed themselves as steeped
in tradition. By 1585, a recognizable shift had occurred.
For example, the indigenous official had clearly become
a *colonial* figure who no longer justified his authority by
calling on his royal genealogy. Similarly, the Spanish
litigant no longer tied himself to the previous indigenous owners. The Spaniard now expressed confidence
in his property rights, gained through purchase or
grant. He expressed indignation at having his title challenged by Indians (see, e.g., AGNT 54–2, 1587; 56–4,
1590; or 58–7, 1595). The emergence of the threatening
Spaniard foreshadows an important theme in late seventeenth-century lawsuits and in the sociocultural system
of that period: the development of a clear-cut racial
hierarchy that in and of itself signaled social characteristics that Spanish or casta litigants and Spanish lawyers intended judges to view as legal impediments.[18]
And after 1585, a new character type entered the cases:

[18]On the subject of race in colonial Mexico, see, e.g., Mörner (1967); Israel
(1975); Chance (1978); and Seed (1982).

the "minor," a child who needed adults, especially either the mother or a legal guardian, to safeguard his or her property rights. But other familiar figures exited the scene: especially the kin-based group as litigants. Other types persist, such as the lone woman defending her rights and the common man suing to protect his own or his wife's property rights.

Further shifts in the portrayals of participants occur after 1650. The stereotype of the hardworking husband is replaced by a new image of a conjugal couple in which the husband strongly defends his wife's smallholding. But the lone woman litigant vanished. The earlier extended kin-based groups were replaced by groups consisting of full siblings. The category of non-Indian litigants expanded after 1650 with the appearance of black, mestizo, and nonelite Spanish plaintiffs or defendants. The non-Indian litigant now used race as a pejorative cultural marker.

Throughout the early colonial period, participants often characterized their adversaries in disparaging terms. As we saw earlier, María Tlaco characterized her adversary, don Luis, as a tyrant and the son of an adulterer, and he responded by calling her a slave's daughter. Nevertheless, sixteenth-century lawsuits tend to contain far fewer negative portrayals than later cases. During the sixteenth century, litigants and lawyers focused their attention on the "facts" of the case, emphasizing specific histories of ownership. Litigants rarely examined the merits of the other side's case.

This is not to say that plaintiffs and defendants drew no pejorative characterizations of their adversaries. Frequently, litigants described their opponents as devious. Sometimes, they claimed that their opponent was being manipulated by a Spaniard (see, e.g., AGNT 30–3, 1570). This accusation was commonly made against female litigants. In one 1576 case, Spanish litigants employed this argument against an Indian barrio government (AGNT 37–2, 1576). This rhetorical strategy was commonly used by litigants who knew their opponents would be perceived by the audiencia as weak and needing of protection.

Another accusation leveled against adversaries was that they were violent and disorderly people. In a number of cases, the participants charged that their opponents had caused altercations and had forcibly usurped property (e.g., AGNT 23–2–4, 1568). The notion of disturbance recurs in descriptions of opposing litigants as "troublesome" (*inquieto*) and as people who enjoyed conflict (see AGNT 20–2–2, 1563; 55–5, 1564; 39–1–2, 1578; 46–4, 1581). Frequently, litigants contrasted the aggressive nature of their adversaries with their own tranquil nature. They described their own property ownership as "quiet and peaceful" and "without contradiction."

Elite Indians frequently mentioned the humble origins of their opponents (e.g., AGNT 19–2–3, 1561; 24–3, 1569; also see Durán 1967: I:11:115). While belittling their adversaries' status, they characterized themselves as charitable and generous. They asserted that they had allowed needy persons to use property that they now unjustly claimed for themselves.

Frequently, in the latter stages of a case, plaintiffs or defendants made specific attacks against their opponents' witnesses, claiming that they were untrustworthy or had received bribes in return for their testimony or had an interest in the case's outcome, for example, that they were relatives of the opposing party (e.g., AGNT 29–5, 1570; 35–6, 1574; 37–2, 1576).

Clearly, indigenous litigants were eager to create certain images of themselves in the eyes of the oidores. They portrayed themselves as peaceful, hardworking, and deserving, desiring only to control what was truly theirs. They claimed that their adversaries not only sought to usurp property wrongfully, without right and often by force but also enjoyed provoking conflict.

During the seventeenth century, derogatory references to adversaries and their witnesses grew more common. Accusations that adversaries had violently removed property or disturbed the peace of a neighborhood or community were supplanted by harsher, more personal attacks. Litigants described their opponents as malicious people with sinister intentions. Increasingly, non-Indian litigants used race to attack their foes by playing on racial stereotypes and accusing Indians of being untruthful.[19] Indians, in turn, asserted that non-Indians did not possess the same legal rights as themselves. Lawyers began to subject the testimony of witnesses to close scrutiny, identifying alleged contradictions and pinpointing inaccuracies.

In short, during the seventeenth century, litigants made a more determined effort to identify and exploit the weaknesses of their opponents' cases. In a number of instances, this took the form of accusing adversaries of illegal acts, such as submitting fraudulent documents. These accusations were designed to influence the oidores, to make them see the opponents not only as engaged in questionable activities but as immoral as well.[20] These shifts are signs of a new interest in the individual characteristics of opponents (i.e., new ways of thinking about and describing social relationships).

Time, History, and the Legal Process

In the cases heard before 1585, the Mexica often referred to two expanses of time: the period preceding and the period following the conquest. In their descriptions of the preconquest period, litigants described specific ancestors, employing a single Nahuatl name. They

[19]In AGNT 101–6, 1645, Juan de la Cruz, a *"chino esclavo,"* accused María de la O, an Indian woman, of offering a "sinister narrative" of their conflict (fol.2r).

[20]This connection was made evident by the procurador Juan Leonardo de Sevilla who refuted a will he viewed as a fabrication by saying that he presented to "God and the cross" the weak claims of his opponents (AGNT 128–2, 1682: fol.13v).

also mentioned specific aspects of pre-Hispanic life, for example, the inheritance of land and the payment of tribute. Indians tended to emphasize the importance of custom during the precolonial period, frequently stating that a particular practice "always" occurred in a certain way. Thus, litigants might state that land was "always" owned and worked by specific families (e.g., AGNT 17–2–1, 1557; 17–2–4, 1559). References to "custom," however, were both subtle and highly context-specific; it appears that the Mexica took the cultural contexts of their practices for granted and did not feel that they needed to be described in detail (the section on colonial symbols below examines seventeenth-century Indian notions of custom).

When litigants wanted to clearly signal that they were referring to the pre-Hispanic past, they identified it simply as "the time before the Spanish came" (e.g., AGNT 55–5, 1564: fol.16r) or they used references to Cortés (e.g., AGNT 23–2–4, 1568: fol.214r). The *causes* of a particular legal conflict, however, never were traced to the precolonial past; litigants only assigned ownership rights to the preconquest period. In their testimony, colonial Mexica tended to represent the pre-Hispanic past as a period of customary rules, rigid hierarchy, kinship, and peaceful ownership. The "present," in marked contrast, was a time of discord, disease, and endless legal wrangling (also see Zorita 1942: 40–41).

Clearly, by the seventeenth century, the pre-Hispanic past had become a symbol rather than a real memory (also see Wood 1991a). After 1600, Nahuas evoked the preconquest period much less frequently and with less detail (the one persistent, though by this time relatively uncommon, reference to the precolonial period was the use of a single Nahuatl name). One of the latest references in the court records to the pre-Hispanic period can be found in a 1613 case. The leaders of the barrio San Antón Acatlan sued to overturn the sale of a solar; they based their action on their traditional title to this property, stating that their ancestors had owned it "before this land was won" (AGNT 95–8, 1613: fol.1r, 4r). Though disconnected from any specific historical or genealogical details rooted in the pre-Hispanic past to substantiate it, the Real Audiencia accepted this notion of aboriginal ownership (see AGNT 103–2–6, 1653).

In structuring their legal narratives chronologically, sixteenth-century litigants often organized their pleadings in terms of a succession of legal actions. For example they frequently cited the orders of the early oidores Ceynos and Zorita as a basis for ownership. In fact, Ceynos and Zorita were the two Spaniards most often mentioned in these texts, and both seem to have been held in some regard by the indigenous population. The pleadings also described at length earlier judicial decisions. Thus, the legal process itself served an important role by providing markers through which Indians constructed linear chronologies and histories in these suits.

After 1600, descriptions of earlier legal decisions appear less often in litigants' pleadings. Instead, participants present a history of ownership, substantiated by wills and documents of sale and transfer. By the mid-seventeenth century, Indians rarely couched property rights in terms of custom or practice. Instead, like Spaniards, they based ownership claims on written documents, such as wills and bills of sale. Spanish law and legal practice had become the standard by which property rights were understood.

Symbols

Embedded within legal narratives, one encounters a number of key cultural symbols that indigenous litigants invoked to influence the decisions of the audiencia's judges. In certain cases, these were Mexica symbols, through which they conveyed notions of status and power, appropriate behavior, and kinship relationships. In other instances, they were Spanish symbols, through which Indian litigants communicated their acceptance of particularly significant Spanish values. Over time, there appeared a new hegemonic set of colonial symbols.

Mexica Symbols: Indian litigants sometimes embraced certain pre-Hispanic Mexica symbols of power to enhance their social status. For example, during the sixteenth century, a number associated themselves genealogically with past Mexica tlatoani, or rulers. The mere reference to a ruler or other high officials such as a cihuacoatl implied some genealogical relationship, however vaguely defined by litigants.

Elites frequently sought to paint a negative portrait of their opponents by calling them macehuales or terrazgueros, terms that symbolized low social status and implied that they should not be awarded property. Disputes over status became increasingly common during the seventeenth century when litigants frequently identified themselves with the term *don,* to suggest high social status. Occupation was also used to denote status; for example, in a number of instances, litigants described themselves as merchants (e.g., AGNT 49–5, 1585).

They also frequently invoked Mexica symbols of order and disorder in their testimony. As we have already seen, in a number of cases from the early colonial period, litigants accused each other of disorderly conduct or of fomenting arguments. In part, this was simply a tactic used to discredit an adversary. But this concern with order and disorder had larger cultural meanings. As Miguel León-Portilla and Louise Burkhart (1989: chap.4) have persuasively demonstrated, Nahuatl culture showed an intense interest in promoting "appropriate and righteous" behavior (León-Portilla 1963: 153) and discouraging disorderly conduct (also see Offner 1983: 242–55). A number of litigants paradoxically relied on Spanish law to quell agitators and to control the behavior of those who were regarded as excessively opportunistic, thus expressing a Nahua cultural concern.

Mexica kinship symbols also recur in the legal narratives. Consider the "autochthonous couple." In the early cases before the audiencia, Indians frequently traced ownership back several generations to a married couple. The idea of the founding couple resonates strongly with a kinship system in which male and female had separate but equivalent rights and responsibilities (Kellogg 1986a, 1988; also see chap. 3). It also corresponds to conceptions of Nahua deities with androgynous aspects who were often depicted in pairs, as married couples (Nicholson 1971: 409, 410–30; Clendinnen 1991: 167–69).

Another example of a recurring kinship symbol in the narratives is the corporate sibling-based kin group. Not only were siblings frequently represented as co-owners of properties, who shared a common inheritance, but litigants sometimes traced property ownership back or through to a "founding group" of siblings, who transmitted rights to an extended kinship group (Kellogg 1980, 1986a). In sixteenth-century litigation, Indians attached a great deal of significance to a litigant's membership either in a particular kinship unit (e.g., AGNT 55–5, 1564) or in a residential group (e.g., BNP 112, 1593). While the use of kinship symbols persisted into the late sixteenth and seventeenth century, their nature underwent an important transformation: litigants increasingly emphasized lineal transmission of property from a single owner, reflecting changes in ideas about both property ownership and kinship. Beginning in the late sixteenth century, married couples or sibling groups were rarely identified as the original owners of Indian properties. By the late seventeenth century, ownership of property was rarely traced more than two generations above a litigant or testator and was traced back to a single owner, not a couple or a sibling group (also see chaps. 4 and 5).

Spanish Symbols: Litigants who wished to appear so-
phisticated or acculturated incorporated Spanish symbols into their legal narratives. Before 1585, such symbols were rare and often awkwardly used; after that
date, explicit use of Spanish symbols became increasingly common. A 1573 case, described earlier in this
chapter, offers an early example of the invocation of a
Spanish legal concept—the quinto, or fifth—in a property suit (AGNT 20–1–3). Another early example of the
explicit use of a Spanish legal concept can be found in
Hernando de Tapia's will in which he lists his *universales
herederos* (AGNT 37–2: fol.92r),[21] a concept that never
became standard in colonial Mexica wills.

Litigants also employed the Spanish concept of dowry. Although Indian nobles had a practice similar to the
European notion of dowry (Cline 1986: 116), it seems
clear that those indigenous litigants and their lawyers
who introduced the concept did so to justify property
rights in Spanish terms (see, e.g., BNP 112, 1593).

Hoping to suggest that they had the support of
Spanish power and authority, litigants frequently invoked the names of early oidores who were said to have
looked favorably on particular claims (e.g., AGNT 2729–
20, 1562: fol.18v). A device that Indians invoked to
indicate their good character was to assert that they used
the property in question to pay Spanish tribute (e.g.,
AGNT 29–5, 1570: fol.10r).

A dispute between the indigenous officials of San
Juan Tenochtitlán and the widow and daughters of
Hernando de Tapia illustrates the way that Spanish legal
and political symbols were manipulated in an effort to
influence the decisions of the audiencia (AGNT 37–2,
1576). The officials argued that the property contested

[21]The concept of a universal heredero referred to the inheritor who inherits
all, most, or the residual parts of an estate (i.e., what is left after individual
legacies). There is a useful discussion of the history and meaning of the concept
in the entry for *heredero* in the *Enciclopedia universal ilustrada Europeo-Americana*
(1958–68: XXI:1151–52).

in the case, a tecpan, was communal and not personal property and that communal ownership rested on both pre-Hispanic tradition and events of the colonial period. To support this argument, the officials invoked a number of potent Spanish symbols (yet combined these subtly with certain trappings of an earlier sovereignty).

> Your royal symbols [coats of arms] are placed in them [i.e., the rooms of the tecpan] and they are accustomed to performing many ceremonies of the community and your oidores, Quiroga and Ceynos, visited the Indian prisoners in them and Don Pablo Yguanici and Don Diego and another Don Diego Vcingui who were governors of [the Indian barrios of] Mexico lived and resided in them as a common house and the priests who were in charge of the church of San Pablo resided in these houses with the consent of the said governors where they had their feather-work and ancient pictures and the tributes belonging to His Majesty. (fol.39r)[22]

Note the officials' implication that the community's claim to the tecpan had been affirmed by earlier Spanish colonial officials as well as by Catholic priests.

The use of Catholic symbols and imagery by Indians became increasingly pronounced after 1585. However, the earliest invocations of Christianity as an emblem of good character date from the early 1570s, when litigants or witnesses began occasionally to describe themselves in their testimony as "good Christians" (e.g., AGNT 20–1–2, 1572: fol.203r).

---

[22]estan puestas en ellas vras armas reales y solian hazerse muchas fiestas en ellas de la comunydad y siendo bros oydores los dotores quiroga y ceynos visitaron a los yndios presos en ellas y don pablo yguanici y don di° y otro don di° de vcingui gouernadores q fueron de la pte de mex^co como en casa comun la abitaron y moraron y los clerigos que tenian cargo de la yglesia de san pablo posaban de consentimi° de los dhos gobernadores en las dhas casas sin pagar por ello cosa algu^a y como en casa de comun se ponian los materiales de las obras publicas de la pte de mex^co y tenian las casas donde tenian su plumeria y pinturas antiguas y los tribut°s pertenencientes a su mag^t . . .

Indian widows, in particular, identified themselves as "good Christians" to bolster their property rights. These women and their lawyers used both Spanish law and religious images. The latter were expressed through increasing use of the phrase "legitimate wife" (*mujer legítima*) in these texts. In 1570, María Tiacapan referred to herself as a "mujer legítima," but this was not a highly elaborated image (AGNT 30–1, 1570: fol.9r). In 1578, Magdalena Ramírez argued that she and her daughter should inherit a part of a house site from her deceased husband, Pedro Luis. Magdalena's documents, especially her interrogatorio, described her as having married "according to the law and with the blessing of the holy mother Church" (AGNT 39–1–2, 1578: fol.33r).[23]

By the 1580s, references to Christian marriage ceremonies had become frequent. And during that decade, children or grandchildren often referred to the marriages of their parents or grandparents in this manner. In a 1583 case, there was an explicit attempt to employ Christian imagery against a litigant (AGNT 48–4, 1583). The plaintiffs argued, probably untruthfully and definitely unsuccessfully, that the defendant was the product of an incestuous marriage. This type of strategy and use of imagery contrasts with earlier tendencies for both sides to cover up relationships that were not licit in Spanish eyes. Just as marriages were increasingly characterized as legitimate, so children were described as their legitimate issue. Thus, the moral character of litigants increasingly was asserted and depicted as flowing from adherence to the Church-sanctioned nuclear family.

Catholic symbols — such as references to marriages as legitimate — continued to be used in seventeenth-century legal narratives, but they grew less common after 1650. Interestingly, two of the seventeenth-century cases

---

[23]"a ley y bendicion de la madre sancta yglesia . . ."

in which Catholic symbols were invoked involved the efforts of Indian barrios to justify the collective owner- ship of land within the barrios on the grounds that the land was used for religious purposes (see AGNT 95–8, 1613; 103–2–6, 1653).

Colonial Symbols: Prior to 1585, indigenous litigants seldom attempted to use Spanish *and* Mexica symbols in combination, to form new and distinctive *colonial* sym- bols. Litigants more commonly used one set of symbols or the other, and when they did appeal to both (as in BNP 112 as described in chap. 1), the appeal was part of purposeful legal and rhetorical strategies, not a rela- tively unconscious interweaving of traditions. But from 1585 to 1650, as a colonial Indian culture developed, new symbols emerged and are very clear in cases heard after 1650. These symbols reflect a hegemonic construc- tion.

One example of such a symbol is the reliance on Nahuatl documentation as a basis for claims of property ownership. Prior to 1585, as described earlier, a great variety of documentation provided to the audiencia was in Nahuatl. This material offered empirical information to the oidores. The indigenous context for the produc- tion of such documents was also stressed, especially the public, communal act of witnessing by a large group (also see Lockhart 1985: 473–75; Horn 1989*a:* 163–69). But over time, Nahuatl documents and Indian witness- ing took on new meanings. The presence of witnesses not only satisfied the requirements of Spanish law but also symbolized the right of Nahua communities to oversee their own property transactions. Nahuatl docu- ments themselves, which became fewer in number and increasingly problematic in legal contexts, also took on new meanings, self-consciously symbolizing the special legal rights Indians had developed.

Another example of a hegemonic symbol is apparent in the invocation of indigenous custom as a defense of property rights. In the mid-sixteenth century, Nahua communities did not advance the argument that Indians possessed special legal rights. Instead, they based claims to ownership of communal properties either by presenting detailed and highly specific arguments based on genealogy and inheritance or by forging alliances with individual Spaniards. During the seventeenth century, in contrast, Indian communities took the position that they held certain special rights. Indian litigants defended the right of these communities and their officials to maintain and protect barrio properties, arguing that this practice was rooted in everyday life in the pre-Hispanic and colonial periods (e.g., AGNT 95–8, 1613; 101–6, 1645; 103–2–6, 1653).

The notion of special indigenous rights rooted in custom could cut two ways. Alongside it arose a new racial consciousness, which tended to explain Indian behavior in terms of an irrational Indian nature. In one case, a procurador explained a seemingly unusual bequest from his client's father by stating that "Indians do not observe the precise law in their ultimate dispositions because they distribute their few goods as they wish" (AGNT 155–9, 1693: fol.14r).[24] In another case, a procurador attacked the credibility of a litigant's witnesses on explicitly racial grounds, commenting, "Each side has presented three witnesses, those for my side are of better quality because among them are a Spaniard and a mestizo; and the three opposing [witnesses] are all Indians, whose nature diminishes the faith that can be given to the witnesses" (AGNT 163–5, 1699: fol.61r).[25]

---

[24]"los indios no obseruan la puntualidad del derecho en sus disposisiones vltimas porq̃ ellos distribuyen sus cortos bienes a su arbitrio . . ."

[25]"cada una [de las partes] ha pressentado tres testigos, los de mis partes son de mexor calidad por auer entre ellos un español, y un mestisso; y los tres contrarios ser todos Yndios, cuya naturalessa diminuye la fee q̃ se deue dar a los testigos."

DECISIONS: RESPONSES TO INDIAN LEGAL TEXTS

How effective were the particular legal and rhetorical strategies used by Indians and their lawyers? How did judges respond to the arguments advanced by indigenous litigants? Because oidores left few descriptions of their experiences (Zorita 1942; Ceynos 1866: 158–64, 237–43), and because these are quite general and offer no special insight into the decision-making processes, we must turn to the texts of actual decisions to consider the effectiveness of particular pleadings. While the decisions tended to be clear-cut—for the plaintiff or for the defendant, with few compromise decisions—the oidores' rulings referred neither to specific laws nor to precedents. Indeed, they frequently reversed earlier decisions issued by indigenous officials (thereby undercutting their authority) (e.g., AGNT 55–5, 1564; 24–3, 1569; also see *CO* 1947).

While decisions generally conformed to the demands of Spanish property law (Markov 1983), the texts of decisions reveal that the early oidores had a special paternalistic concern with overseeing the affairs and regulating the conduct of Indians. The decisions of oidores hearing cases through the mid-1580s tended to be both protective and paternalistic. Ceynos, for example, issued the following order:

> When someone disturbs her [one Ana Xoco to whom Ceynos had given possession] in her ownership of the entrance to the said houses and chinampas, they should appear before His Honor and, having appeared, justice will be done to them. (AGNT 35–1, 1573: fol.16r)[26]

Judicial paternalism took a number of forms. At times, oidores sought to minimize disorder among Indi-

[26]"quando alguna persona le perturbaren en la posesion de la entrada de las dhas cassas y camellones de tierra parezca ante su md y parescidos les hara just[a]."

ans. In a number of decisions from the early colonial period, they demanded that the litigants granted possession of property not be disturbed by their adversaries. In cases in which there had been a break in ownership (e.g., where property had been abandoned during the conquest) the decisions reveal a desire to protect the property rights of the original owners. The oidores overturned later sales and grants (even when these had been made in good faith) and evicted then-current residents from rooms and house compounds (see, e.g., AGNT 55–5, 1564; 22–1–5, 1567). In the earliest cases, the judges frequently requested additional information from litigants, suggesting that they had a real interest in the specific circumstances surrounding litigants' stories (see AGNT 20–2–2, 1563: fol.123r; 32–1, 1575: fol.12v, 21r).

After 1585, the texts of decisions manifest appreciably less interest in the actual circumstances of litigants; for example, the oidores issued fewer requests for information. This may reflect in equal parts the increasing bureaucratization of the colonial court system, the widening social distance between the judges of the audiencia and the Indian litigants who came before them, and the development of a more rigid racial hierarchy.

But shifting patterns of decision making after 1585 also suggest an attempt by the oidores to reinforce the legitimacy of property sales. A 1589 case illustrates the concern with supporting property claims based on purchase (AGNT 55–6). Cristina de la Cruz, an Indian woman, bought a house site from another Indian, Rafael Xuárez, for forty-five pesos. The parties agreed that the purchase price would be divided into three payments of ten, twenty and fifteen pesos. Cristina had already paid thirty pesos when a mestizo *solicitador*, Toribio de Alcaraz, tried to return her money on the grounds that Xuárez no longer wished to sell the property. Xuárez later testified that he sought to return the funds because the sale had caused his wife pain (fol.5v).

79

Agustina Ana, Rafael Xuárez's wife, then explained that the house site was actually hers because she had inherited it from her parents. She claimed that her parents had originally purchased the site and that her husband had forced her to sell it against her will (fols. 6r–7r). She further described how she had given Alcaraz thirty pesos and implored him, in front of witnesses, to return the money to Cristina de la Cruz. Perhaps because she was unable to furnish documents proving that her parents had purchased the site and bequeathed it to her, Agustina Ana was not able to persuade the audiencia that she was indeed the legitimate owner of the property.

It seems likely that Agustina Ana was truthful in her claim that she, not her husband, was the house site's owner. Her husband acknowledged that it was she who was opposed to the sale. Additionally, it was she who pursued a lengthy series of fruitless appeals to overturn the court's decision to award the property to Cristina de la Cruz. Nevertheless, neither the alcalde ordinario nor the audiencia ever accepted her argument. The alcalde ruled that the sale was valid and ordered Cristina to pay the last installment to complete the purchase of the property. He also ordered Alcaraz, the mestizo solicitor, not to interfere with Cristina's ownership and to move out of the barrio. In strictly legal terms, the decision about the property was out of line with Spanish law. According to the *Siete Partidas,* a sale did not take place until the full purchase price had been paid (P3.T28.L46). It seems that in this case the court's primary concern was to sanction the validity of agreements to sell property. This decision contrasts with the more paternalistic and protective concerns of the oidores in the sixteenth century.

After 1600, and especially after 1650, there were several other noteworthy changes in judicial decisions. For one, the texts of decisions grew longer as they began to include brief summaries in which the judges identified what they perceived as the key issues raised by litigants. In a 1613 case, in which the barrio of San Antón Acatlan successfully overturned a sale to a Spaniard of property that the community claimed to have traditionally controlled and used for religious purposes (in this case, for Catholic, not Mexica, rites), the case summary suggested that the oidores were persuaded by the the barrio's claim based on customary rights over the property (AGNT 95–8, 1613: fols. 78v–79r).

A second innovation is that the phrase *autos y méritos* appears in seventeenth-century decisions, suggesting that oidores wished to emphasize that they considered both laws and rules *and* the merits, or particularities, of individual cases in rendering decisions. Perhaps judges were attempting to demonstrate their impartiality at a time of increasing friction with viceroys, who began to take an increasing role in judicial decision making beginning in the 1590s (also see Borah 1983: 80–9, 113–14). Because of the penchant of viceroys to make judicial decisions in individual cases, the audiencia was forced sometimes to rule either for (e.g., AGNT 183–4, 1607: fol.53r) or against them (AGNT 157–6, 1694: fol.49r) when decisions were appealed.

During the seventeenth century, one of the primary grounds for judicial decisions involved the introduction by litigants of documents indicating that a valid property transfer had occurred (see AGNT 1720–7, 1633: fol.53r; 103–2–6, 1653: fols.115r, 242r–242v; 128–2, 1682: fols.54r–55r; 157–6, 1694: fol.49r). But while such decisions appeared to be impartial, there is reason to believe that the judges' racial beliefs influenced decision making. It was not uncommon for the judges of the audiencia to reject much Indian documentation as false (e.g., AGNT 128–2, 1682: fol.54r) even when they accepted from Spaniards documentation that appears to have been equally flawed (e.g., AGNT 103–2–6, 1653: fols.115r, 242r–242v).

CONCLUSION

In analyzing shifts in legal narratives and strategies, forms of argumentation, rhetorical devices, and judicial decision making, we have observed a process of mutual accommodation. The forms of legal argumentation and rhetoric were particularly revealing of the largely unconscious shifts occurring in colonial Mexica conceptualizations of conflict and social relationships. On the one hand, Spanish notions of property, ownership, and legal process were establishing their hegemony over more traditional Mexica modes of thought, ideas of ownership, and mechanisms for resolving disputes. On the other hand, the Spanish legal framework was relatively plastic and malleable. It offered Indians a variety of ways of describing common social dramas and asserting their claims, which they proceeded, energetically, to use. Furthermore, we have seen that while New Spain's legal system did not emphasize case law or precedent in the way that the Anglo-Saxon system did, informal precedents arose which allowed indigenous individuals and communities to claim special rights.[27] This ethnographic interrogation of legal texts illustrates the essential point that Indians, through their strategic, rhetorical, and symbolic efforts, were able to exert a significant influence on the outcomes of specific lawsuits. Yet the practices and procedures involved in presenting cases before the audiencia, especially the shifting rhetoric for portraying social dramas, provided equally strong influences on Mexica conceptions of property, personhood, time, and kinship.

[27]But these rights were not so much syncretic (i.e., unconscious blends) as hegemonic, developing out of accommodations between Spanish law and the realities of colonial Mexica circumstances.

PART TWO

The Social History of Everyday Life

CHAPTER 3

Law and the Transformation of Women's Roles

During the early colonial period, Tenochcan Mexica women participated in legal processes to a degree almost without parallel in other areas of colonial domination in the New World. More than Maya women in southern Mexico or women in most other parts of Spanish America, Tenochcan Mexica women engaged in litigation.[1]

This raises a number of significant scholarly questions. Why were indigenous women so active as litigants? Did Mexica women and men participate in the colonial legal process in the same way? Did they present similar legal arguments before the audiencia? And most important, how did women's legal status change over time, and how were these changes linked to other cultural transformations?

In chapter 1, we saw that well over half of all sixteenth- and seventeenth-century Indian property litigation included women as plaintiffs and defendants. And it was suggested that there was a pronounced gender difference in the kinds of property under litigation; that over time fewer women initiated lawsuits independently; and that by the seventeenth century, husbands had become the primary parties in lawsuits. This chapter accounts for those characteristics; it also probes how changes in gender roles were related to the growth of Spanish cultural hegemony.

---

[1]Andean women also participated in litigation (Silverblatt 1987; Zulawski 1990), but it is difficult to assess their rates of litigation in comparison with Andean men or Mexica women and men in Mexico City.

The preceding chapter examined the legal arguments, rhetorical strategies, and narrative structures
that indigenous litigants employed before the Real Audiencia to uncover underlying cultural assumptions, attitudes, and perceptions. In this and the succeeding chapters of the book, the documents that litigants submitted
to the audiencia are treated as sources for cultural and
social history, which allows us to reconstruct everyday
structures and customs of Mexica life and the ways these
were transformed between the late pre-Hispanic and
early colonial periods. I will argue that the roots of
Spain's hegemonic colonial social system lay in the ac-
cretion of sometimes small, sometimes more dramatic
changes in everyday life and, ultimately, in patterns of
cognition, thought, values, and ideologies.[2]

The second half of this book seeks to address a lacuna
in our knowledge of the internal structure and organization of the Indian barrios of Tenochtitlán-Tlatelolco
during the early colonial period, drawing on the statements of litigants and witnesses and the various forms of
documentation that they introduced before the audiencia as well as chronicles and parish records. Unlike other
ethnohistorians, who generally adopt a "top-down" approach, starting with the largest, most encompassing
organizational units (see Calnek 1976 and Clendinnen
1991 for especially well written and authoritative uses of
this approach), I will utilize a "bottom-up" approach,
which asks how individual Indians saw themselves as
connected to families and kin groups and broader economic and political structures.[3]

Among the structures through which the colonial
Tenochcan Mexica organized their everyday lives were
gender, inheritance, and kinship. This chapter focuses

[2]On the importance of the "everyday" for uncovering both structures and
resistance, see Certeau (1984). Also see Bourdieu (1978) and Ortner (1984).

[3]I have something organizationally different in mind with the distinction
between "top-down" and "bottom-up" approaches than does Cohn (1987: 39–
42) in his discussion of "proctological history."

on transformations in gender roles and ideologies; chapter 4 analyzes changing inheritance patterns; and chapter 5 investigates shifting kinship patterns. We will discover that gender played a critical role in the emergence of a colonial social order in New Spain because the transformation of Mexica men's and women's relationships bore a dialectical relationship to key aspects of Mexica society: politics, economics, religion, and kinship and family organization. That is, the organization of practices and ideologies in each of these domains of activity helped to shape and was in turn shaped by gender relations. As political organization, economic activity and labor organization, and religious beliefs and practices underwent far-reaching transformations, so, too, did gender relations. Yet shifts in gender relations initiated further changes in other areas of human activity.

Why were sixteenth-century Tenochchan Mexica women actively involved in property litigation? In part, their engagement was rooted in pre-Hispanic patterns of gender relations, which gave Mexica women certain property rights and endowed them with "jural adulthood."[4] It also rested, in part, on the demographic upheavals of the early sixteenth century, which unbalanced sex ratios and generated numerous property disputes. By the seventeenth century, however, as pre-Hispanic gender ideologies declined and demographic conditions stabilized, the legal status of Mexica women

[4] I define "jural adulthood" as the capacity to take social and legal responsibility for one's self as an *adult,* even if the concept of adult personhood is thoroughly "genderized" as it was among the Mexica (i.e., the adult woman was treated as one kind of human being, whereas the adult man was another). Those societies in which women were treated as jural adults differ from those in which they were treated as jural minors under the social and legal protection of men (whether these men were fathers, brothers, or husbands). I draw in a general way here on feminist anthropological literature, which examines how women are defined as persons in a variety of societies. This literature is summarized in Moore (1988: 38–41). Note also the depictions of pre-Hispanic court scenes in the *Codex Mendoza* where both male and female litigants were depicted as seated before the judge (1992: III:fols.68r, 69r).

declined. A new notion of separate but unequal gender spheres developed among Nahuatl-speaking peoples, including the descendants of the Mexica. Indian women were reduced to the status of "jural minors."[5] Yet, as late as the seventeenth century, even as Indian women lost overt legal status, they continued to challenge the colonial state through legal and extralegal means.

PARALLEL AND EQUIVALENT: GENDER RELATIONS DURING THE LATE PRE-HISPANIC PERIOD

In the late pre-Hispanic period, "gender parallelism" characterized Mexica society; that is, there were parallel social structures and cultural configurations for males and females. Gender parallelism, it must be stressed, does not connote equality; particularly in the realm of politics, gender parallelism was compatible with some degree of gender hierarchy. It does mean, however, that the Mexica placed a high cultural value on women's roles. It also means that in diverse realms of Mexica life, women and men played parallel or complementary roles.

The elaborate rituals surrounding birth are an important source of information for the ethnohistorian interested in understanding how gender functioned in Tenochcan Mexica society in the late pre-Hispanic period. The Mexica rites marking the birth of a child reflected the great value this society attached to fertility and reproduction. Let us analyze this rite to examine how gender was used as a symbol of and a vehicle for the construction of ideas and practices that underlay and enacted the basic organizational units in Mexica society.

The ceremonies that surrounded a birth were only the culmination of a series of rituals and feasts that followed a woman's discovery that conception had oc-

---

[5]After this chapter was written, two works that make a somewhat similar argument (though for very different and more egalitarian peoples) came to my attention. See Anderson (1991) and Devens (1992).

curred (*FC* 1950–82: VI:chaps. 25–27; also see chap. 5). Following a birth, a series of rituals then took place which can be divided into three ritual complexes and which can be envisioned as connecting the Tenochcan infant to progressively wider circles of significant others.

The first ritual complex took place immediately after birth; this was the most private ceremony, and it was performed by the midwife who delivered the newborn child. She first bathed the child and cared for the umbilical cord. The cord of a female infant was buried within the household, near the hearth, where she was born. A male infant's umbilical cord was sent to be buried on a battlefield (ibid., IV:1:3–4; VI:31:171–73; also see Burkhart in press). As the cord was cut, the midwife spoke of some of the fundamental tenets of Mexica belief—especially the centrality of work and the fragility and brevity of human life—and these explanations were offered in a way that stressed the distinct types of work performed and the lives led by Mexica men and women. The burial of male and female umbilical cords in different *places* is a critical symbol of the sites most closely identified with maleness and femaleness and was therefore symbolic of the realms in which the primary activities of each were carried out and most fully expressed.

A second complex of birth-related rites involved the ritual bathing and naming of a child. The Spaniards regarded this aspect of Indian birth ceremonies as most similar to their own practices. Thus, Spanish observers referred to this set of rites as the "baptism" (see, e.g., Mendieta 1945: I:117). The Indian ritual, however, involved not only bathing but also naming. Soon after birth, the infants' parents or other relatives consulted astrologers ("*in tonalpouhque, in tlamatinjme*" [*FC* 1950–82: VI:36:197]) who would read the day signs of the child's birth to assess its future and decide which day would be most propitious for the naming ceremony. This ritual usually took place four or five days after birth (Durán 1967: I:5:57; *FC* 1950–82: VI:36:198).

The midwife conducted this ceremony also, and it took place in the household's courtyard (*FC* 1950–82: VI:37:201). Unlike the earlier ritual cutting and burial of the umbilical cord, other kin were also present at this ceremony (ibid.; Motolinía 1971: 47). After adorning the infant with the gender-appropriate accoutrements (a shield and bow and arrow for elite male infants, insignia of future occupations for nonelite male infants [Durán 1967: I:5:57], and spinning equipment and female clothing for a girl), the midwife bathed the child and again spoke about certain Mexica beliefs, especially focusing on water symbolism and the value of work (*FC* 1950–82: VI:37:202).

The child was then given a name, the "earthly name" ("*jtlalticpactoca*" [ibid., 203]). While names were frequently calendrical in nature and were derived from the day of birth (Motolinía 1971: 47; *FC* 1950–82: IV:1:3), other sources of names included one's relatives (*FC* 1950–82: IV:1:3, VI:37:204), deities, and animate or inanimate objects in the natural world (Mendieta 1945: I:117; Torquemada 1975: II:455–56). Women also frequently received birth order names (*FC* 1950–82: X:1:3; also see Cline 1986: 117–19). Many of the names that did not come from these sources may have been second names given on the presentation of the infant to a temple, or school. Children of rulers and the high elite also acquired a third name signifying office (Motolinía 1971: 48). Based on early colonial legal texts, it appears likely that these names generally passed from adult male relatives (usually fathers) to sons.

The bestowal of a second or third name leads us to the third and final complex of rites related to birth. These were the most public of the birth-related ceremonies because officials and/or priests of the *telpochcalli* (school for commoner youths emphasizing military affairs and public works) or *calmecac* (religious school primarily for young noble males) participated (*FC* 1950–82: VI:39: 209–10). At least part of the ceremony may have taken place, not within the household, but at these respective institutions. These rites centered on the dedication of a child to the telpochcalli or calmecac and took place anywhere from twenty days (*CM* 1992: III:fol.56v) to three months (Motolinía 1971: 48) after the birth. Officials or priests of the appropriate sex oversaw the dedication of infants to these institutions (Sahagún 1975: VI:39:401–2). While it was apparently usual for both male and female children to be dedicated in this way (*FC* 1950–82: VI:39:209)—either to the calmecac or the telpochcalli—the proportion of female children that attended them later is unknown.

Taken together, the complex of rituals surrounding birth indicates that from the moment of birth, gender was recognized as crucial to an individual's identity and future experiences. These rites also suggest the parallel nature of male and female gender roles in late pre-Hispanic society. Gender provided a symbolic basis for parallel structuring of institutions, ceremonies, and leadership roles.[6]

In diverse realms of life, women and men played parallel or complementary roles. Women, like men, held administrative authority in the *cuicacalli,* or houses of song, in the *tlaxilacalli,* or wards, and in the *tianquiztli,* or markets. Gender parallelism can also be discerned in the religious realm. Temples had both female and male priests, and the inhabitants of Tenochtitlán worshiped female deities as well as male deities during the eighteen monthly calendrical ceremonies. Gender parallelism in the political, economic, and religious realms existed within a gender hierarchy in which males held the highest-status positions. Nevertheless, in everyday life, responsibilities and ceremonies were structured so that

[6]For a definition of gender parallelism, see Silverblatt (1987: chap. 3). Also see Kellogg (1988: 673–76) and Clendinnen (1991: 170).

men and women had semiseparate activities and organizations. The organization of production, politics, and religious practices ensured that women had at least limited access to positions of authority.[7]

Thus, in late pre-Hispanic Tenochtitlán, gender roles and gender relationships consisted of both complementary and hierarchical elements; in general, however, these separate but equivalent aspects of gender roles outweighed hierarchy. The complementary aspects of gender relations expressed themselves in a variety of ways including genealogy and kinship, labor and work, politics, and religion. Complementary gender relations were also frequently expressed through parallel structures of thought, language, and action in which males and females played different yet parallel and equally necessary roles.

The basis for Mexica gender parallelism lay in both Mexica forms of culture and thought and Mexica kinship beliefs and structures. The former prominently featured dualities and complementarities that sometimes emphasized contrast and opposition and sometimes merged the differences into a higher unity (Burkhart 1989: 36–39; León-Portilla 1963: 36, 82–83, 90–96; López-Austin 1980; Nicholson 1971). The kinship system was rooted in an ideology of descent from men and/or women (or cognatic descent [see chap. 5]) that structured the conceptualization and organization of kin and family groupings (Calnek 1974a, n.d.; Carrasco 1971; Kellogg 1986a; cf. Offner 1983: 163–213; Lockhart 1992: chap.3). The Mexica believed that both the mother and the father contributed bodily fluids that formed a fetus; and the new child was considered to be the descendant of ancestors related through both the mother and the father (see chap. 5). Gender parallelism

[7]For recent discussions of the roles, status, and experiences of pre-Hispanic women across the Valley of Mexico, see Brumfiel (1991); Clendinnen (1991: chaps. 6–8); Kellogg (1984, 1988); MacLachlan (1976); McCafferty and McCafferty (1988, 1991); Nash (1978); and Rodríguez (1988, 1990b).

also rested in part on a utilitarian division drawn both in ideologies and in practices between a male domain of activity centered around war, battlefields, and male forms of work and a female domain centered on households and female forms of work.

Further, under the Mexica cognatic system of descent, both women and men could acquire property through inheritance (Kellogg 1986*b;* also chaps. 4 and 5). Early colonial Tenochcan wills indicate that Mexica men and women held roughly equivalent inheritance rights in three distinct categories of property: houses, land and movable property (Kellogg 1980: chap.3, 1986*b,* also chap. 4 herein; Cline 1986: 65–77). Siblings, male *and* female, inherited equivalent shares of property owned by their fathers and mothers. In the precolonial period, women's ability to activate their inheritance rights, especially their rights to land, may have been constrained by the tendency of the eldest male in a sibling group to act as a guardian. The ability to activate inheritance rights was also limited by scarcity of land as a resource (Cline 1986: 116). Nevertheless, even though women's rights to land often remained residual, those residual rights could be passed on to their children and/or other relatives and descendants.[8]

In the late precolonial period, women's access to property—whether gained through dowry, inheritance, gift, or work—meant that women possessed independent resources that allowed them to function somewhat autonomously from their husbands. For example, the property that women brought into marriage remained separate from that brought to the marriage by men (Durán 1971: I:5:57). Further, the Mexica distinguished between those household goods that belonged to men and those that belonged to women (*FC* 1950– 82: VII:12:31). Women

[8]This pattern is suggested by the will of Hernando de Tapia, AGNT 37–2, 1576: fols.78v–94r, and the litigation over part of de Tapia's estate by his niece, doña Barbara Marta, AGNT 46–4, 1581.

also had access to separate space within domestic house structures, including sleeping and work spaces apart from men's (ibid., IX:9:41; Pomar 1891: 68). Women's customary access to property underlay their legal status and jural independence in the early colonial period.

Women's contributions to production further bolstered their property rights. In the late pre-Hispanic period, extra-household institutions organized many of the productive activities of women. Female administrators, who will be discussed further below, frequently oversaw their tasks. Husbands thus appear to have had only limited control over their wives' work.

In addition to performing essential productive tasks within the household—including cooking, cleaning (which had both sanitary and religious implications [Burkhart 1989: chap.4]), caring for children, marketing, spinning, weaving, and carrying out the daily round of household rituals—women also performed a variety of activities outside the household, in palaces, temples, markets, schools, and craftsworkers' organization. Women served as priestesses, teachers, merchants, healers and midwives, and professional spinners, weavers, and embroiderers.[9] Thus, women—like men—provided labor necessary to sustain their families and fulfill the labor, tribute, and ceremonial obligations of their households (Brumfiel 1991). Men valued this labor and were reluctant to abandon polygamy in the early colonial period precisely because of its value (Motolinía 1971: 189).

Indeed, among the traits associated with "good women," especially commoner women, in the *Florentine Codex* are labor and a capacity for hard work. The "good mother," for example, is described as constantly working, as are the "middle-aged" woman (*iiolloco cioatl*) and

[9]The single most useful ethnohistorical source on Mexica women's labor is the *Florentine Codex*. This material is ably summarized in Hellbom (1967: 126–45).

the "mature" woman (*omacic cioatl*) (*FC* 1950–82: X:1:2, 3:11–12). Noblewomen also could be described as hard-working. One such description of the *cihuatecuhtli,* or "noble" or "ruling woman," states that she not only works hard and uses resources carefully and well but also "governs" and "leads" (*tlapacho, tepachoa*) (ibid., 13:46).[10]

Given women's property rights and labor contributions, it is not surprising to find that adult Mexica women were considered to be autonomous beings and not the dependents of men. The day sign discussions in Book IV of the *Florentine Codex* strongly support such an interpretation. In the description of the very first day sign, Ce Cipactli, or One Crocodile, Fray Bernardino de Sahagún's informants suggested that women as well as men had the capacity to merit or earn the good fortunes due them for being born on this day. Male nobles or commoners would be rulers or brave warriors; women would prosper and be able to feed others.

> She would have food and drink available. She would have food for others to eat; she would invite others to feast. She would be respectful. She would be visited by others; she would revive and refresh the spirits and bodies of those who lived in misery on earth. . . . [O]f her fatigue and effort, nothing would be in vain. Successful would be her dealings around the marketplace in the place of business; it was as if it would sprinkle, shower, and rain her wares upon her. (Ibid., IV:1:2)[11]

But men and women also shared equally the capacity to destroy their good fortune by neglecting their responsibilities. Women born under the fourth sign, Ce Xo-

---

[10]For examples of women rulers (*cihuatlatoque*), see Schroeder (1991: 183–85) and Gillespie (1989: 18–20).

[11]Oniez in qujz, in qujquaz, tetlaqualtiz, tecoanotzaz, tetlacamatiz, ipan calacoaz, qujtechieltiz in atl, in tlaqualli: ypal ihiiocujoaz, ypal ceviz in jiollo, in jnacaio, in tlaihiiovitinemj tlalticpac . . . in jçiaviz, yn jtlapaliviz, atle nenvetiz, vel motitianqujz in tianquiznaoac, in nentlamachoian: iuh-qujn pipixaviz, ipan tepeviz, ipan tzetzeliviz in jtiamjc.

chitl, or One Flower, were said to be skilled embroiderers. But this sign was described as "indifferent," and
thus in order for a woman to be skilled in embroidery,
she had to do penances, fast, and draw blood. If she did
not perform her penances, she would harm her sign and
thereby merit "complete poverty and misery" (ibid., 7:
25).[12] She would then fall into poverty and sell herself
into prostitution.

In addition to being viewed as economically autonomous, women passed on the fruits of their economic
hard work and good fortune to their children, as shown
by the discussion of the ninth sign, Ce Coatl, or One
Serpent, a special sign for merchants. For example,
women merchants born on this day were thought to be
particularly successful.

> She would be quite rich, she would be a good provider; she
> would be well-born. She would look to and guard the
> services and the property of our lord. She would be a
> guardian and administrator. Much would she gather, col-
> lect, save, and justly distribute among her children. (Ibid.,
> 15:59)[13]

Thus, women—like men—were capable of influencing
their own economic well-being and could contribute to
the economic welfare of their descendants.

In the war-oriented society of the Tenochcan Mexica,
women's labor possessed additional significance. Wom-
en, whether noble or commoner, often had to manage
households and productive activities in the absence of
men.[14] In fact, the daily demands placed on women
appear to have been quite heavy (Brumfiel 1991: 226,

[12]"çan moch icnoiotl, netoliniliztli . . ."
[13][Auh intla cioatl,] vel motlacamatiz, vel motlaiecoltiz, vel motlacatiz, qujt-
taz, qujpiaz in jteicneliliz, in jcococauh totecujo, tlaçaloanj, tlapachoanj iez,
vel qujntlaçalhujz, qujntlapachilhujz, qujntetzontiz, qujntlatlamachiz in
jpilhoan,
[14]Durán describes the customary rituals practiced by women when their
husbands went off to war (1967: II:19:164–65).

234–36; 239–43). Large numbers of men were frequently absent from their households for prolonged periods due to frequent warfare and the expansion of the empire of the Triple Alliance (Hassig 1988: chaps.2–4). Moreover, the Mexica birthrate appears to have been high, since during the precolonial period the population of the Valley of Mexico grew rapidly as did population density (Sanders, Parsons, and Santley 1979: 184–86). Not only were women bearing and caring for these children but large amounts of their labor time must have been spent in productive activities (as opposed to reproductive) for households and crafts groups that had to both feed their own members and meet the increasing demands of palaces, temples, and the state.

One way that Tenochcan Mexica women may have had help in meeting all the demands placed on them was to buy prepared or semiprepared foods, called *tianquiztlaqualli*, in local marketplaces. An enormous number of cooked foods, many of which were meat or fowl with a variety of seasonings, were available in marketplaces (ibid., VIII:13:37–38; Cortés 1932: I:99–100). Even when men went off to war, the food supplies appear to have been provided primarily through the markets (*FC* 1950–82: VIII:19:69).

In the marketplace, women were not only buyers and vendors but also administrators (*tianquizpan tlaiacanque*), an occupation they shared with men (ibid., 67–69). The responsibilities of the market administrators included ensuring the fairness of the prices of goods, overseeing the production of war provisions, and assigning tribute. Thus, female administrators oversaw certain of women's productive tasks.

Supervisory positions in marketplaces were not the only economic posts held by women. A ceremony described in Diego Durán's *Historia* (1967: I:13:130), performed to increase the number of sacrificial victims offered to the goddess Cihuacoatl, featured important women crafts producers and merchants. This ritual involved taking the cradle of a child and placing a stone knife in it, then delivering it to "*la más principal joyera,*" who then took it to the market to "*la más principal mercadera.*" This passage alludes to women holding official and hierarchically ranked positions, either within women's divisions of guilds or within parallel women's guilds.

The term *tlaiacanque,*[15] as used in "tianquizpan tlaiacanque," recurs in another context in the *Florentine Codex,* suggesting that it also applied to women who held administrative authority in the cuicacalli, which were part of the royal palace, according to the *Florentine Codex,* or attached to major temples, according to Durán (*FC* 1950–82: VIII:18:43; Durán 1971: I:21:190; also see Calnek 1988). During the month of Uey tecuilhuitl (Great feast of the lords), couples living in concubinage (*nemecatiliztli*) were brought for judgment before the cuicacalli. A man would be punished by having his possessions taken, and he was beaten, burned, and expelled from the cuicacalli. Sahagún's informants then explained that the "mistress(es) of women" (*cihuatetiachca-huan*) expelled the woman. "Nevermore was she to sing and dance with the others; nevermore was she to hold others by the hand. Thus the girls' matrons [*ichpochtlaia-canqui*] established; thus they resolved" (*FC* 1950–82: II:27:103).[16] *Ichpochtlaiacanqui* means "administrator or director of young women" and in conjunction with the term *cihuatetiachcahuan* is similar to the paired terms *teachcahuan* and *telpochtlatoque* used for the male teachers in the telpochcalli.

The existence of parallel structuring of male and female barrio leadership roles is further suggested by Durán in his chapter on the "schools of dance" (his term for the cuicacalli) in his volume on rites and ceremonies.

---

[15]The term *tlayacanqui* is related to the verb *yacana,* which means "to guide another or govern a *pueblo,*" as well as to the term *tlayacati,* which refers to being first or in front (Molina 1977: pt. 2:fols.30r, 120v).

[16]"aoqujc no teoã cujcoianoz, aoqujc no tenaoaz, ic qujcennaoatia, qujcen-macaoa, yn ichpuchtlaiacanquj."

In order to collect and bring these young men to teach them [to dance], there were old men, assigned and chosen only for that office, in all the barrios, who were called *teanque*, which means "men who go to collect young men." In order to collect the young women there were old Indian women, appointed by all the barrios, who were called *cihuatepixque*, which means "women guards" or "mistresses." (1967: I:21:189)[17]

Early colonial legal documents for both Tenochtitlán and Culhuacan indicate that women were included among the *tepixque* (generally referred to as *cihuatepixque*, or women guards) and *tlaxilacalle* (referred to as *cihuatlaxilacalle*, or women ward elders) (also see Cline 1986: 54; Lockhart 1992: 44).[18]

It needs to be stressed that parallel structuring did not extend to the higher levels of administration or governance; these positions were virtually always held by men. Warfare and the warrior hierarchy also excluded women, though Mexica ceremonies drew a symbolic equivalence between females giving birth and males taking a prisoner. Mexica rituals also drew a parallel between dying in childbirth and being killed or captured in battle (Burkhart, in press).

Yet even if the highest levels of governance precluded women's participation, the Mexica, nevertheless, used a language of politics that drew gender parallels. The ruler of the Tenochcan Mexica was referred to as the

[17]Para recoger y traer estos mozos a enseñarse, había hombres ancianos, diputados y electos para solo aquel oficio, en todos los barrios, a los cuales (ancianos) llamaban *teanque*, que quiere decir "hombres que andan a traer mozos." Para recoger las mozas había indias viejas, señaladas por todos los barrios, a las cuales llamaban *cihuatepixque*, que quiere decir "guarda mujeres," o amas.

[18]These women's titles were occasionally attached to indigenous women who witnessed wills in Mexico City as in, for example, Marina Tiacapan's will, written in 1561, in AGNT 2729–20: fol.3v or in the Spanish translation of Francisca Tecuchu's will, dated 1560, in AGNT 42–5: fol.3r. A third example comes from Juana Antonia's will, written in 1595, found in AGNT 59–3: fol.18r. Note also the interesting discussion of female *cofradía* officers by Lockhart (1992: 226–28).

tlatoani and his second-in-command and closest adviser was called the cihuacoatl (woman serpent). The female deity who was associated with the "rain-moisture-agricultural fertility" complex of deities (Nicholson 1971: 414–24) also went by the name Cihuacoatl. The cihuacoatl as political persona would not replace a tlatoani who died (i.e., he was not a successor), but he could substitute for him at ceremonial occasions. One noted scholar of Nahuatl believed that the use of the term *cihuacoatl* embodied the representation of a "female principle" at this highest level of government.[19] The tlatoani himself was spoken of in a way that suggests he carried male and female qualities or at least paternal and maternal responsibilities. Thus, he was frequently described metaphorically as the parent, as the "father and mother" of his people (Kellogg 1993; Haskett 1991: 100, 199; Clendinnen 1991: 160). The Mexica envisioned leadership as combining paternal and masculine qualities with maternal and feminine ones.

Gender parallelism as an organizing theme can also be discerned in the religious realm. The major deities of sustenance, dedicated to maize (Xilonen, Iztac Cinteotl, Chicomecoatl), salt (Uixtociuatl), and maguey (Mayahuel), were all female, as was one of the water deities, Chalchiuhtlicue, the wife of Tlaloc. Other female deities, Toci and Cihuacoatl, represented earth and fire. All of these deities were worshiped during the eighteen monthly calendrical ceremonies, and some were also worshiped in their own temples (Hellbom 1967: 36–42; 44–47; also see Brown 1983: 121–22; Kellogg 1988: 672–73; Klein 1988; Sullivan 1982).

[19]In the edition of Durán's *Historia* edited by Father Garibay (II:Glossary:584), he provided a glossary of Nahuatl terms. Garibay made the following comments about the term *cihuacoatl*: "Es el representante del 'principio femenino.' De ahí su nombre, que puede traducirse 'Mujer serpiente' o mejor 'Comparte femenino.' Es el que sustituye al rey, como la mujer al marido en casa."

Temples had both male and female priests called *tlamacazque* and *cihuatlamacazque*.[20] The term *tlamacazque* generally was used for lower-status priests and the term *quacuiltin*, along with *cihuaquacuiltin*, for higher-status priests (Nicholson 1971: 436–37). Parents could offer their infant daughters to the calmecac to become priestesses, though in contrast to male priests, relatively few women remained as such for their whole lives (*FC* 1950–82: II:app.:246–47). Priestesses trained women in religious service and oversaw their education and well-being (Clavijero 1976: VIII:206). Males held the highest-status priestly positions and carried out human sacrifice, while women helped prepare sacrificial victims (see, e.g., *FC* 1950–82: IV:7:25). But women priestesses may be depicted in the *Primeros memoriales* as sacrificing a female victim during the month of Ochpaniztli (Sweeping the Road) (Brown 1983: 127).

While the cihuatlamacazque lived in temples and helped carry out calendrical ritual, the cihuaquacuiltin were older priestesses of higher status. The holder of one particular title, the Iztaccihuatl cihuaquacuilli, watched over those women who swept and kept the fire at Toci's temple, Atenchicalcan; this position was likely one of some authority. "And any who made supplications [to the goddess] spoke to the Iztac ciuaquacuilli. This one pronounced judgement on all that was done here at [the Temple of] Atenchicalcan" (*FC* 1950–82: II:App.:211).[21]

We should not neglect the other roles played by women in education and life-cycle rituals. The *ichpochtiachcauh* in the telpochcalli was in charge of young girls (ibid.,

---

[20]The term *tlamacazqui* relates to both the verb *maca* ("to give") and *tlamaca,* which Molina defines as "seruir a la mesa, o administrar la comida y manjares" (1970: pt. 2: fol.125r).

[21]"Yoan in aqujn vmpa monetoltiaia, iehoatl conilhujaia in cihoaquacujlli iztac cihoatl, muchi eihoatl quitzontequja in tlein vncan muchivaia atenchicalcã" This passage and the one immediately preceding (on the "Ciuaquacuilli") suggest that there was a hierarchy of priestesses.

VI:39:210). As described earlier, the cihuatepixque delivered girls for teaching and ceremonies at the cuicacalli. And a midwife not only delivered babies but, as noted earlier, officiated during the ceremonies conducted after a child was born. Women also played key ceremonial and strategic roles at marriage. Several older women, called *cihuatlanque,* negotiated a marriage once the bride had been selected by the groom's family (ibid., 23:128; *CM* 1992: III:fol.61; also see chap. 5). Their role in the marriage was symbolized during the wedding ceremony when they tied the shirt of the groom to the skirt of the bride after the bride and groom had been presented gifts by their respective mothers-in-law. The matchmakers then placed the couple in a chamber and, according to Sahagún's informants, "put them to bed" (*FC* 1950–82: VI:23:132).[22]

In the symbolic realm, women could be depicted in negative as well as positive terms. Female mythicohistorical figures, collectively referred to as "women of discord" by Susan D. Gillespie, were associated with historical periods of great political change (1989: chaps. 1–4). Cowardice or defeat in warfare were also symbolically associated with women, as when female clothing or material items used by women in production were given to enemies deemed unworthy of respect (see, e.g., Durán 1967: II:10:92; also see Nash 1978: 356). But women could also engage in highly inflammatory and warlike behavior, as when Tlatelolcan women taunted Tenochcan forces during the siege of Tlatelolco by exposing their nude bodies and expressing breast milk and sprinkling it on the Tenochcan Mexica warriors (Durán 1967: II:34:263). Likewise, female deities could convey powerfully negative images even when associated with basic values of Mexica culture (Klein 1988: 237–46). Across these realms of politics, warfare,

---

[22]"qujmonteca in cioatitici." Note the use of the term *ticitl* in the matchmaking context.

and religion, we find that symbolic images of womanhood often connoted female power. While a certain degree of sexual antagonism may be read into some of these examples (Clendinnen 1991: 171–73), they do not represent perceptions of women as weak, dependent, or polluting (ibid., 164–67, 206). The powerful drive in Mexica thought and culture to unite complementary yet opposed forces was stated through gender symbols and helped to structure everyday life and social arrangements.

In daily life, the Mexica structured responsibilities and ceremonies so that men and women had semiseparate activities and organizations. The organization of production, politics, and religious practices ensured that women had access to positions of authority. While women did not serve in the very highest levels of political administration or governance and were excluded from the warrior hierarchy, women, like men, held administrative authority in markets, temples and houses of song, and neighborhoods. The frequent absences of men in warfare and merchant and trading activities reinforced the existence of semiseparable domains, male and female, which both conceptually and practically served to organize and differentiate women's and men's experiences.

The pre-Hispanic Mexica conception of parallel and complementary spheres for women and men did not survive the transition to colonial rule. The new regime brought a gradual but clear decline in the status of Mexica women. In the early colonial period, women's formal access to positions of authority decreased and the older division between male and female realms, semiseparable and autonomous, gave way to a new, more hierarchical division between male and female realms that resulted in a clear reduction of women's formal status. A key feature of the colonial system was a rigid, more hierarchical conception of gender roles and relations.

THE CONQUEST AND ITS IMMEDIATE
AFTERMATH FOR MEXICA WOMEN

During the sixteenth and seventeenth centuries, Spanish colonizers successfully introduced a court system, a legal code, and inheritance customs that over time served to redefine the legal status of Mexica women. While according women limited legal rights, Spanish practices tended to reinforce the centrality of the conjugal couple and the nuclear family, eroding Mexica women's independent jural identity.

The gender complementarity that played such a crucial role in the conceptual and social structures of the Tenochcan Mexica did not fare well during the postconquest era. Nevertheless, the shape of the new system of gender relations did not emerge immediately. The social conditions of the immediate postconquest period actually enhanced women's access to property and reinforced certain property rights that underlay their legal status and jural independence in the pre-Hispanic period.

From about the 1530s to the 1580s, Nahua women's status, particularly in urban areas, rose somewhat for two reasons. First, the postconquest demographic imbalance in sex ratios resulted in women outnumbering men (Gibson 1964: 141). In consequence, many women succeeded to positions of authority within households, kin groups, and political units.[23] Second, the introduction of a highly malleable law code and legal system reinforced women's autonomy *in the short run.*

Spaniards used the law as a colonizing tool when they arrived in the New World. Neither Castilian legal codes nor those formulated in the New World, such as the *Recopilación de leyes de los reynos de las Indias,* dealt specifically with *Indian* women, but peninsular codes—espe-

[23]Women's access to household headship—in the absence of males—appears to have been a significant cause of litigation among Indians during the sixteenth century. The relationships among gender, kinship, and litigation were dealt with in chap. 1; also see Kellogg (1992: 34–35).

cially the *Siete Partidas* and the *Leyes de Toro*—did elaborate the legal rights of Spanish women. Still, it would be a mistake to assume that one can determine women's status on the basis of formal codes of law. Legal codes and actual practice often diverge profoundly. Nevertheless, Spanish legal codes do provide insight into the beliefs and attitudes about women's property rights held by male colonists.

In Spain and its colonies, women had both access to and control over property (Arrom 1985*a:* chap. 2; Lavrin and Couturier 1979; also see Bernal de Bugeda 1975; Arrom 1985*b;* and Couturier 1985).[24] Dowry and inheritance constituted women's major routes of access to property. The law protected women's dowries and allowed women to sell or otherwise alienate such property (Arrom 1985*a:* 67; Lavrin and Couturier 1979: 282). While husbands could use dowries' earnings as they wished, women could recover their dowries on the event of their husbands' death or if they received an ecclesiastical divorce. When a wife died before her husband, her dowry would be divided among her children, or if she had no children, it was returned to her parents (Arrom 1985*a:* 67–68). Thus, Castilian law placed certain legal limits on the patriarchal authority of fathers and husbands.

Spanish bilateral inheritance laws also reinforced these limits. According to both the *Leyes de Toro* and the *Siete Partidas,* the spouse and children were the preferred heirs whose claims had to be satisfied before those of parents, siblings, or others (see these codes as reprinted in Martínez Alcubilla 1885: vol. #1).[25] While testators

[24]On women in early modern Spain, see Pescatello (1976); Bilinkoff (1989); and Perry (1990). On the experience of Spanish women and women of other ethnic identities in colonial Latin America, see several of the essays in *Presencia y Transparencia* (1987) as well as Gonzalbo (1987).

[25]These law codes are reprinted in this volume. Inheritance laws are treated in laws 7 to 10 of the *Leyes de Toro* and *Partida* 6 covers inheritance laws in the *Siete Partidas.*

could leave one-fifth to one-third of their estates to spouses or children through a *mejora* (specific bequest), the law protected the inheritance rights of both male and female children. A significant feature of Spanish inheritance law, however, was that "wom[e]n in practical terms [had] an economic edge over the potential rights of the children" (Lavrin and Couturier 1979: 287).

Yet none of these property rights established male and female equality. In fact, the law made women's inequality explicit. It expressly prohibited women from formal participation in the political and religious affairs of Spanish society. It also prohibited women from serving as judges, lawyers, or priests; nor could they hold political office or vote. Still, women did have legally sanctioned access to certain roles: they could serve as guardians for children or grandchildren, and they could speak for elderly relatives in court if husbands or other appropriate male relatives were not available. In addition, women could participate in a broad set of legally defined economic activities, including buying, selling, renting, or inheriting property (Arrom 1985*a:* 58–62). "They could lend and borrow money, act as administrators of estates, and form business partnerships. They could initiate litigation, be their own advocates in court, and appear as witnesses (except in wills)" (ibid., 61).

Spanish women's legal rights involved an awkward balance of restrictions and protections in the context of a patriarchal society in which law fundamentally supported the power and authority of fathers and husbands. Single children, whether male or female, remained under the father's authority unless they were explicitly emancipated. Fathers exercised primary authority over key aspects of their children's lives, including their educations, legal affairs, and property transactions (ibid., 56–57, 69). While in New Spain, women often served as executors of their husbands' wills and guardians for their children, husbands legally and practically did have great control over their wives' property and transactions

(Lavrin and Couturier 1979: 287; Arrom 1985*a:* 66). And while a wife required her husband's permission to undertake legal activities, the reverse did not hold. In practice, however, the codified requirements for women participating in legal affairs were not always obeyed. Colonial Indian women initiated legal actions before the courts despite the obstacles erected by formal law codes, and they frequently served as witnesses when the dying made wills.

Since the Spanish Crown encouraged New Spain's aboriginal population to use colonial legal institutions to settle disputes, it provided an arena in which conflicting cultural conceptions of gender would be contested and redefined. As we saw in chapter 1, women crowded the legal arena. Indeed, I would suggest that indigenous women were compensating for a loss of power and authority in other realms of their lives. During the early colonial era, a wide range of institutions in which women held positions of authority—temples, calmecac, and cuicacalli—disappeared. Simultaneously, the pre-Hispanic notion of formal parallel institutional structures for men and women began to collapse, along with the religious, political, and economic institutions and forms of organization that both supported and expressed this parallelism. For example, after the 1530s, control of the large markets in Mexico City passed from Mexica to Spanish hands as Spanish alguaciles, always male, took over the duties of the tianquizpan tlaiacanque, a position that had been held by both males and females (Gibson 1964: 355, 569 n.144; Hassig 1985: 229). The formal religious role of women also declined as the parallel structuring of Mexica priests and priestesses rapidly atrophied. Even the symbolic expression of parallel and equivalent gender roles, as expressed in the ceremonies carried out at birth, declined.[26]

[26]The practices associated with and meanings attached to Christian baptism are fundamentally different from the practices and meanings of Mexica birth

Women's active participation in colonial courts attracted comment from sixteenth-century Spanish jurists. One Spanish judicial official[27] with extensive experience in central Mexico during this period wrote,

When some Indian has a dispute, though the Indian may be very important, able and skilled, he will not appear before the court without bringing his wife with him, and they inform and speak that which by reason of the lawsuit it is necessary to say, and the husbands are very timid and

ceremonies. For Catholics, the sacrament of baptism represents "the death and resurrection of Christ" (*New Catholic Encyclopedia* [hereafter referred to as *NCE*] 1967: II:62) and as such is more concerned with the individual's acceptance of Christ and relationship with Christianity. If Christian baptism symbolizes incorporation of the individual—child or adult—into the Church, Mexica birth ceremonies symbolized incorporation of the infant into the family and other higher-level social institutions. While Christian baptism of infants featured the sprinkling or pouring of water as did part of the Mexica practices, the other aspects of Catholic baptismal ritual were quite different and included giving the cross, exsufflation (exhaling or breathing on the infant), placing hands on the infant, and the offering of salt (ibid., 61). The adult baptism was fundamentally similar, only lengthier (ibid.). Note also that gender symbolism was not highly elaborated in Catholic baptisms.

As these practices were brought to the New World, several problems and issues developed. For the early period, these are most clearly discussed by the priest Toribio de Benavente (or Motolinía). Among the problems he noted were the diverse ways of baptizing practiced by the different orders, sometimes not baptizing in native languages, and some tendency not to perform any baptisms (especially for "children and people who were ill" (1971: 123–25; also see Mendieta 1945: II:115–17; and Burkhart 1989: 112–17).

An early eighteenth-century treatise (*Farol indiano*) giving advice to priests suggests that by this time different problems had developed. One was that not all parents belonged to parishes yet still brought their children to be baptised (Pérez 1713: 3). Another was that some baptisms were being conducted in Indian households rather than in churches (7–8) and even in Nahuatl (8–15). The shift in attitude from Motolinía to Manuel Pérez, author of this treatise, is apparent in the way that Motolinía assumed that for baptisms to be valid, they *had* to be conducted in native languages whereas Pérez debated whether a baptism conducted in Nahuatl *was* valid and concluded that it was not. Pérez's primary reason was that Latin concepts could not be translated exactly into Nahuatl.

[27]Gómez de Cervantes had been an *alcalde mayor* in several towns in the Valley of Mexico, including Tlaxcala where he also served as gobernador. The observations he makes throughout his text suggest a man especially knowledgeable about law and economic conditions in the central portions of New Spain (also see Warren 1973: 82).

quiet; and if the court asks something that it wishes to know, the husband responds: "here is my wife who knows it"; and in such manner it has happened to me upon asking one Indian or indeed many, "what is your name?", and before the husband responds, his wife says it; and thus in all other things; thus they are men who have submitted to the will of the woman. (Gómez de Cervantes 1944: 135)[28]

The courts codified gender roles, stipulating that women could only serve as litigants or witnesses. Nevertheless, women did make a significant contribution to litigation heard in colonial New Spain's legal system during the sixteenth century.

Women and men initiated litigation at about equal rates; similarly, women were just as likely as men to be defendants in civil disputes. Compared to men, however, women served as witnesses at far lower rates (see chap. 1; Kellogg 1984). Women participated in a broad range of legal activities: they made wills; served as witnesses for wills (for both female *and* male testators, though female witnesses did so more often for female testators); bought, sold, and inherited property; and acted as legal guardians for children and grandchildren when fathers or parents were not available.[29]

Yet legal transactions preserved certain subtle gender differences. For one thing, Mexica women served as legal guardians for children more often than did men (AGNT 30–1, 1570; 49–5, 1585). Second, Mexica men

[28]The original passage reads:
> Cuando algún indio tiene algún pleito, aunque el indio sea muy principal, hábil y entendido, no parecerá ante la Justicia, sin llevar consigo a su mujer, y ellas informan y hablan lo que en razón del pleito conviene hablar, y los maridos se están muy encogidos y callados; y si la Justicia pregunta algo que quiere saber, el marido respone: "aquí está mi mujer que lo sabe"; y esto en tal manera, que aún me ha acaecido preguntar a un indio y a muchos,"¿cómo te llamas?" y antes que el marido responda, decirlo la mujer; y así en todas las demás cosas; de manera que es gente que está rendida a la voluntad de la mujer.

[29]These observations are based on legal documentation as cited extensively in chaps. 1 and 2.

had a wider range of options for claiming access to or transferring property. In addition to buying, selling, and inheriting property, which women also did, though at lower rates than men, men received property through dowry (see, for example, AGNT 20–1–3, 1573); they acquired property through mercedes (see, e.g., AGNT 55–5, 1564; AGNT 55–2, 1589; BNP 112, 1593); and they also rented property, especially houses (e.g., AGNT 24–1, 1568; 54–2, 1587). Women did not participate in any of these latter kinds of transactions. A third gender difference was that women claimed ownership to property through inheritance much more often than men. In contrast, men were no more likely to claim ownership on the basis of inheritance than on the basis of any other form of property transfer, including sale, dowry, or grants.

Perhaps more so than men, women attempted to control the disposition of their worldly goods, movable and immovable, after they died. Extant lawsuits suggest that during the sixteenth century, the courts received more female than male wills to bolster legal cases. The submission of wills was thus a gendered strategy. Twenty-five of thirty-three surviving wills were submitted to the courts during litigation. Women offered sixteen (six female plaintiffs, ten female defendants), men nine (five male plaintiffs, four male defendants) (see chap. 4).

However, in one area of everyday Nahua life, production and work, continuity outweighed change in women's roles, especially for commoner women. While Mexica women's participation in higher-status crafts did decline as Indians, men and women alike, lost control over elite crafts during the course of the colonial period (Gibson 1964: 350), women continued to participate in extra-familial forms of production and employment throughout the colonial period (see below).

They did this work to help support their families and to help make tribute payments. From an early date, Spanish authorities commanded from women in agricultural areas "specified amounts of cotton cloth" in tribute (Gibson 1964: 198; also see Villanueva 1985).[30] By the second half of the sixteenth century, Spanish authorities had extended the obligation to make tribute payments to the indigenous population of Mexico City, stipulating that these payments take the form of money. During the second half of the sixteenth century and the seventeenth century as well, widows and unattached women were pressed to make tribute payments (Gibson 1964: 203). An eighteenth-century Spanish legal scholar stated that Indian women in New Spain regularly paid tribute, though in lower amounts than men (Solórzano y Pereyra 1776: I:161–62; also see Arrom 1985a: 308 n.81).[31] Not until 1758 did the law formally exempt unmarried women from making tribute payments, and not until the nineteenth century were all women excused (Gibson 1964: 207, 394).

SEPARATE AND UNEQUAL: INDIAN WOMEN IN MEXICO CITY IN THE SEVENTEENTH CENTURY

By the seventeenth century, the status of Mexica women had visibly declined. In the legal realm, Indian women initiated far less property litigation than in the sixteenth century. While they continued to appear as witnesses for wills and property sales, women no longer served as legal guardians of minor children in lawsuits. In the economic realm, the rates at which women bought, sold, or inherited property fell significantly below those of the sixteenth century.

[30]Fernández de Oviedo commented about how nonurban women commonly performed agricultural labor (1851: III:536–37).

[31]Ixtlilxochitl suggested that even noble women, at least in Texcoco, were helping to supply tribute (1975–77: I:393). In 1620, the Juzgado de Indios ordered that no one impede the work of one Juana María, a *mulata* married to an Indian, Juan Vázquez, so that she could continue to supply "sustenance and the payment of tributes" (AGNI 7–475, 1620: fol.228r). Married Indian women were also occasionally described as tribute payers in census records dating from the early 1690s for Indians living inside the traza (AGNH 413–1).

Two developments account for women's declining status. First, by the seventeenth century, Indian women's legal identity had become increasingly intertwined with that of their husbands. Seventeenth-century legal records reveal that husbands were the driving force behind lawsuits undertaken by their wives, even in cases in which the property had been inherited by the wife. In short, by the seventeenth century, men routinely acted as intermediaries between women and the legal and political realms. Of eighteen *Tierras* cases dating from the seventeenth century, only two included female litigants who did *not* have men to play the major role in the lawsuit. Husbands usually spoke for their wives; occasionally, brothers represented their sisters; in one case, a nephew represented his aunt in litigation (AGNT 163–5, 1699).

A 1607 case illustrates the emerging tendency to treat women as legal minors (AGNT 183–4, 1607) (see fig. 16). Diego Nunciales and his wife, Marta María, residents of the barrio of Santa Lucía in Santiago Tlatelolco, sued Francisco Pablo and his wife, Beatriz Francisca, residents of the barrio of Tezcatzonco in Santa María la Redonda, over a plot (*suerte*) of land measuring 100 by 20 brazas in the district of Santo Tomás Petlachiuhcan. Diego claimed that his wife inherited the land from her father, Jusepe Ximénez, who had purchased the property in 1542. In response, Francisco insisted that his wife had inherited this same land from *her* paternal grandmother, Juana Xoco, who had received the property from don Diego de Mendoza as restitution for another plot of land that Mendoza had usurped from Juana's father, Chimalteuhtzin. Both the plaintiffs and the defendants rested their ownership claims on inheritance by the wife. Yet all the legal documents submitted to the courts listed the husbands' names before those of their wives or listed only the name of the husband.

The second source of women's declining legal status lay in the rapid breakdown of the social institutions in which women had held power and authority. Many of the religious, political, and economic institutions that had given tangible expression to gender parallelism had collapsed, replaced by new structures of authority.

Although work and production formed the area of greatest continuity in the lives of Mexica women, changes also occurred in this realm. Women continued to engage in extrafamilial forms of employment and production throughout the colonial period, even as their access to skilled crafts and other high-status forms of production declined. In urban areas, Nahua women worked in the marketplaces and received assigned places in the city's major markets (AGNI 4–194, 1590: fol.60v; also see Gibson 1964: 198). Indian women also provided various types of personal service (Zavala 1984–87: I:300–303, 320–21).

At first, men and women performed parallel kinds of labor, perhaps reflecting pre-Hispanic gender divisions in the world of work (see, e.g., *CO* 1947: 339).[32] Over time, the forms of personal service provided by men and women diverged. The censuses of 1753 and 1811 reveal very high rates of labor force participation by Mexico City's Indian women; in 1811, almost half of all Indian women (46%) listed an occupation (Arrom 1985*a*:157–61). Not surprisingly, Indian and casta women were far more likely than Spanish women to be employed. But even in work, one sees the growth of male authority. Instead of working in autonomous female institutions, an increasing number of Indian women were employed in households as servants. According to census data, domestic service, food preparation, and selling at markets were the most common forms of female employment (ibid., 158–59). Urban Indian women also worked in crafts, textile production, and, in the late colonial period, tobacco processing (Gibson 1964: 394; Johnson 1986: 243–44).

[32]In this description of a drawing of work done, probably for the viceroy, ten men were said to sweep the tecpan and ten women were said to prepare grain.

113

One of the most potent forces for change in indigenous women's lives during the sixteenth and seventeenth centuries was a religious ideology that laid a new stress on female honor and purity. Mexica goddesses, depicted by images rich in associations with fertility, power, and sexual symbolism (Sullivan 1982: 15–19; Burkhart 1989: 92–93; Clendinnen 1991: 167–69, 177–80, 198–200), had little in common with Catholic images of Mary and other saints.[33] New religious doctrines repeatedly depicted Mary as pure of body and soul and as a perpetual virgin (Burkhart 1989: 128–29). As early as the 1520s, the daughters of elite Mexica families began to attend schools that advanced the doctrines of "Christian womanhood" (Gallagher 1978: 150).

While the early priests encouraged celibacy and virginity for both young men and young women, Mexica religious texts of the early colonial period associated virginity specifically with women and female deities (Burkhart 1989: 154–56). This ideology helped to demarcate a domestic domain for confining women in both a physical and a social sense. One text states that girls should follow the example of Mary.

> Do not go about passing by people, do not go about from house to house. Do not linger in the marketplace, do not sit here and there among people, do not stand in the road, do not address men, do not smile at people. (Anunciación 1577: fol.165r [quoted and translated in Burkhart 1989: 137])

In another text, Sahagún contrasted Saint Clare with the activities and ways of life of Mexica noblewomen, stressing the saint's plainness, simplicity, and virtue. The noblewomen, in contrast, were

[33]Burkhart suggests that there was some continuity between Eve and Cihuacoatl, i.e., "the woman who first sinned, and who like Cihuacoatl, had serpent associations" (1989: 93). While Eve was discussed in a variety of early colonial texts, she does not appear to have become a major syncretistic symbol (Burkhart 1988: 74–78).

continually going out, they follow the roads about, they pass out among the houses, they go around in front of people in the marketplace, thus do the women make people desire them. They wish to be seen. *But Saint Clare just enclosed herself.* (Sahagún 1583: fols.146v–147v [quoted and translated in Burkhart 1989: 139])

Priests were instructed on how to explain the responsibilities of each partner to married couples. Husbands were to be responsible for the material sustenance of their wives and children; wives were to help guard and care for property and carry out household tasks and were told explicitly to be or stay in the house (Molina 1565: fols.64v–65r). Priests were also advised to explain to husbands their spiritual responsibilities for the members of their households including knowledge of doctrine, confessing, hearing mass, and attending important fiestas (León 1611: fol.113v). Thus, priests emphasized that husbands had both material and spiritual responsibilities for the members of their nuclear families. Of course, Mexica women could hardly embed themselves rigidly within the domestic sphere; their labor was too valuable for their families and the colonial economy. Yet as one chronicler observed, even in the "Babylon" of contrasting classes and mixed races that was Mexico City, numerous Indian women—including those who bought and sold in the markets—were able to keep their chastity (Mendieta 1945: III:72).

The new ideology of purity and enclosure undermined women's ability to hold formal positions of authority. In the passage just referred to, for example, Fray Gerónimo de Mendieta explicitly contrasts young Indian women who must interact outside of their households with young Spanish women ("*las muy encerradas hijas de señoras españolas*" [the very enclosed daughters of Spanish ladies]), who he described as being placed "behind twenty walls." This new and restrictive ideology had its greatest effect on Mexica society and culture after 1585

115

and particularly during the seventeenth century when new, specifically colonial, forms of Indian cultural and social practice emerged.[34]

Another indicator of indigenous women's declining status was a subtle, yet real, shift in their names across the sixteenth and seventeenth centuries. Between 1585 and 1600, the names (first and sometimes second) borne by Indian women began to change as parents increasingly assigned their female children what I term "feminized masculine names." While names such as Juana and Francisca had been commonly used by urban Indian women in the decades after the conquest, by 1600, women's names had become more varied. Included among these that began to appear regularly in legal and parish records were names, often of saints, such as Bernabela, Blasina, Diega, Felipa or Felipiana, Josefa, Manuela, Melchora, Micaela, Nicolasa, Pascuala, Simona, and Tomasa or Tomasina.

If female testators' names are examined (see tables 2, 5, and 8), we see that the percentage of feminized masculine names increased. In the years prior to 1585, both women and men generally carried two names, with the second frequently being a Nahuatl name or title. The second name might be another Spanish first name, however. Thus, the fourteen female testators of that period had a possible twenty-eight names; in the wills from the 1540s through the first half of the 1580s, only five names were feminized masculine names. For the period from 1585 to 1649, of eighteen possible names, nine were; and for the period from 1650 to 1700, seven of sixteen were. This pattern is further demonstrated by reviewing the names of female witnesses in lawsuits and Indian birth records for Mexico City.[35] This shift in

---

[34]The daughters of nobles were made special targets of such indoctrination early on (Cuevas 1914: 56–57).

[35]If the names of women witnesses in lawsuits are compared for three decades, the 1560s, 1590s, and 1690s, the following numbers of such names appear: none of ten possible names for the 1560s; four of eight for the 1590s;

names reflects the creation of a more male-centered culture and one in which Christian values (as expressed in sources for names) were clearly demonstrated.

By the seventeenth century, the precolonial system of gender parallelism, rooted in complementary male and female domains, had been transformed. The formal religious, political, and economic organization that had given tangible expression to gender complementarity and parallelism lay weakened and an ideology emphasizing the patriarchal authority of husbands and fathers, tied to beliefs that stressed the need for women's sexual purity and honor, was expressed clearly and repeatedly by both religious and legal institutions (Arrom 1985*a:* 63–78; Seed 1988: chaps. 4, 6; Gutiérrez 1991: chaps. 5–7).

To state that Indian women's status was declining is not to claim that these women had no voice in political, religious, or economic affairs. A few clues suggest that indigenous women continued to play some role in political organization. Throughout the seventeenth century, women still served as witnesses in property litigation and often in wills. Their participation in legal affairs suggests that they held some institutionalized position(s) through which they were called upon as witnesses. Male witnesses in wills and legal cases were often low-level barrio officials; perhaps some of these women represent

---

and five of fourteen for the 1690s. Parish records are spotty but show similar patterns. Birth records for Tlatelolco for 1590 show eight such names for twenty-one infant girls, whereas birth records for the barrio of San Sebastián show for 1640, sixteen of twenty-six; for 1660, nineteen of thirty-eight; for 1680, thirty-three of fifty; and for 1700, twenty-four of forty. Birth records for Santa Cruz y Soledad show for 1660, seventeen of thirty-five; for 1680, forty of seventy-three; and for 1700, twenty-eight of sixty-three (the figures for 1700 are not complete because of several illegible pages). These records come from the parish records microfilmed by the Church of the Latter Day Saints. The Tlatelolco records are on roll 0037–031; the records for San Sebastián are on roll 0037–375 and 0037–376; those of Santa Cruz y Soledad are on roll 0195–534. Also on colonial naming patterns of Indians, see Cline (1986: 117–22); Horn (1989*b*); and Lockhart (1992: 117–30). For an interesting discussion of surname patterns among "plebians," see Cope (1994:58–63).

the equivalent.[36] Women also continued to function as matchmakers during the early colonial period in defiance of Church policy (Gruzinski 1989*b:* 109) and played some role in cofradía (lay religious association) governance (Lockhart 1992: 226–28).[37]

They also figured prominently in counterhegemonic activities expressing opposition to both male domination and the domination of the colonial state. Spanish and casta women acknowledged Indian women for possessing special medical and ritual knowledge (Behar 1989: 192). Women of other ethnic groups used this special knowledge for sexual witchcraft intended obliquely to counter male domination (ibid., 201). Indian women also employed these practices within their own communities (Ruiz de Alarcón 1984: 65–66, 131–39), and, as already noted, they continued to serve as matchmakers. Ruth Behar (1989:199–200) has argued that women's ritual practices denoted limited power, circumscribed by male domination and women's consequent ability to exercise authority only in the private domain. But while the fall in women's status is clear (symbolized most sharply by women's decline to being treated jural minors and by the restrictive ideology that drew sharp boundaries between male public, political, and economic activities and female private and domestic activities), they were able to draw on their domestic roles in overtly political contexts.

Women frequently participated in colonial rebellions. Indeed, on occasion, they led them. William B. Taylor has written that across a broad range of Indian communities in central Mexico,

[36]A set of documents from the early seventeenth century, tracing the ownership of a house site in Tlatelolco, refers to the deceased owner, doña Elena Cortés, as an *yndia casica* (BNMAF, *Caja* 80–1303, #15: fol.11r). While this designation might be thought of as reflecting her marital status, in an earlier sale document—from prior to her marriage—she was referred to as a *principala soltera* (fol.6r).

[37]Serna (1892: 24) also mentioned that midwives frequently indulged in syncretistic, and therefore superstitious, practices. He himself referred to these practices, not as "syncretistic," but as resulting from "mixing."

118

militiamen called in by the Spanish authorities were likely to encounter nasty mobs of hundreds of women brandishing spears and kitchen knives or cradling rocks in their skirts, and young children and old people carrying or throwing whatever they could manage, as well as better-armed groups of adult men. "The whole community" and "multitudes" of armed villagers of all ages are descriptions constantly repeated in the reports and testimony. The place of women is especially striking. Perhaps because men were more often traveling outside the community or working fields several miles from town, more women than men usually took part. In at least one-fourth of the cases, women led the attacks and were visibly aggressive, insulting, and rebellious in their behavior toward outside authorities. (1979: 116; also see Tutino 1983: 380–81; Haskett 1991: 39, 84, 199)

Similar events took place in Mexico City. Indigenous women, along with men, violently protested when Spanish authorities imposed tribute payments on the indigenous residents (Chimalpahin 1963–65: II:18). Accounts of the Mexico City uprising of 1692 assign Indian women a prominent role in initiating it. Letters describing the unfolding of the uprising go on to suggest that Indians plotted to simulate the trampling and death of "*una anciana*" to foment further rebellion. One of the sites attacked early in the second day of the attack was the viceroy's *wife's* balcony at the royal palace (Gonzáles Obregón 1952:408–10; also see Guthrie 1945: 247–48; Gibson 1964: 384; but see Cope 1994:157–58). Indigenous women in the colonial period thus had a long history of confronting the colonial state in a variety of ways, though their sources of power shifted from formal to informal ones.

CONCLUSION

The period stretching from the late pre-Hispanic era to the end of the seventeenth century witnessed a marked decline in the legal status of Tenochcan Mexica women. During the late pre-Hispanic period, gender parallelism coexisted alongside gender hierarchy, structuring many aspects of Mexica life, including the realms of religion and work. In turn, the notions of complementarity and exclusiveness embodied in gender roles and relationships exerted a powerful effect on Mexica conceptions of rulership and religious authority. Mexica notions of gender parallelism did not, for the most part, survive the transition to colonial rule, and women lost a large measure of economic and social autonomy.

During the sixteenth and seventeenth centuries, indigenous women, especially nonelite women, found themselves increasingly circumscribed in a more rigid and narrowly defined "woman's" domain, which was rooted symbolically in the family and household but which extended outside the home into forms of labor that usually took place under male supervision and control. By the seventeenth century's end, urban Indian society had a more clearly defined domestic sphere, subordinate to a public sphere in which Spanish and Indian men played virtually all significant formal political, economic, and religious roles. Gender relations among Mexico City's indigenous residents were not identical to those found among Spaniards, but more and more they tended to be shaped by Spanish legal and religious models.

CHAPTER 4

Wills, Property, and People

Mexica concepts of property and ownership under-went a profound transformation during the early colonial period as a growing number of Indians sought in Spanish law justifications for forms of property transmission contrary to common practice prior to the conquest. Many of these litigants were elites, descendants of pre-Hispanic ruling and noble families. Yet elites did not have a monopoly on these new notions of property and its ownership and transmission. Over time, Mexico City's indigenous population began to conceive of forms of property and their ownership and transmission in new ways—ways that reflected strong Spanish influence. Nevertheless, colonial Indians' concepts and practices in regard to property did not mirror exactly Spanish concepts and practices; they reflected the complex conditions of social, cultural, and material change that both enveloped and were shaped by the colonial Mexica.

The new custom of writing wills exerted a strong influence on changing concepts of property. Encouraged by priests, will writing served as a vehicle through which Nahuas could direct the movement of their property and goods after their deaths. Will writing also played a significant role in introducing and reinforcing Spanish religious beliefs and notions of property. This chapter describes both pre-Hispanic and colonial inheritance practices. It analyzes new conceptions of property and ownership as well as shifting patterns of property transmission, which themselves illuminate innovations in social relationships within Indian society. I begin by examining funerals, forms and categories of property ownership, and means of property transmission during the late preconquest era.

PROPERTY AND INHERITANCE AMONG THE LATE FIFTEENTH-CENTURY MEXICA

Following an individual's death, several factors determined the conduct of mortuary rituals and the manner of cremation or burial of the body. Class and occupation, gender, and the nature of the individual's death each played a role in shaping funeral rites. Rulers, nobles, and merchants had the most elaborate rites (Motolinía 1971: 304–7; *CM* 1903: fol.64v–67r; Torquemada 1975: II: 521–23; *FC* 1950–82: III: App., chap.1:45–46). Nonelites and the poor had simpler ones (Motolinía 1971: 307; Durán 1967: I:5:56). Along with the body of the deceased were burned gender-specific symbols, objects associated with war for men and with weaving for women (*FC* 1950–82: III: App., chap.1:43).

In preparation for cremation and burial, the body was first bathed and then clothed with the person's most elaborate dress or a variety of decorative items. Mourners gathered for up to four days to express grief, singing or chanting lamentations for the dead and holding ritual feasts. At funerals of elites, people gave gifts such as *mantas*, cloaks (Durán 1967: I:5:56). The bodies of those who died from certain specific causes—such as drowning, lightning strikes, or diseases associated with water deities (leprosy, dropsy, or gout)—were buried (ibid., App., chap.2:47), as were the bodies of women who died in childbirth (ibid., VI:29:161). Others were cremated, and their ashes were buried either in the household or in the barrio temple (ibid., III:App., chap.1:45).

According to Mexica belief, class, gender, and the cause of a person's death determined where a person's soul spent the afterlife. The souls of warriors and women who died in childbirth rose up into the sky and for four years traveled with the sun. The souls of warriors then became hummingbirds or butterflies and returned to earth. The *mocihuaquetzque,* the heroic women who had died in childbirth, in contrast, carried the sun to Mictlan, the "place of the dead," and became joyful, if occasionally troublesome, spirits (ibid., III:App., chap. 3:47; VI:29:161–64). Those who had died in water or from diseases associated with water deities went to Tlalocan, the heavenly paradise associated with certain rain deities (Nicholson 1971: after 408, 409). Other Mexica, the majority, traveled to Mictlan. These souls endured a difficult and dangerous four-year journey through nine layers of the afterlife, accompanied by a yellow dog, symbols of one's possessions, and food (FC 1950–82: III:App., chap.1).

Class and gender also determined the transmission of property on death. The discussion of property transmission in Book XI of the *Florentine Codex* and the earliest colonial wills written by Indians indicate that the pre-Hispanic Mexica, like the Spanish, distinguished among three major categories of property: land, houses, and movables. Ownership of land was complicated by the variety of classifications of land (by soil type, location, and use [ibid., XI:12:251–56; Cline 1984, 1986]) as well as by distinct forms of land tenure that gave multiple groups of people rights to the same plots of land (Caso 1963; Gibson 1964: 257–70; Kirchhoff 1954–55). It appears that in the late pre-Hispanic period, an increasing amount of land was becoming "privately" owned (i.e., the land was not attached to temples or offices and was both heritable and sellable [Gibson 1964: 263; Cline 1986: 152]), though this ownership may often have been by kin groups, not individuals (LAL/FSC AGI Patronato 181–8:fols.53r–59v). Yet even these "private" lands, known either as *pillalli* or *tecuhtlalli,* were worked by retainers who held certain customary rights that they asserted in early colonial lawsuits (Gibson 1964: 263; also see, e.g., AGNV 255–1, 1562; 255–2, 1562).

123

House ownership was more widespread than land-ownership, but it, too, was characterized by a pattern of multiple, overlapping, and residual rights. Houses, or calli (which meant both "room" and "house"), were distinguished by function, status, or architectural style. The elite — rulers, nobles, and wealthy merchants — lived in palaces (tecpan) and two-story houses (*calnepanolli* [*FC* 1950–82: XI:12:274]); the nonelite lived in "ordinary houses" (*Çaçan ie calli*), "houses of the *maceualli*, or commoners" (*macehualcalli*), or "humble houses" ("*icno-calli*") (ibid., 269–72; also see Robertson 1974: 159–63). There were also a number of stylistically varied huts and plank houses, which may represent either geographically distinct house types or merely individual or household preference (ibid., 273–74; also see, in the same volume, house illus., nos. 888–920). Mexica terminology distinguished among distinct types of rooms and areas within houses, including the "women's room" (*cihuacalli*), the "small room" (*caltepiton* or *caltontli*), the "patio" (*ithualli*), or the "upper story" (*acocalli*) (Kellogg 1993).

The records of the late pre-Hispanic Tenochcan Mexica reveal an extremely diverse array of movable property, particularly smaller manufactured items used for a variety of purposes. All Mexica, regardless of class, gender, and occupation, appear to have owned an assortment of movable items (though, of course, type, quantity, and quality of goods would have varied markedly), but the movable articles owned by men and women differed significantly. The term *cihuatlatquitl*, or "women's property," referred to the tools used by women to weave and to perform other kinds of work (*FC* 1950–82: VI:29:163; Cline 1986: 113; also see, e.g., the will of Juana Mocel, 1596, AGNT 70–4: fol.16r).[1] People passed these goods on to their survivors and heirs.

[1] Note also that Cline found the parallel term "*oquichtlatquitl*" in a Culhuacan will in which one testator referred to his "men's things," which appear to have included his boat, chest, *tecomate,* bed, and some small planks (quoted and translated in Cline 1986: 227 [n. 13]).

Ethnohistorical evidence suggests that Tenochcan Mexica inheritance practices were bilateral and partible, placing roughly equal emphasis on lineal (to descendants) and collateral (primarily to siblings) patterns of transmission. In the next chapter, I argue that these inheritance patterns are congruent with a cognatic kinship structure and with a complex household organization structured around lineal ties among parents, grandparents, and descendants and lateral ties among siblings.

Both chronicles and early colonial testaments indicate that males and females, noble and non-noble, inherited property. According to the *Florentine Codex,* one of the responsibilities of a father was to accumulate wealth "to protect and divide justly among his children" (IV:38: 127; also see FC X:1:1).[2] Fray Toribio Motolinía called attention to the customs regulating property division in central Mexico when he stated that although

> the will was not the custom in this land, nevertheless, they left the houses and estates to their children, and the eldest, if he were male, possessed it, and was in charge of his brothers and sisters, as the father did in his life. The siblings growing and marrying, the older brother divided with them according to what he had; and if the children were to marry, the siblings themselves became entitled to divide the estates and did with their nephews [and nieces?], as I have said the older brother did with the other property. (1971: 134–35)[3]

During the early colonial period, Mexica testators commonly left real and movable property to both sons and

[2]"qujtetzontia, qujntlapachilhuja, qujtlatlamachia ympilhoã."

[3]el cual testamento no se acostumbraba en esta tierra, sino que dejaban las casas y heredades a sus hijos, y el mayor, si era hombre, lo poseía, y tenía cuidado de sus hermanos y hermanas, como lo tenía el padre en su vida. Yendo los hermanos creciendo y casándose, el hermano mayor partía con ellos, según tenía; y si los hijos eran por casar, entraban en las heredades los mismos hermanos, y hacían con sus sobrinos, como he dicho que hacía el hermano mayor, de la otra hacienda.

daughters (Kellogg 1980: 59–66, 1986*b*: 317–20; Cline 1986: 83). The bilateral inheritance practices likely marked a pre-Hispanic pattern and not a postconquest innovation. S.L. Cline, too, has observed that "women's control of property does not appear to have been a postconquest innovation" (1986: 84). Daughters had access to land through inheritance and dowry. Durán noted that wives customarily brought property to marriages and that both the parents and barrio leaders (*señorcillos de los barrios*) kept records of the property both spouses held when a marriage took place (1967: I:5:57; also see Cline 1986: 115–16).

Nevertheless, gender influenced modes of transmission, access to, and actual use of real property, with women at some disadvantage, especially in regard to land. Sons retained household headship, thereby guarding and having greater use rights to property inherited from parents and grandparents (López de Gómara 1943: II:222–23, 246; will of Hernando de Tapia, 1555, AGNT 37–2:fols.78v–94r).

During the pre-Hispanic period, inheritance appears to have been partible, with real property, both house compounds and land, frequently divided among a testator's children, siblings, and nephews and nieces (Kellogg 1980: 59–66; Cline 1986: 79–82). Mexica landed estates were not unitary; they were fragmented (Gibson 1964: 263–64; Cline 1986: 125; also see wills from period one referred to below). Inheritance practices in which testators divided their holdings among both lineal and collateral kin reinforced the dispersed character of landholdings (Kellogg 1980: chap. 3; Cline 1986: 83).

Early colonial Indian wills, especially those wills made before 1585, frequently granted siblings shares of houses or plots of land in Mexico City (Kellogg 1980: 72–78). In his 1555 will, don Hernando de Tapia stated that his father had held nine plots of land in Atlixuca, now shared by his children.

Which said lands belong to me and my siblings, we who are still living to myself and Juan and Pedro and Diego and Toribio and doña Juana my niece, daughter of doña Juana my sister, and don Andrés my nephew, son of doña Juana my sister, who are two siblings and likewise my sister doña María de Tapia wife of don Pedro lord of Izquincotlapilco such that we are six living siblings among whom are divided the said lands among us in the said paper and paintings [that] above is mentioned. I say we are six inheritors to whom belong the said lands because doña Juana my niece and don Andrés siblings are one inheritor together and thus they are given their lands in the said painting. (AGNT 37–2: fols.86v–87r)[4]

Tenochcan succession patterns within the ruling family also emphasized brother/sibling transmission patterns as opposed to the more lineal patterns found in Texcoco (Offner 1983: 207–8).

Early colonial wills also indicate that lineal and collateral relatives inherited most property, with spouses acquiring less property through inheritance than did these other relatives. Thus, spousal rights to inheritance were limited. The earliest surviving colonial wills, especially those dating from the 1540s to 1585, show that spousal inheritance generally entailed the transmission of use rights only. Most often this involved husbands transmitting use rights of house compounds to their wives (Kellogg 1986b: 320). The available ethnohistorical evidence suggests that during the late pre-Hispanic period, women's property rights derived not from their husbands or

[4]las quales dhas tierras pertenesçen a mi y a mis hermanos los que agora somos a mi y a joan y a pedro y diego y a toriuio e a dona joana mi sobrina hija de dona ju[a] mi hermana y a don andres mi sobrino hijo de dona joana mi hermana que son dos hermanos y asimesmo mi hermana dona maria de tapia muger de don P[o] senor de yzquincotlapilco por manera que somos seis hermanos y hermanas bibos entre los quales estan repartidas las dhas tierras entre nosotros conforme al dho papel y pinturas de que arriba se haze minsion digo que somos seis herederos a los que le pertenescen las dhas tierras porque dona joana mi sobrina y don andres hermanos es un heredero ambos a dos y asi les dan sus tierras en la dha pintura.

from their husbands' households and kin groups but rather from their own households and kin groups and their positions as daughters and siblings within them.

The Mexica bilateral inheritance system bore certain superficial similarities to the Spanish inheritance system. Both systems were bilateral, permitting sons and daughters alike to inherit from their parents and their parents' families though both systems exhibited variation geographically. In theory, the Spanish inheritance system, like that of the Mexica, was partible; in practice, however, a number of strategies existed, including the entailing of estates through the practice of *mayorazgo*, by which landed properties remained intact (Ladd 1976: 71–76). Moreover, in the Spanish system, spouses and children enjoyed far stronger rights than adult siblings (*Siete Partidas*, P6.T13.5). Certain characteristics separated Tenochcan Mexica inheritance practices from those of the Spanish: a greater emphasis on partibility of inherited property and consequently more dispersed landholdings; the importance of lateral modes of property transmission; and somewhat less emphasis on spousal or affinal ties as a route of property transmission.

Not only were the rules that organized indigenous inheritance practices distinct from those that underlay Hispanic practices but examination of wills suggests that the content of wills made by Mexica and Spanish residents of Mexico City during the sixteenth century also differed. Whereas sixteenth-century Spanish wills tended to concentrate inheritances within the nuclear family,[5] Indian wills placed greater emphasis on inheritance among a wide circle of kin, including collateral relatives and grandchildren (also see Anderson, Ber-

---

[5]To facilitate comparison, I collected a small group of wills made by Spaniards from the Archivo de Notarías and the *ramos Tierras* and *Bienes Nacionales* of the AGN. Most of these wills (twenty-four in total) were written between the years 1570 and 1599, with thirteen by women and eleven by men. In addition, brief summaries of thirty-four wills made by Spaniards may be found in Millares and Mantecón (1945–46).

dan, and Lockhart 1976: 6). In part, this reflected past Mexica practice. But it also reflected greater Spanish desire to prevent estates and other property holdings from becoming overly fragmented (Altman 1989: 156–58, 163) and the fact that recent Spanish immigrants to the New World had not yet produced dense kinship networks. A variety of pieces of evidence suggest that sixteenth-century Spaniards were more interested than the Mexica in maintaining unified property holdings. Spanish wills rank order inheritors in categories of spouses and descendants, followed by ascendants and, last, collaterals. Likewise, while in the sixteenth century Indians rarely left a "universal heredero," Spaniards almost always did. Over time, Spanish wills, especially those left by elite families, became more complex as Spanish family structures and kinship networks in New Spain grew denser and families devised strategies to deal with demographic vagaries and to keep estates from fragmenting (Couturier 1978; Tutino 1983). Nevertheless, important differences with Indian wills persisted.

Indians wills are an important source of information about the social history of the early colonial period. They indicate that the material basis for the class structure of Mexica society became severely weakened during the early colonial period and that a gradual transformation took place in the nature of their kinship networks and family and household structures—a subject that chapter 5 examines in depth. The remainder of this chapter offers a close textual analysis of Indian wills that survive from early colonial Mexico City, tracing indigenous responses to the far-reaching changes that occurred in the social and material conditions of their lives.

TESTAMENTS AS TEXTS

Why did Indians begin to make wills in the sixteenth century? I argue that they were not simply mimicking Spanish inheritance rules and practices; rather, they were adapting this Spanish custom, sometimes forced on them, for their own purposes.

In the late sixteenth century, Gonzalo Gómez de Cervantes insisted that parish priests preyed on ill and dying Indian men and women, ordering them to make wills. He claimed their motive was to enrich the Church.

An Indian man or woman becomes ill, and being in danger, the friars in charge of his [or her] *doctrina* order him [or her] to make a will in which, although he [or she] might have and leave many legitimate children, he [or she] leaves them disinherited, and the few goods, houses and lands that he [or she] has he [or she] gives to the Church that unforgivably seizes them, and leaves the children without anything. (1944: 185–86)[6]

Early ecclesiastical writings, in contrast, which include two "model wills,"[7] dating from 1565 and 1611, respectively, imply that parish priests held a range of motives for encouraging or pressuring Indians to write wills and that they cannot simply be reduced to a desire to enrich the Church.[8]

[6]Enferma un indio o india, y estando en peligro, los frailes a cuyo cargo es su doctrina mándanle hacer testamento en el cual, aunque tenga y deje muchos hijos legítimos, los deja desheredados, y los pocos bienes, casas y tierras que tiene los manda a la Iglesia, que irremisiblemente los aprehende, y quedan los hijos sin ninguna parte.

[7]I define a "model will" as one written in Nahuatl for the instruction of natives though this instruction was mediated by both priests and native scribes. The reader should note also two important differences between these texts. Molina's will offers both a Nahuatl version and directly below it, on each folio, a Spanish translation. León's text is only in Nahuatl. Second, while Molina explicitly addresses his text to male or female testators, León envisions his testator as male, as his will discusses the testator's wife (fol.140r).

[8]The description of Catholic funerals in the *NCE* (VI: 225–26) makes it clear that Catholic funerary practices were less elaborated than those for birth and marriage. Furthermore, the influences of class, gender, and manner of death on funerary practices was more muted for Spaniards than for Indians. When friars wrote about their experiences or gave advice to other friars, they emphasized birth, marriage, confession, and the making of wills more than death itself or funerals (e.g., León [1611] and Pérez [1713]).

The *Confesionario mayor, en lengua mexicana y castellana* by the learned linguist of Nahuatl, Fray Alonso Molina, contains a detailed discussion of the Catholic sacraments, including a section describing the formal religious acts surrounding death (also see Lockhart 1992: App. B). Among other concerns, Molina wanted Indian scribes to make valid wills under proper conditions and without undue pressure (1565: fol.60r). He instructed scribes not to force Indians to make wills or to influence the allocation of bequests (fol.60r). Molina also stated that Indian testators should understand that the act of making a will would prevent their belongings from being misused, squandered, or destroyed (fols.59r–59v). But it did not escape Molina's notice that the preparation of a will offered an ideal opportunity to reinforce both Christian beliefs and Spanish practices concerning property. While Molina himself advised that the witnesses should keep secret the contents of wills (fol.60v; also see Lockhart 1992: 471–72), the texts of wills indicate that the documents were often written and signed in the presence of family, friends, and local officials. Molina instructed scribes to ask testators to describe their religious history and whether their children had been born after they were married by the Church (fol.60r). Thus, the will-making process actually provided a semipublic vehicle for drawing attention to Catholic beliefs about marriage, legitimacy, death, the soul and the afterlife, and property transmission. But wills, especially those written during the sixteenth century, continued to express the orality, kinship connections, and patterns of property transmission characteristic of Mexica culture (insofar as these could be expressed within rapidly changing circumstances).

Martín de León's confession manual, *Camino del cielo*, published in 1611, contains another set of instructions for the writing of wills. Less concerned than Molina with scribal procedures or with the use of the will-making process to reinforce Catholic belief and practice, León advocated will making on more practical and pragmatic grounds: so that Indian souls would not suffer from their earthly debts and so that children would know what belongs to them (fols.136v–137v). Yet despite their general disavowal of priests influencing Indian bequests, both Molina and León did in fact discuss how Indians should divide and allocate their goods.[9]

Their instructions explicitly followed Spanish edicts, though in a highly simplified form that reduced inheritance law to its bare essentials. Both men emphasized the importance of bequeathing goods to one's children. Both also referred to other possible heirs, including parents, grandparents, or spouses (Molina 1565: fol.61r; León 1611: fol.138r). In the text of his sample will, Molina listed two specific charitable contributions, one for "the poor," the other for "the hospital" (*ymmotolinia, los pobres; ospital, hospital*) (Molina 1565: fol.63r). His only suggested bequest to the Church consisted of payment for the burial and the recitation of some masses (fol.62r). León, by contrast, explicitly stated that four-fifths of an estate should go to the testator's children and one-fifth to the Church (1611: fol.138r). If Gómez de Cervantes's belief that priests sought to use wills to enrich the Church was oversimplified, it is also clear that the motivations of early priests like Molina—concerned with testators' souls, legitimacy of procedure, and the reinforcing of newly introduced practices—gave way by the beginning of the seventeenth century to greater material concerns that children and the Church each receive their due.

Molina's spiritual, procedural, even ideological, interests were reflected in the organization of his sample will. The longest sections of the will dealt not with the distribution of property but with the presentation of a "reli-

<hr />

[9]It is interesting that Molina's concern with possible religious coercion and pressure is echoed in Chimalpahin's brief discussion of Indian wills (1963–65: II:66) but not in León's.

gious formula"—a lengthy statement of basic Catholic beliefs and doctrine.[10] In fact, the section of the will dealing with property bequests was quite short. It suggested that the testator leave his or her property in the following way:

> My four houses, my three fields, my gold, my precious stones (they were truly my belongings when I married). And I say that the belongings of my spouse (they were already his/her belongings when we married); he/she should take everything. And everything that has increased, in all the time that we lived together, which I will state here (it is necessary that everything be told), should be divided, one part apart [for the spouse], my children will take [the other part]. (Molina 1565: fol.62v)[11]

The will's final section listed the testator's own debts, money owed to the testator, the names of the testator's children, and the names of the individuals charged with

---

[10]In this opening section, the wills often stated that while the testator was ill, \ his or her mind was sound and that as he or she was awaiting death, he or she was making a will. This section always states the testator's belief in God and the Holy Trinity and often asks for forgiveness for his or her sins. Instructions about burial and masses were included here as well. Specific bequests to pay for these would also be listed (also see Kellogg 1986*b*: 316; Cline 1986: 19–21; Anderson, Berdan, and Lockhart 1976: 23,26).

[11]The Nahuatl passage reads:
> yn nocal nauhtetl, yn nomil etetl, yn noteocuitl, yn nochalchiuh (yn vel naxca catca, yn iquac ninonamicti) Auh yzcatqui, nicteneua yn uel yyaxca nonamic, yn nochantlacatl (yn iyaxca ytlatqui [vel] mochiutica yn iq̄c titonamictique) mochi q'cuiz. Auh yn ixquich yc otlapiuix, yn yxquichcauitl toneuan otinenque, yehuatl in ye nicā nicteneua (monequi quitoz yn quexquich) tlacoxelihuiz, cētlamantli yz cecni, quicuizque yn nopilhuan.

Molina's Spanish version reads:
> Quatro casas, y tres heredades, mi oro y plata y piedras preciosas (las quales yo tenia y posseya antes que me casase) y declaro tābien aqui, la hazienda propia de mi muger y huespeda (la qual truxo cosigo, quandonos desposamos y casamos) la qual toda, tomara ella. Y todo lo que se ha multiplicado, e todo el tiempo que emos ambos biuido jūtos que es lo que aqui dire (conuiene que lo declare todo) se partiera en dos partes, la vna de las quales tomara ella y la otra parte, tomara mis hijos.

Also note that while the Nahuatl version is gender neutral, the Spanish translation provided by Molina assumed a male testator.

overseeing the children. This model will named two individuals, both male, to care for the children and the distribution of the testator's property. Neither appears to have been envisioned as a member of the testator's family or indeed of his immediate kin group. The will also listed the names of five male witnesses and the scribe and stated further that only bequests specifically made in the will should be honored (fol.63v). While in Molina's view, a testament was a legal document disposing of a person's property and estate after death, it also declared the individual's spiritual principles.

Likewise, León's model will contained a statement of religious principles, including a lengthy discussion of the testator's belief in the tripartite divinity and an expression of concern for his or her soul in the afterlife. But León, unlike Molina, gave more attention to institutionalized Church practices—such as the bequest of money for specific types of masses and the individual's cofradía (fol.138v)—and to the disposition of goods. The model will listed property including houses (calli), land (*milli*), and various movables such as maguey (*metl*), cloaks or blankets (*tilmatli*), precious stones (*chalchihuitl*), and money, in tomines and pesos (fol.140r). León's testament, like Molina's, clearly distinguished between the testator's property and the property brought to the marriage by his wife. León suggested that this individual leave his property to his children, or, if they died prematurely, to his grandchildren, parents, or grandparents, with a share of what had increased during the marriage going to the wife (fol.140v). And like Molina, León concluded with a statement that the will was freely made and signed before four witnesses (fol.141r).

The writing of wills was probably an adopted—and not a pre-Hispanic—practice.[12] The earliest surviving wills date from the 1540s. This suggests that will making

---

[12]Cline makes the very reasonable suggestion that prior to the conquest, the Mexica may have "publicly bequeathed property through oral declarations" (1986: 16; also see Durand-Forest 1962).

began just prior to the 1550s and became a more common activity during the following decade, remaining so throughout the colonial period (also see Loera y Chávez 1977; Cline 1986; Wood 1991*b*). Some were made under the auspices of either parcialidad or barrio officials (e.g., will of Diego Tlacochcalcatl, 1566, AGNT 48–4; will of Martín Lázaro, 1551, AGNT 20–1–3); some reflected the guidance of Indian cofradías and cofradía officials (e.g., will of Angelina Martina, 1585, AGNT 49–5); others were produced under the auspices of Indian church officials (e.g., will of Juana Micaela, 1685, NL/Ayer 1481F[9a]).

All together, this chapter analyzes sixty-three wills from various repositories made by Indians resident in Mexico City during the period from 1550 to 1700. Men executed thirty-one of them; women, thirty-two.[13] In format, the wills follow the general form of Molina's and León's sample wills. But in many particulars, they differ from the samples. The indigenous wills, like Molina's and León's models, began with a religious formula—a statement of faith invoking God and the Holy Trinity. The testators then stated their names, their places of residence (including their parcialidad and tlaxilacalli), and the date that the will was executed. Next, the testators declared their intention to make a will, frequently adding that they did so freely and without duress. Bequests for masses, burials, and charities follow. Some of these masses were for themselves; others were for relatives who had already died. Early wills contained few bequests for masses for spouses. Deceased parents and siblings were preferred for this honor. By 1650, however, testators regularly left bequests for masses to be said for predeceased spouses and even in-laws.

[13]Most of the wills come from the AGN; a significant number, especially of the later wills, come from the Ayer Collection at the Newberry Library. Note also that two women appear to have drafted five wills during the late sixteenth century.

Only then did the testators describe the disposition of their properties. Usually, the wills listed houses first, followed by landed property and movable goods. Debts came last, along with the names of the *albaceas* (executors) asked to carry out the will's provisions and the witnesses present at the will's signing. Up to 1650, wills followed this general format with minor variations in order and detail (in a few wills, movable property was listed before houses and landed property), though the types and amounts of property owned by testators varied greatly.

In four specific ways, the actual wills produced by sixteenth-century Mexica differ from the models of Molina and León. First, the wills employed much shorter religious formulas. While some included model statements of religious piety (see, e.g., the will of Hernando de Tapia, 1555, AGNT 37–2, or the will of Ana Tiacapan, 1566, AGNT 35–6), others contained *no* religious formula at all (e.g., will of Martín Lázaro Pantecatl, 1551, AGNT 20–1–3) or only a highly abbreviated formula (see the will of María Xocoyotl, 1569, AGNT 35–6). Second, these wills referred to a wider range of kin than do the models. Third, the descriptions, categorizations, and bequest patterns (particularly for real property) were complex and reflective of both pre-Hispanic forms of property ownership and the changing economic and social situations of Indians during the early colonial period. Finally, sixteenth-century Mexica wills, unlike the model wills, generally did not clearly distinguish between the testator's property and the spouse's property, or between goods owned prior to marriage and those acquired during a marriage.

The surviving seventeenth-century wills provide vivid contrasts to their sixteenth-century counterparts. Religious formulas were even more abbreviated than in sixteenth-century wills. Further, bequests of land appear far less frequently. Unlike the sixteenth-century testaments, which are often lengthy and complex documents encompassing a wide variety of social relations and material goods, seventeenth-century wills are more truncated. There are, however, two respects in which the later wills, especially those written after 1650, resemble the models of Molina and León: in their clear emphasis on children and spouses and their corresponding de-emphasis of other kin.

TYPES OF GOODS AND BEQUEST PATTERNS

1546–1584

Twenty-three wills have been found which were written between 1546 and 1584: nine by men, fourteen by women. Tables 1 and 2 identify these wills by the date on which they were written, the name of the testator, the language in which the will was inscribed, and the archive in which the will is currently located.

Table 1
Men's Wills, 1548–1577

Source/ Location	Year	Name of Testator	Language[a]
AGNT 35–1	1548	Juan Tehuitzil	S
AGNT 20–1–3	1551	Martín Lázaro Pantecatl	N/S
AGNT 37–2	1555	Hernando de Tapia	S
AGNT 49–5[b]	1555	Don Diego de Mendoza	S
AGNT 48–4	1566	Diego Tlacochcalcatl	N/S
AGNT 1595–4	1569	Antonio Quahuitencatl	N/S
AGNT 38–2	1576	Francisco Hernández Quauhçequi	N/S
AGNBN 293–1	1576	Francisco Xochpanecatl	N
AGNT 39–2–-1	1577	Martín Jacobo	N/S

[a]N = Nahuatl; S = Spanish.
[b]Only a partial text is extant.

137

Table 2
Women's Wills, 1546–1581

Source/ Location	Year	Name of Testator	Language[a]
AGNT 35–1	1546	Angelina Poqui	S
AGNT 42–5	1560	Francisca Tecuchu	S
AGNT 22–1-5	1561	Magdalena Tiacapan	S
AGNT 2729–20	1561	Marina Tiacapan	N
AGNT 35–6	1566	Ana Tiacapan	N/S
AGNT 35–6	1569	María Xocoyotl	N/S
BNP 112	1570	Beatriz Papan	S
AGNT 56–8	1574	Juana Hernández	S
AGNT 42–5	1576	Francisca Tlaco	N/S
AGNT 48–4	1576	Juana Francisca	N/S
AGNT 56–8	1576	Juana de Santana	S
AGNT 56–8[b]	1579	Angelina de la Cruz	S
AGNT 49–5	1580	Angelina Martina	N/S
NL/Ayer 1481B(1a)	1581	Elena Angelina	N

[a]N = Nahuatl; S = Spanish.
[b]Only a partial text is extant.

What kinds of material items did these testators leave to their inheritors? Their properties fall into the categories identified by Molina: residential property, land, and movables, usually in that order. Residential properties, or what we might term "house compounds," were frequently described room by room, with each room listed separately and described by function, location, orientation, and/or who had previously used or owned it. In wills, compounds varied from one to five rooms, with the greatest number of compounds containing three. Six house structures had one or two rooms (though the majority of these had two), and thirteen had three, four, or five rooms (five more had two or more rooms but were not precisely described).[14]

[14]These numbers agree well with the range suggested by house plans and descriptive material in other legal texts (see Calnek 1972, 1976; Kellogg 1992b).

Testators provided very precise descriptions of each room within a house compound and detailed information about who should inherit it. An example of such descriptions can be found in a will made by María Xocoyotl in 1569.

> The first thing I declare, first of all, that which leads the way, is the *cihuacalli,* which faces towards Xochimilco and a small upper-story room faces east and a small room faces west and there is a passageway there at the door that is there. I truly understand that it is my house because my husband, Domingo Temmolonqui, left it to me. And, second, I declare that I have three children there, the first is named María Tiacapan who was married in Xochimilco. The other two are not yet married. The first is named Marcharita Tecuhccho and the other is named Quidelia Xocoyotl. I promised four rooms, I give them to my two children. And the patio, they should use it together. And the oldest, truly the first, is there in the house of her husband, in Xochimilco. However, I bestow money [upon her]. (AGNT 35–6:fol.8r)[15]

The wills identify three kinds of landed property commonly left by the testators. One form of landed property was the site on which house compounds were built, usually referred to as *tlalli* in Nahuatl (e.g., Martin Jacobo's will, AGNT 39–2–1) and *solar* in Spanish. Although the dimensions of compound plots were precisely measured in sale documents (e.g., documents of sale

[15]The Nahuatl passage reads:

> Ynic centlamantli yn niquitova achtopa yevatl y yacattiuh in cihuacalli xochmilcopa ytzticac yvan acocaltontli yquiçayanpa tonatiuh ytzticac yvan caltontli ycalaquiampa tonatiuh ytzticac yvan ocaltontli ycac oncan quix-ovayan puelta oncan ycac huel noyollo quimati ca nocal oncan nechcauhtia ȳ nonamic̄ Domingo temmolonqui. Auh occeppa niquitova ȳ nevatl ca oncate nopilhuan yeintin ynic ce ytoca maria tiacapan omonamicti ompa xochmil-co Auh yn oc ome ayamo monamictia ynic ce ytoca marcharita tecuhccho auh yn oc ce ytoca quidelia xocoyotl yn onicteneuh yn calli nauhtetl çan niquincemmaca yn ome nopilvan Auh çan icemitval çan cenquicazque Auh in yacapantli canel ycoya ca onca ycal yn inamic yn xochimilco tel nictlaoco-liz tomintin.

collected in AGNHJ 298–4, 1592–93), the descriptions included in wills of the compounds themselves were much more elaborate than those of the plots of earth on which they were built.

A second kind of landed property was an urban raised or floating garden connected to a house site, known as a chinampa. Descriptions of these gardens, like those of house sites, were vague, and their dimensions were often not given. While all male and female testators left house property during this period, only nine testators left chinampas: five (of fourteen) women and four (of ten) men. The typical number of chinampas bequeathed was three.

Testators also left rural fields, categorized in a variety of ways. The most commonly used terms were *milli* (field), *huehuetlalli* (old or inherited land, translated as "patrimonial land" in Spanish documents), and *tlalcohualli* (bought land). Less frequently, land was referred to as *tlalmilli* or *tlalmantli*.[16] Testators identified the location of lands through the use of toponyms or boundary markers, most often others' fields (also see Cline 1986: 126; Horn 1989a: chap.4). Wills also frequently described the sizes of rural fields by designating length and width or only length (also see Cline 1986: 129).

Conspicuously missing from the wills are terms referred to in chronicles dealing with pre-Hispanic land tenure: *tlatocatlalli,* office land; *teotlalli,* temple land; *tecpantlalli,* palace land; and *calpullalli, calpulli* (community) land (also see Cline 1986: chap.8; Lockhart 1992: chap.5).[17] Of course, wills may not offer a full picture of early colonial Indian landholdings, given the small number of wills, especially the scarcity of those left by men (since they tended to own more land than women). Or it

---

[16]According to Molina, tlalmilli consisted of "tierras o heredades de particulares que están juntas en alguna vega" (1971: II:fol.124r). Tlalmantli consisted of "tierra allanada o ygualada" (fol.124r; also see Cline 1986: 137).

[17]Note that there are occasional references to *pillalli* (noble land); see below for an example.

may well be that certain precolonial categories of land were already ceasing to exist by the time Indians began to write wills. Another possible explanation for the absence of terms denoting pre-Hispanic forms of land tenure may be that Indian landholders who wrote wills during the early colonial period wanted to emphasize *how* they had obtained land by stating whether it was inherited or bought rather than emphasizing its civil classification.

All together, just three female testators left land apart from house plots or chinampas, compared to six male testators. While native women could and did transmit, buy, and inherit land during the early colonial period, they did so less frequently than men. For both men and women, the ownership of land signaled greater wealth and higher socioeconomic status.

While only a few individuals left rural land, virtually all left some type of movable property. Only two male testators listed no movables; all female testators passed along this type of property. The most common items identified in the wills, named in descending order of amount by item, were money, household and work-related goods, clothing, and religious objects (including candles, crucifixes, and, in a single will, an image of the Virgin Mary).

Testators bequeathed money for a variety of purposes: to pay debts and to pay for religious masses, burials, and items like candles. Money also substituted for shares in real property, especially for close relatives who could not receive equal shares for some reason (see, e.g., María Xocoyotl's will, passage translated above) or who had moved away (see, e.g., will of Martín Jacobo, 1577, AGNT 39–2–1). Small money bequests might also be given to distant kin or to nonkin who had provided services to the testator. While men tended to leave greater amounts of money, most individuals, male or female, included some monetary bequests.

Among the household items and work-related objects passed on in bequests were the *metates* that women used for food preparation and the *ollas* and *tecomatl* that women and men used for storage. Textiles, thread belonging to women, and tools used by men also would be given away—most often to testators' children. Both men and women frequently bequeathed clothing to heirs as well.

Although Indian wills include itemized lists of property, they should not be regarded as mere inventories. In addition to furnishing a catalog of property holdings, wills are important cultural documents. By analyzing how Indians allocated their property, it is possible to reconstruct certain aspects of the changing nature of Mexica family and kinship relations. In the paragraphs that follow, we will seek to understand the factors that influenced bequests.[18] As we will see, gender, demographic circumstances (such as who of an individual's circle of kin was alive and in reasonable proximity), and how a particular piece of property had been acquired (not to mention the quality of particular interpersonal relationships) all influenced bequests. Table 3 enumerates bequests for distinct categories of property by gender.

Three significant patterns emerge from tables 4.1 through 4.3. The first is the wide range of kin who received shares in property: children, siblings, and nephews and nieces as well as grandchildren and great-grandchildren (also see Anderson, Berdan, and Lockhart 1976: 6; Cline 1986: 65–77). Siblings and their children were especially likely to receive shares of houses or land that the testators, male or female, had themselves inherited. This property was often referred to as *huehuecalli* or *huehuetlalli* (Kellogg 1980: 73–78; 1986*b*: 323–25). Property that a testator had purchased rarely went to siblings or nephews and nieces; it most often was left to children and grandchildren.

The second significant inheritance pattern is a ten-

---

[18]For the impact of interpersonal relationships on bequests, see the will of Francisco Xochpanecatl, 1576, AGNBN 293–1: fol.243r; also see discussion of bequest patterns in the next period for a negative example.

Table 3
Number of Wills Showing Bequests to Relatives,
by Gender and Property Type, 1546–1584[a]

Men	sp	so/da		bro/sis		gso/gda		ne/ni		af/o[b]	
Houses	7	1	5	1	2	2	0	1	1	1	2
Land	4	1	3	2	2	2	0	2	2	1	1
Movable property	4	1	1	1	2	1	0	1	1	0	2
Women											
Houses	0	2	7	1	3	2	4	1	1	2	2[c]
Land	1	1	4	0	0	2	2	2	0	4	3[d]
Movable property	0	2	5	0	0	3	2	1	0	3	0
All											
Houses	7	3	12	2	5	4	4	2	2	3	4
Land	5	2	7	2	2	4	2	4	2	5	4
Movable property	4	3	6	1	2	4	2	2	1	3	2

[a]In each table of this type in this chapter, the following abbreviations will be used: sp = spouse; so = son; da = daughter; bro = brother; sis = sister; gso = grandson; gda = granddaughter; ne = nephew; ni = niece; af = affine; and o = other. The category "other" includes individuals not identified as kin or distant kin that cannot be accommodated on this chart.

[b]In one will, an inheritor was the testator's father's father's brother's child's son (will of Martín Jacobo, 1577, AGNT 39–2–1).

[c]One will includes bequests to a great-grandson and great-granddaughter (will of Angelina Martina, 1580, AGNT 49–5).

[d]One will left a small plot of land to a servant; another left land to a great-grandson and great-granddaughter (will of Ana Tiacapan, 1566, AGNT 35–6, and will of Angelina Martina, 1580, AGNT 49–5, respectively).

dency for women to favor female inheritors, especially for houses and movable property. Women willed little property to their husbands. No husband inherited house property from a wife; only one husband received a small share of an urban solar (will of Magdalena Tiacapan, 1561, AGNT 22–1–5). Likewise, no wife acquired land from a husband, although wives frequently received shares in house compounds. In an example of gendered inheritance practices, women tended to leave daughters and granddaughters the greatest shares of their proper-

143

ties—sometimes to the exclusion of living male relatives. The notable exception was landed property; here women to some degree favored male relatives (Kellogg 1986*b*: 322).[19] Angelina Martina (1580, AGNT 49–5), for example, left her grandsons a disproportionate share of her landed property, while her granddaughters inherited greater shares of her houses and movable goods.

A third pattern embedded in the wills is that sons received strikingly few bequests. This pattern probably reflects high rates of male mortality (Gibson 1964: 141) and male absence from family groups, barrios, or even Mexico City. Several legal cases contain references to male relatives who were absent, having married elsewhere (e.g., AGNT 21–1–2, 1565) or left the city (e.g., AGNT 20–1–3, 1573; 39–2–6, 1577). It seems likely that the absence of male relatives was socially disruptive and was one of the causes of litigation as women and children turned to the courts to enforce their property rights.

1585–1649

Property bequests underwent subtle transformations during the late sixteenth and the early seventeenth century. Among other things, the wills reveal a marked change in the kinds of material entities left and in the

[19]Cline has argued—in relationship to houses—that women in Culhuacan "did not seem to have a preferred class of heirs" (1986: 80). There is, however, some evidence in her data of gender differences in bequest patterns. When discussing sibling inheritance patterns, she notes, for example, that "while men mentioned sisters as frequently as brothers, women mainly mentioned sisters" (75). She also states that certain categories of land "were generally not bequeathed to spouses but seem to have been given to heirs of the same sex, often lineal descendants—children and grandchildren" (82). Cline also found that women felt less "constrained to bequeath residences to living heirs" (79), i.e., that they were freer in their bequest patterns, often choosing to sell houses for masses. While geographic variation and sample size (my smaller number for the sixteenth century) may account for some differences in our findings, time may also be a significant factor. That is, the majority of her wills date from the years 1580 and 1581, which is close to the time when significant changes in bequest patterns and kinship arrangements were becoming routinized as part of larger cultural adjustments.

category of kin receiving bequests. These developments, I will argue, were closely tied to the emergence of a more "mature" colonial urban Indian culture in the seventeenth century. Among the important shifts taking place were the decline of extended family households and kin groups and the increasing impoverishment of Mexico City's indigenous population. Twenty-one wills date from the period 1585 to 1649. Twelve wills were executed by men and nine by women. Tables 4 and 5 summarize the information contained in these testaments.

Table 4
Men's Wills, 1587–1642

Source/ Location	Year	Name of Testator	Languageᵃ
AGNT 442–5	1587	Pedro Doçan	N
AGNT 59–3	1588	Pedro Jacobo	N/S
Gates. Coll. box 1, folder 21ᵇ	1590	Don Gaspar de Buena Bentura	N
AGNT 1595–4	1591	Joséph Ramírez	N/S
AGNBN 1455–5	1604	Martín Xochitl	N
AGNT 95–8	1607	Antón Jacobo	S
AGNT 157–7	1615	Juan Matías	N/S
AGNT 1586–1	1618	Don Melchor de Mendoza	S
AGNT 1592–1	1630	Gaspar de Mendoza	S
AGNT 1720–7	1632	Sebastián Francisco	N/S
AGNBN 339–8	1634	Baltasar Bautista	N/S
AGNT 101–2	1642	Joséph Melchior	N/S

ᵃN = Nahautl; S = Spanish.

ᵇThis will is probably a forgery, written about one century later. It has certain characteristics in common with the Techialoyan Codices, seventeenth-century texts containing maps and claims to town ownership of certain lands to the south and west of Mexico City, and is not included in the analysis herein. Important discussions of the Techialoyan texts may be found in Galarza (1980), Harvey (1986a), Wood (1984), and Borah (1991) as well as Lockhart (1992).

Early seventeenth-century Indian wills indicate a downturn in Indian life, most notably, a growing impoverishment and economic compression. Fewer wills made

Table 5
Women's Wills, 1587–1642

Source/Location	Year	Name of Testator	Language[a]
AGNT 54–5	1587	Isabel Ana	N/S
AGNT 56–8	1591	Juana Hernández	S
AGNT 59–3	1595	Juana Antonia	N/S
AGNT 70–4	1596	Juana Mocel	N/S
AGNT 1595–4	1606	Magdalena Ramírez	S
AGNT 128–2	1609	Juana Agustina	N/S
AGNT 101–2	1616	Juana María	N/S
BNP 299[b]	1623	María Alonso	N/S
NL/Ayer 1481F(5)	1642	Ana Melchiora	N

[a]N = Nahautl; S = Spanish.
[b]This will was transcribed and translated into French by Durand-Forest (1962).

bequests of landed property. House sizes had diminished, as had the average number of rooms in each house compound. The modal number of rooms (which range from one to seven) was still three, but house sites with one or two rooms were now more numerous than the larger ones. Wills themselves had grown simpler by the early seventeenth century. No longer did they describe the functions of particular rooms in a household compound. Baltasar Bautista's will (1639, AGNBN 339–8) offers an example of the simplified manner in which houses were now depicted; he referred to a large house structure with five rooms (*caltzitlin macuiltemanin* [fol. 2r]), with each room then identified only by orientation.

A few wills mention urban house sites (usually referred to as either tlalmantli [e.g., will of Joséph Ramírez, 1591, AGNT 1595–4] or tlalli [e.g., will of Baltasar Bautista, 1639, AGNBN, 339–8]). A number of others refer to chinampas; four wills mentioned chinampas associated with house sites, one with three chinampas (will of Joséph Ramírez, 1591, AGNT 1595–4; will of Juan Matías, 1615, AGNT 157–5), two others with two (will of Juana Antonia, 1595, AGNT 59–3; will of Juana María, 1616, AGNT 101–2).

Only four wills list nonurban agricultural land, two executed by men and two by women. Two wills were written by a father and daughter (Joseph and Magdalena Ramírez), and both included land that can be traced one generation farther back to Joséph Ramírez's father-in-law, Antonio Quahuitencatl. Antonio left four fields, milli, to his son-in-law, Joséph Ramírez Mahuito, in a will written in 1569 (AGNT 1595–4). In 1591, Joséph Ramírez bequeathed to his children, Andres and Magdalena, three milli, each of which was clearly located where Antonio Quahuitencatl had described them in his will, two were exactly the same size, and one field was larger. By 1606, when Joséph Ramírez's daughter, Magdalena Ramírez, dictated her will (which survives only in Spanish), one field had been divided into two pieces (*es en dos pedassos* [will of Magdalena Ramírez, 1606, AGNT 1595–4: fol.15r]) and she no longer owned another one of the plots. But she did have a third field that she perhaps had bought as she referred to having "papers and a drawing" (*papeles y pintura,* fol.15r]). Significant landholdings consisting of five separate plots were listed in Juana Agustina's will of 1609 (AGNT 128–2), located in or near a small community that was a sujeto of Santiago Tlatelolco.

The only other notable rural landholdings were those mentioned in the 1618 will of don Melchor de Mendoza Guaquaupitzahuac.[20] Don Melchor, the son of don Diego de Mendoza de Austria y Montezuma, left major landholdings to his two sons, don Gaspar Diego and don Juan, as well as to his grandchildren, don Juan de Santa María and don Diego de Santa María. This will is particularly interesting because while Mendoza listed twelve separate pieces of land ranging in size from forty brazas

[20]His brothers were don Baltasar de Mendoza Montezuma and don Gaspar de Mendoza Axayacatl (will, 1618, AGNT 1585–1: fol.24r). He identified them but left them no property.

to over one thousand brazas,[21] his other possessions were quite minimal. He mentioned the house he owned in Santiago Tlatelolco which had two rooms and an *oratorio*, a small chapel where religious statues were kept (AGNT 1586–1: fol.24r). In describing the smaller items, he stated that "All that is in my house, consisting of not many boxes and *petates* [bundles], must go to my children and my wife" (fol.25r).[22] His lands, by contrast, were far more extensive, and he described them in much greater detail. He gave the location and a measurement for each piece of land, and he often stated the name(s) of an official in a *cabecera* (head town) or a nearby pueblo who could verify that the property belonged to him. He left six plots to his grandsons, two to his sons, one to a "doña Agustina" (without clarifying who she was in relation to him), and three with no instructions about who was to inherit them. He identified five plots as "*tierras de cacicazgo*" (lands associated with Cacique rule), three of which he bequeathed to his grandchildren, two of which he did not specify who should inherit.[23]

These wills illustrate that while Indian landowner-ship was declining, a small number of Indians still had access to rural property through inheritance or purchase. But mainly, the wills offer a record of urban Indians selling off their landholdings. In 1588, Pedro Jacobo, for example, gave two pesos from the sale of "our huehuetlalli" (*tohuehuetlal* [AGNT 59–3: fol.17r]) to his aunt for safekeeping so the money could be used to pay for his burial.[24] As Tenochcan Mexica landholdings

---

[21]Note that for most of his lands he gave only one measurement (also see Cline 1986: 129; Horn 1989a: chap.4).

[22]"Todo lo que hay dentro de mi Casa que no son muchas Caxas y petates, ha de ser para mis hijos y mi muger."

[23]If these plots that had no inheritors specifically listed also went to his sons, that would mean his sons and grandchildren would receive roughly equal shares in his real property with his grandchildren receiving six pieces of land and his sons receiving five pieces of land plus his house.

[24]A sale of huehuecalli was also mentioned in the will of Pedro Doçan (1587, AGNT 442–5: fol.8v) who described how his wife had sold "her huehuecalli

declined, the Nahuatl terminology for land became less elaborated during this period. By 1600, there were no longer any references to huehuetlalli, neither were there references to tlalcohualli. The only terms I have found are *milli* or *tlalli*. The number of testators owning chinampas or other types of land is far smaller than in the period 1546–1584.[25]

Movable properties assumed a new importance in wills written between 1595 and 1649. In the wills of Juana Mocel (1596, AGNT 70–4) and Pedro Jacobo (1588, AGNT 59–3), for example, movables—including money and other items—were listed directly after the testators' own dwellings, with small pieces of real property along with other presumably less valuable items recorded later. Objects mentioned in wills included money, household and work items, religious items, and clothing. New kinds of storage objects, such as boxes or baskets, also appeared. Religious objects were included more frequently and in greater numbers than in earlier wills (including crucifixes, figures or images of the Virgin Mary, and saints' images [the latter mentioned first in the testaments of Baltasar Bautista, 1634, AGNBN 339–8, and Joséph Melchior, 1642, AGNT 101–2]). Clothing was listed relatively infrequently in these wills, but three new items appeared: women listed pans (e.g., *bayla,* will of Juana Mocel, 1596, AGNT 70–4: fol.13v), maguey plants were occasionally mentioned (e.g., will of Juana Antonia, 1595, AGNT 59–3), and one will referred to livestock (will of Baltasar Bautista, 1634, AGNBN 339–8, refers specifically to pigs).

While the listings of movable properties included in wills illustrate the growing impoverishment of Mexico

because she was getting old" and presumably needed the money.

[25]Note that Juana Agustina's will (AGNT 128–2, 1609) has certain irregularities that suggest it is a composite of one will dating from approximately 1609 plus a fragment of a second, later will. Although it was being used to bolster specific land claims, because its language and bequests are not markedly different from those of this period, I have included it in the analysis of wills whereas Gaspar de Buena Ventura's will (see table 4) was not.

THE SOCIAL HISTORY OF EVERYDAY LIFE

City's indigenous population, such inventories also show the existence of some degree of economic differentiation, with Indian society based on entrepreneurship or craft skills. Antón Jacobo, for example, listed six separate house sites that he owned with instructions that five of them be sold, some for sizable amounts (in one case, 200 pesos, and in another, 110 [1607, AGNT 95–8: fols.17r–17v]); he also mentioned owning nine looms, seven of which were to be sold (fol.19r). The wills of Juana Mocel (1596, AGNT 70–4), Magdalena Ramírez (1606, AGNT 1595–4), and María Alonso (1623, BNP 299) illustrate that occasionally Indian women amassed fairly sizable amounts of money, clothing, and other small objects, perhaps based on their marketplace activities (see chap. 3).

Clear changes took place in the categories of kin to whom bequests were made. Table 6 summarizes changes in bequest patterns and suggests changes in family and kinship structure as the Indian population underwent economic and demographic decline.

Three patterns are evident in these wills. First, testators placed an increasing emphasis on lineal and nuclear relationships. In contrast to the early colonial period, few siblings, nephews, and nieces received property. As we shall see in the next chapter, extended family households and kin units were gradually being replaced by smaller units.

Second, there was a growing impoverishment of Indians. Not only did testators leave less landed property but they had to sell houses and movable property to pay for debts or to provide care for parents, children, or grandchildren. In his will, Joséph Melchior (1642, AGNT 101–2) referred openly to his need to sell his house ("caltzintli") because he owned six years of tribute payments (*niquitlacotica tlacalaquihli 6 xihuitl* [fol.2r]).

Third, there is evidence of marital and familial stress. For example, two male testators left so little to their wives as to suggest that the spouses were either deeply

Table 6
Numbers of Wills Showing Bequests to Relatives,
by Gender and Property Type, 1587–1642

Men	sp	so/da	bro/sis	gso/gda	ne/ni	af/o
Houses	5	7 3	1 1	0 0	0 0	2 1
Land	0	3 1	0 0	1 0	0 0	0 1
Movable property	4	4 0	0 1	1 0	0 0	3 3[a]
Women						
Houses	0	1 3	1 1	1 3	0 0	4 1[b]
Land	0	1 2	0 0	0 1	1 0	0 0
Movable property	1	3 3	1 0	0 2	0 1	3 2[c]
All						
Houses	5	8 6	2 2	1 3	0 0	6 2
Land	0	4 3	0 0	1 1	1 0	0 1
Movable property	5	7 3	1 1	1 2	0 1	6 5

[a]Two men left their mothers money shares from the proceeds of sales of their houses (will of Pedro Jacobo, 1588, AGNT 59–3; will of Juan Matías, 1615, AGNT 157–7).

[b]One woman left a room in her house to a small boy who had been orphaned and whom she was raising (will of Juana Agustina, 1609, AGNT 128–2).

[c] One woman left her *comadre* a metate (will of Magdalena Ramírez, 1606, AGNT 1595–4).

estranged or physically separated (will of Pedro Jacobo, 1588, AGNT 59–3; will of Juan Matías, 1618, AGNT 157–7). In his will, Pedro Doçan spoke of his painful estrangement from his daughter to justify his bequest of all his property to his son. This daughter appears to have been a troubled, perhaps alcoholic, woman with whom Doçan had long had a frustrating relationship (1587, AGNT 442–5). In another will, a woman left money from the sale of her house site for masses for a son and daughter who had died and left only a crucifix to a son who was still alive (will of Isabel Ana, 1587, AGNT 54–5). That they lived apart is probable, and they may also have been emotionally estranged from one another.

151

The quality of social relations as reflected in these wills appears more troubled than that found in the earlier period.

1650–1700

Nineteen wills date from the second half of the seventeenth century; ten are executed by men and nine by women. The earlier trends toward impoverishment and toward a narrowing of kinship and family structures continued. Tables 7 and 8 summarize basic descriptive information about these wills.

By the late seventeenth century, very clear shifts had occurred in the types of goods inventoried in testators' wills. The amounts of real property, especially land, had declined dramatically. As fewer testators were able to leave landed property, movable properties made up a greater proportion of the bequests; but by the late seventeenth century, most movable property was in men's hands. A century before, women had left the major proportion of movable items; later, men did.[26] Moreover, religious items made up an increasing proportion of all movable property. This reflects some success in Christianizing the indigenous population, however much this provoked both ambivalent responses and creative interpretations and practices (Klor de Alva 1982; Burkhart 1989; but see Lockhart 1992: chap.6).

The increasing impoverishment of this population is apparent in the terms they use to describe their houses. The most commonly used Nahuatl term for residences was *caltzintli* (see chap. 2 for a discussion of this term). In 1679, Juan de la Cruz referred to a small house (or possibly room) he owned as a *xacaltotli* (NL/Ayer 1481B [3d]: fol.1v). A *xacalli* was a shack or house made of only semipermanent building materials such as mud and

[26]This pattern actually emerged during period two but becomes much more striking after 1650.

Table 7
Men's Wills, 1659–1693

Source/ Location	Year	Name of Testator	Language[a]
NL/Ayer 1481B(3b)	1659	Don Matías Xuares	N
AGNT 2776–18	1662	Francisco Antonio	N/S
AGNT 163–5[b]	1672	Felipe de Santiago	S
AGNT 165–4	1675	Felipe de la Cruz	N/S
NL/Ayer 1481B(3d)	1679	Juan de la Cruz	N
AGNT 163–2	1691	Francisco Agustín	N/S
AGNT 155–9	1692	Don Felipe de la Cruz	N/S
AGNC 592–1	1692	Don Francisco de San Pedro	N/S
NL/Ayer 1481B(3l)	1693	Don Juan de Santiago	N
AGNC 1828–5[b]	n.d.	Francisco de Luna	S

[a]N = Nahautl; S = Spanish.
[b]Only a partial text is extant.

Table 8
Women's Wills, 1652–1699

Source/ Location	Year	Name of Testator	Language[a]
AGNT 1595–4[a]	1652	Juana Francisca	N
NL/Ayer 1481B(3e)	1677	Micaela Angelina	N/S
NL/Ayer 1481B(3f)	1683	Diega Nicolasa	N
NL/Ayer 1481F(9a)	1685	Juana Micaela	N
AGNC 1763–2	1693	Juana de los Angeles	N/S
AGNC 1828–5	1693	Ana María	N
AGNC 592–1	1695	Teresa de Jesús	N/S
NL/Ayer 1481B(3a)	1697	Gerónima Verónica	N
NL/Ayer 1481B(3l)	1699	Melchora de Santiago	N/S

[a]N = Nahuatl; S = Spanish.
[b]Only a partial text is extant.

straw. The number of rooms in house compounds referred to in wills continued to decrease. Only one house
had as many as six rooms, while six houses had just one
or two rooms (four house compounds had three or four
rooms). While the rooms within houses were not described in much detail, one house did have a second
story (an *acocalo*) [will of Micaela Angelina, NL/Ayer
1481B[3e]: fol.1r]) and two houses had oratorios.[27]

Twelve of nineteen testators explicitly cited land in
their wills; seven were male, five were female. But the
only land the majority of these testators described was
the solar (referred to in Nahuatl either as tlalli or tlalmantli or by the Spanish loanword *sitio*). Four of these
testators also mentioned chinampas, numbering from
one to five.

Four testators referred to landholdings other than his
or her own site or chinampas. Two were male, and two
were female. Two of these testators, a man and a woman,
owned more than one urban solar. Felipe de Santiago
owned two solares (will, 1672, AGNT 163–5), and Juana
de los Angeles left five pieces of tlalmantli (translated as
sitio in the Spanish translation of her will [1693, AGNC
1763–2: fols.3r–3v, 4r–4v]). Two other testators were a
father and his daughter, don Juan de Santiago and
Melchora de Santiago, who each referred to tlalli in San
Juan Cochtocan. Don Juan left the property, which he
described simply in terms of its location near San Juan
Cochtocan, to this daughter and her husband (1693,
NL/Ayer 1481B[3l]: fols. 3r, 4v).

His daughter, Melchora, discussed the same property
in her 1699 will, but her attention was drawn more to the
income produced by this "*tlalli cazicazgo*," as she called it
(ibid., fols.5v, 7r). From the twenty pesos that came

---

[27]A variety of terms was used for this part of a domestic structure. The term
teopa calli occurs in the will of Francisco Agustín, 1691, AGNT 163–2: fol.2r, and
in the will of Juana de los Angeles (1693, AGNC 1763–2: fol.3r), she refers to the
totecuio ychantzinco. Note that a reference to an oratorio also occurs in the 1618
will of don Melchor de Mendoza.

yearly from this property, in the year of her death the money was to be used to pay for her burial and related expenses. In later years the money was to be divided, with part to be used for a mass sung by a priest and singers during the Feast of the Purification and the rest to be divided equally, half for masses and half for a girl she had raised as a daughter (fols.5v–6r, 7r–7v).

Most property listed in late seventeenth-century wills consisted of movable items, notably religious articles. Sixteen of eighteen testators left movable property; eight were men and eight were women. Of these sixteen testators, over half—or nine—left *only* religious items in their wills, and of these nine, seven were men.[28] Whether Indians of this period were more pious or simply practiced or expressed their religious beliefs in different ways is not known (also see Wood 1991*b*). But these individuals, especially men, clearly expressed an affiliation and loyalty to Catholic belief and practice through their household objects which was not evident earlier. Thus, a marked trend toward predominance of religious over secular items is clearly present in these wills.

Religious items increased not only in number but in variety as well. The wills describe religious artifacts in great detail. In a text that appears to be a fragment of an inventory listing the contents of an oratorio, more than twenty-five *echuras* (sometimes referred to as *echuras de bulto;* figurine, statuette [in the round]; also see Wood 1991*b:* 270) and *lienzos* (canvas paintings) were listed (will of Francisco Agustin, 1691, AGNT 163–2: fol.4r). Both were identified by the saint or other subject that was portrayed, and lienzos were further described by a measurement (a *vara* [0.84 m], *vara y cuarta,* or *vara y media*).

[28]Wood remarks on a similar finding in late colonial Indian wills from Indian towns in the Valley of Toluca. She states that "when ownership and inheritance patterns [of saints' images] are examined, men emerge as the more numerous owners of images, and images are bequeathed to male relatives more often than to female relatives" (1991*b:* 277).

Other wills listed from two to ten figures or lienzos. The figures and paintings were of both male and female saints as well as Christ and various forms of the Virgin Mary. Echuras or lienzos of the Virgin of Guadalupe are mentioned in three wills, and Christ appeared in five wills. Saints who were frequently listed included San Antonio, San Nicolás, San Juan, and Santa Catalina. That these objects carried both spiritual and material value is intimated not only by their prominence in the wills of this period but by the suggestion in one will that they could be pawned (will of Francisco Antonio, 1662, AGNT 2776–18: fol.18v). Testators also repeatedly voiced the concern that the images be cared for by their children or grandchildren (see, e.g., the will of Francisco Agustín, 1691, AGNT 163–2: fol.2r).

The numbers of secular objects in all categories decreased in proportion and number in the wills from the period 1650–1700. Even in a will that only consisted of movables (will of Ana María, 1693, AGNC 1828–5), secular objects declined in number and included only a few items such as some clothing, jewelry, and a cover (*cubija* [fol.13v]). Few men left work items, though one left a canoe (*nacali*) and a pan (*huispayla*) (will of Don Francisco de San Pedro, 1692, AGNC 592–1: fol.8v). One woman bequeathed a *tornillo* (screw, bolt or vise) (will of Micaela Angelina, 1677, NL/Ayer 1481B[3e]: fol.1v), and several women passed on clothing or jewelry. Only two testators mentioned money to be given for other than explicitly religious purposes. These testators might list money or other things owed to them, but, in contrast to the first two periods, they listed few debts that they themselves owed.

Bequest patterns in these wills resembled those seen in the preceding period with a few subtle differences. The clearest shift was the increased tendency to make bequests to children-in-law, especially sons-in-law. Overall, lineal and nuclear bequests clearly predominated. Table 9 summarizes changes in bequest patterns.

156

Table 9
Number of Wills Showing Bequests to Relatives,
by Gender and Property Type, 1652–1699

Men	sp	so/da		bro/sis		gso/gda		ne/ni		af/o	
Houses	2	5	6	0	0	0	0	0	1	2[a]	0
Land	0	0	1	0	0	0	0	0	0	1	0
Movable property	1	4	5	0	0	1	1	0	0	2	1[b]
Women											
Houses	2	2	1	0	1	0	0	0	0	1	1[c]
Land	0	0	1	0	0	0	0	0	0	1	1[d]
Movable property	1	3	2	1	0	0	1	1	0	1[e]	1[f]
All											
Houses	4	7	7	0	1	0	0	0	1	3	1
Land	0	0	2	0	0	0	0	0	0	2	1
Movable property	2	7	7	1	0	1	2	1	0	3	2

[a]The testator Francisco de San Pedro directed that his son and son-in-law share his house "as if they were brothers" (1692, AGNC 592–1: fols.8r, 14r).

[b]An echura was given by Felipe de Santiago to his *prima* (1672, AGNT 163–5).

[c]Melchora de Santiago left her house to a girl she had raised as a daughter (1699, NL/Ayer 1481B[3l]).

[d]Melchora de Santiago also left a share of the income from land she owned to the girl she had raised (1699, NL/Ayer 1481B[3l]).

[e]A lienzo of San Miguel was given by Gerónima Verónica to her daughter-in-law (1697, NL/Ayer 1481B[3a]). This was the only example for this period of leaving property to a daughter-in-law. All other affines inheriting goods were sons-in-law.

[f]Several different kinds of movables were left to the girl raised by Melchora de Santiago (1699, NL/Ayer 1481B[3l]).

The wills of colonial Indians were not static; nor did they merely derive from Spanish models. On the contrary, Nahua testaments underwent a process of change and transformation, and by the late seventeeth century, they reflected and embodied broader shifts that had occurred in indigenous society as the result of a century of Spanish colonialism. At the end of the seventeenth century, bequests were more lineal and more nuclear in nature than they had been in the mid-sixteenth century. Colonial Mexica had begun to emphasize relationships among nuclear family members and children's spouses, especially sons-in-law, and to deemphasize relations with testators' siblings and the siblings' children. In contrast to earlier times, wills rarely mentioned siblings; if they did, it was usually in the context of directing them to carry out some provision of a will (see, e.g., will of Juana Micaela, 1685, NL/Ayer 1481f[9a]: fol.1r). For the first time, wives left significant amounts of property to their husbands. And a growing number of spouses bequeathed sums of money to be used to pay for masses in honor of deceased spouses—again reflecting the heightened stress placed on the conjugal relationship and on the nuclear family.

CONCLUSION

At first glance, the introduction of written wills in six-teenth-century New Spain would appear to be a relatively insignificant development in the history of the early colonial Mexica. Yet the adoption of this practice proved to be an important vehicle of cultural conversion and Spanish cultural hegemony. Writing such a document represented a different kind of social drama than did litigation. Not necessarily forged from conflict, will writing represented the dying person's desire to balance significant social relationships with material resources and to influence the future material well-being of those to whom he or she felt close. The writing of testaments was encouraged by priests and was not always voluntary. Although not an unconstrained adaptation by all Indians, will writing did prove useful for distributing goods in a society in which customary practices could no longer hold and in which written texts such as wills had both a social *and* a legal value. Wills also have high value as a source for social and cultural history because they offer a detailed glimpse into individuals' life histories and their wishes for their descendants.

The surviving wills reveal a number of transformations in indigenous life over the course of the sixteenth century and early seventeenth century. For example, they record the growing impoverishment of Mexico City's indigenous population—evident in a decline in the number of rooms per house structure and an increase in the value that Indians placed on the land occupied by houses. They also show the growing success of Spanish efforts to Christianize the urban indigenous population—a success made obvious by a significant rise in the ownership of religious articles, especially relative to ownership of nonreligious pieces of movable property, and in the fact that an increasing number of male testators, for the first time, owned religious items.

These shifts are all aspects of a more fundamental transformation—a transformation in cultural values and social practices that will be described in greater detail in the following chapter. During the late sixteenth and early seventeenth century, Tenochcan Mexica household and family structures became noticeably smaller and less complex. Family relationships within the household (and among members of larger kin units) experienced change. Men and women no longer fulfilled parallel roles of authority or occupied parallel spheres across the domains of existence. The increased subordination of Mexica women indicates not merely that their status was declining but also that the organization of key social and cultural institutions in daily life were undergoing fundamental changes.

CHAPTER 5

Law and a
Changing Family Structure

Of all the factors contributing to the consolidation of Spanish hegemony in central Mexico, none was more important than the introduction of new conceptual and cognitive models of social relationships. The preceding chapters examined Spanish colonial authorities' success in diffusing and disseminating new conceptions of legal process, gender roles, inheritance, and property ownership. This chapter traces changes in Mexica kinship and family relations. As we shall see, the texts of Indian wills and lawsuits reveal a series of shifts in Mexica kinship and family arrangements during the early colonial period: a new emphasis on the nuclear family as a social and moral unit; a shift away from a cognatic kinship system, formed around sibling and intergenerational ties, toward a patrifilial emphasis; and the emergence of more hierarchically ranked and gender-defined domains.

No terms exist in classical Nahuatl that precisely correspond to the married couple or what we customarily mean by the family (i.e., the unit consisting of a parent or parents and children). Instead, Nahuas used a variety of terms to refer either to the household or to groupings of kin. Lawsuits and other texts from the early colonial period suggest that pre-Hispanic Tenochcan Mexica society was loosely divided into groups of kin who traced their descent back to a founding husband and wife couple. The precolonial kinship system was cognatic; that is, descent could flow through either the male or female line. As we saw in chapter 3, descent through women was important in late pre-Hispanic and early colonial Mexica society.

As in other societies with cognatic systems, the Mexica kinship system was loosely structured. Precisely because they allow a high level of individual choice, cognatic systems tend not to form clearly bounded units.[1] Thus, the Mexica kinship system, unlike the kinship systems found among some North American Indian groups, was not a lineal descent system and did not consist of lineages or clans. The flexibility of the pre-Hispanic Mexica kinship system is evident in marriage practices. The Mexica did not necessarily practice endogamy or exogamy, and individual Mexica were permitted to marry close relatives beyond the nuclear family (Motolinía 1971: 324–25).[2] Class, status (i.e., placement within the nobility), and occupation all had a strong influence on marriage practices. For nobles especially, kinship relationships appear to have influenced marriage patterns (Carrasco 1984).

For the precolonial Mexica, kinship affected many important aspects of everyday life. As we have already seen, kinship groups held certain rights over the property of their members. Kin groupings played a critical role in organizing a wide array of economic and ritual activ-

[1]Cognatic descent systems have been the subject of some anthropological controversy because they are very different from the patrilineal, matrilineal, or double descent systems traditionally studied by anthropologists (Davenport 1959; Errington 1989: chap. 7; Firth 1963; Goodenough 1955; Murdock 1960; Keesing 1975; Scheffler 1964, 1965). Societies with cognatic descent have concepts of descent-based entitlement, and descent-based corporate units can be formed by tracing descent through male *and/or* female links (Keesing 1975: 91–92). Cognatic societies differ from societies characterized by bilateral kinship (such as contemporary North American society, for example) in two ways: first, there is strong interest in ancestors and tracing relations of descent from them; second, there are units formed (no matter how flexibly they may be bounded) which have some sense of common identity based on descent and through which rights and obligations are held. Cognatic descent systems are compatible with social and economic hierarchy (Murdock 1960; Ortner 1981).

[2]There were also certain prohibitions on marriage between in-laws and step-relatives, though, again, these were narrowly defined.

ities. The kinship system also provided models of and idioms for both complementarity and hierarchy as these principles were enacted and put into practice throughout the realms of Mexica life.

During the first 150 years of colonial rule, the Mexica kinship system underwent certain far-reaching transformations. Extended kin ties grew less important; household composition became less complex; and within the nuclear family itself, relations grew more hierarchical, as women no longer were regarded as parallel figures of authority with men. How and why these changes occurred is the major theme of this chapter.

CONCEPTUALIZING KINSHIP
AND FAMILY RELATIONS DURING
THE LATE PRE-HISPANIC PERIOD

In late precolonial Mexica society, the couple and their children were deeply embedded within the context of broader kinship groupings. A variety of Mexica life-cycle rituals proclaimed the importance of these groups. From the moment a woman realized that she was pregnant, celebrations and ceremonies took place in which the kin of both the mother- and father-to-be participated (*FC* 1950–82: VI:24–27:135–58; also see Sullivan 1974). These occasions witnessed a series of lengthy speeches, designed to instruct the parents-to-be, especially the mother, of their duty to behave circumspectly and to follow the many rules and customs that this natalist culture emphasized to protect the baby.[3] The husband and wife were reminded at length, probably tiresomely, of their obligations as parents. These occasions, like so many other ceremonial occasions among the Mexica, took place amid a large group of kin, the

[3]See Durán (1967: I:7:77) on the value placed on fertility and fecundity by the Mexica.

162

"mothers, the fathers, the relatives of the woman [and] of the man" (*FC* 1950–82: VI:24:135).[4]

Those who spoke at these occasions prior to the birth of a Mexica child seized the opportunity to make explicit the connections between the new child and previous generations. When kin welcomed a newborn child, these ties were restated in still more precise terms. At the naming ceremony, usually a propitious day several days after the child's birth (see chap. 3), the baby was told of the bonds joining him or her to the broader circle of kin and ancestors. Newborn children heard of their physical resemblance to their ancestors, especially to their "great-grandfathers and great-grandmothers" (ibid., IV:35:114).

Wedding customs and speeches also illustrate these themes. Kin of both the bride and the groom participated in the selection of a mate and attended the feast and ceremonies (ibid., VI:23:128–29). The bride and groom were each reminded rhetorically that their kin encouraged and oversaw the marriage. And the in-laws (especially the mothers-in-law) who gave speeches stressed to the new partner the newly formed kinship relationships (ibid., 132–33; Durán 1967: I:5:57; also see Gruzinski 1980).

Both wedding and birth ceremonies underscore a number of important aspects of Mexica kinship beliefs and practices. First, kinship provided an important *idiom* or vocabulary for describing the connection between the Mexica individual and preceding generations of Mexica society which in these examples was pictured as a family writ large. As we shall see, the Mexica used kinship concepts to express the meaning and content of relationships outside the realm of kinship including ties between or among deities and between deities and humans as well as the bonds between rulers and leaders and subjects and followers.

---

[4]". . . in tenaoan, in tetaoan, teoaiulque, in jtech cioatl, in jtech oqujtli."

Moreover, kinship ties provided children's earliest and longest-lasting social ties, and kin instructed them into culturally sanctioned roles. Children lived, interacted, and worked with other members of the kinship network. Furthermore, kin relationships provided many of the people with whom one participated in the endless rounds of ceremonies (both calendrical and life cycle) through which so many aspects of Mexica belief, history, and ritual were enacted and repeated over and over (Clendinnen 1991: chap.11).

Idioms of Connection and Relation

It is clear from sources such as the *Florentine Codex* that the Tenochcan Mexica viewed the individual as equally related and tied to his or her father *and* mother. Conceptually, the Mexica gave these maternal and paternal ties an equal, or bilateral, weight. They viewed both the father's semen and the mother's blood as necessary substances for forming a new life (*FC* 1950–82: X:27:130, 132). If his semen impregnated and fattened the woman or made or completed the baby's form (ibid., VI:27:156), her blood strengthened and animated the baby (ibid., X:27:132). Repeated intercourse was necessary for semen to form the baby,[5] but once this occurred (in the Mexica view, by the third month), intercourse was supposed to cease, lest the baby be born covered by a white film, which would signal the parents' excessive carnal activities (ibid., VI:27:156–57). As described by the Mexica, the newborn possessed the "blood, color, and essence" of both father and mother ("in motatzin, in monantzin in timezio, in tintlapallo, in timoxijo" [ibid., 40:216]). The baby also embodied the parents' positive and negative traits; as the *Florentine Codex* observed, a

---

[5]Note the Nahuatl riddle quoted in the *FC* (1950–82: VI:43:239): "Çaçan tleino, ça cemjlhvitl otzti. Malacatl." What is that which becomes pregnant in only one day? The spindle.

child could carry the "the blotch, the filth, the evil" of both the mother and the father ("in jtliltica, in jcatzaoaca, in jaquallo" [ibid., 32:175]).

The newly conceived and then newborn child clearly belonged bilaterally to both the parents and through the parents to other kin. These included living kin and those who had died—who were nevertheless considered significant in a variety of ways. The Mexica as a group saw themselves as the descendants of distant ancestors who had emerged from Chicomoztoc; and these ancestors were thought to have a living presence.[6] On the individual level, each person was regarded as the partial embodiment of ancestors who had never fully disappeared since their influences reappeared in living descendants (ibid., 30:168; also see Read 1988: 48–49).

As we have already seen, the rhetoric of life-cycle ceremonies stressed the ties of the living to earlier kin, especially to the "grandmothers and grandfathers" and/ or the "great-grandmothers and great-grandfathers" who were deceased. Thus, the Mexica sense of history written both large and small was described through ties to ancestors who came before and whose lives and actions shaped the character and nature of their descendants.

Relatives of both parents participated not only in ceremonies marking pregnancy and birth but in rituals marking a child's entrance into the calmecac or telpochcalli (*FC* 1950–82: VI:39–40:209–18). Similarly, kin related through both parties' father *and* mother took part in marriage ceremonies (ibid., 23:127–33; Motolinía 1971: 318). Funerals, like other life-cycle rituals, occurred in the presence of an array of kin. At funerals and mortuary ceremonies for women who had died in childbirth or warriors who died in battle, the kinship tie between the deceased and their "mothers," "fathers," and other relatives was reaffirmed (ibid., 3:12; 29:165).

[6]". . . y todos son vivos los que dejaron vuestros padres, sin haberse muerto ninguno, remozándonos cuando queremos" (Durán 1967: II:27:222).

The Mexica frequently used kinship connections and terms as conceptual devices for ordering and describing relationships outside the realm of the everyday. Kinship ties provided a rich symbolic vocabulary on which broader social and political links were modeled. For example, even though "no integrated 'family of gods' structure appears to have ever been worked out" (Nicholson 1971: 409), the Mexica described their major deities as consanguineally or affinally related to each other. While deities do not appear to have been addressed with kin terms, the living representation of a deity could be spoken to in such terms. When captives playing the roles of certain deities were adopted before being sacrificed, both male and female captives/deities were designated and treated as sons or daughters (e.g., *FC* 1950–82: II:21:47, II:30:119). It is noteworthy that the hierarchy of the deity-human relationship was reversed in this context (also see Kartunnen and Lockhart 1987: 45; Kartunnen 1992: 250–53).

Within the political realm, the Mexica used the parent-child relationship to describe the bond between ruler and subject. In this context, the ruler became the parents and the subjects became the children. "As one lieth crying, saddened, longing for his mother, for this father, so the governed desire to be ruled" (*FC* 1950–82: VI:11:57–58).[7] Indeed, Mexica rulers frequently described themselves as the metaphorical fathers and mothers of their subjects (e.g., ibid., 15:79; also see Kellogg 1993; Haskett 1991: 100, 199). Like parents, rulers fed, taught, and punished (Kellogg 1993).[8]

---

[7]". . . ca ynan, ca jta qujnequi, ca chocatoc, ca tlaocuxtoc, ca mopachollanj in tlatquijtl, in tlamamalli": This phrase in its literal meaning—using the terms *tlatquitl* and *tlamamalli,* which liken subjects to property and cargos or burdens, respectively—draws on images of parents and rulers as carrying burdens to be discussed below.

[8]Note also that colonial indigenous political histories that described supreme leaders were rooted in both a chronological *and* genealogical discourse (see, e.g., Chimalpahin [1963–65] and *Crónica mexicáyotl* [1975]).

Thus, parents and rulers performed parallel responsibilities. Both were responsible for protecting and supporting their "children," an image that the Mexica frequently conveyed through images of parents and rulers as shade trees and carrying frames. A pregnant woman had the duties of parenthood described to her in the following terms:

> Still ye take from them the bundle, the carrying frame; ye help carry the bundle for those who already reside beyond, those whom our lord hath destroyed, hath hidden: our forefathers, those who bequeathed, who as they departed placed on your backs, on your shoulders the bundle, the carrying frame, the burden, that which is to be carried, that which is to be borne, the duty of motherhood, the duty of fatherhood. (*FC* 1950–82: VI:25:145)[9]

Rulers were likened to cypress trees (ibid., 43:252), and they were also instructed that they would be carrying "a bundle of people, a carrying frame load of people" (258). The macehualli were described as children who would be "put on one's lap; [they] are borne, are shouldered, are led, are governed; they go in the cradle of one's arms" (246).[10]

Similar ideas of duty and responsibility for dependents defined the relationship between older and younger siblings. The Mexica expected the older brother to be a guide and provider for his younger siblings (ibid., X:2:9). Sibling or age terms, in turn, were frequently extended and used as titles for certain political or religious positions in which care and guidance of younger

---

[9]Oc anqujnqujmjlpatla, anqujncacaxpatla, anqujnqujmjlcevia in ie nachca onmantivi in oqujnmopolhvi, in oqujnmotlatili in totecujo, in totechiuhcaoan in oamocujtlapantzinco, amoteputztzinco concauhteoque, contlaliteoaque in qujmjlli: in cacaxtli, in tlamamalli, in tlatconj, in tlamamalonj, in nantequjtl, in tatequjtl.

[10]"cuexanalo, itco, mamalo, iacanalo, pacholo, temamalvazco ietiuh in maceoalli: amo monomaiacana."

members of Mexica society was the primary function. Thus, male functionaries in the telpochcalli were known as tiachcahuan (elder brothers) and telpochtlatoque (rulers of young men). Female functionaries in the cuicacalli were referred to as cihuatetiachcahuan (literally, female elder brother) and as ichpochtlaiacanqui (guide of young women) (also see chap. 3).[11]

TIES TO THE SOCIAL WORLD

From a Mexica infant's first days of life, the family and kin group bore the responsibility of instilling cultural values. Whether noble or commoner, male or female, a child first experienced life within the domain of family and kinship, a largely female realm in both symbolic and social terms. Let us look now at the ways that family groups and kin units were structured and organized and examine the kinds of kin relationships that young Mexica experienced.

[11]Because I have stressed kinship terms as providing a set of concepts by which certain nonkinship relationships could be named and imbued with kinship symbolism and meaning, I have not discussed Nahuatl kinship terminology more generally. There are several extensive treatments of this subject. The interested reader should see Rammow (1964), Carrasco (1966), Romney (1967), Calnek (1974a), Kellogg (1980), Gardner (1982), Offner (1983), and Lockhart (1992). This literature makes two important points about the terminology. First, like other Uto-Aztecan languages, the kinship terminology is most similar to a Hawaiian system in which siblings and cousins are referred to by the same terms. Siblings and cousins were differentiated by sex and age, however. Second, many of the terms were extended to collateral kin though collaterals may have been distinguished by certain modifying terms. These characteristics of the kinship terminology may correspond to certain aspects of Mexica behavior. The emphasis on generation, age (as in older and younger siblings), and sex appear related to Mexica cultural and behavioral patterns with their emphasis on hierarchy, deference, and the strong symbolic and social distinctions made between men and women. The lack of distinction between siblings and cousins also correlates well with the complex family structure described in this chapter. Like other aspects of Mexica kinship, flexibility and inclusion were stressed over genealogical precision. It is not surprising that the complex Nahuatl sibling terms were among those that showed the earliest and most far-reaching changes (Arenas 1611: 49–50; Lockhart 1992: 82–84).

Family and Household Groups

Young Tenochcan Mexica, whether elite or nonelite, began their lives as members of a small community that offered daily interactions with an extended circle of kin including parents, siblings, aunts, uncles, cousins, and perhaps grandparents and other kin of older generations. While Mexica infants were born into nuclear family groupings consisting of parents and children, Tenochcan Mexica nuclear families operated in a larger world of multifamily household groups (Calnek 1972, 1976, n.d.; Kellogg 1980: chap.2, 1986*a;* 1993).

Although the Mexica lacked a term that corresponds to what we mean by a nuclear family, they had a clear conception of the household. Classical Nahuatl conceptualized the household as a culturally and socially significant unit, the terms for which express the importance of both where family life took place and the oneness and common identity of the inhabitants. Pedro Carrasco has shown that

> Nahuatl words for family are mostly descriptive terms that refer to common residence and thus correspond more exactly to the English "household": *cencalli* ("one house"), *cemithualtin* ("those in one yard"), *techan tlaca* ("people in someone's dwelling"), *cenyeliztli* (literally, "one stay"). (1971: 368; also see Kellogg 1993; Lockhart 1992: 59)

The Mexica version of the household grouping was most often a multifamily or complex family unit. Typically, two, three, or more married couples shared a household compound (Calnek 1972, 1976, n.d.; Kellogg 1980: chap. 2, 1986*a,* 1993).[12] Three kinds of ties that

---

[12]These statements should not be construed as meaning that every person who resided in Tenochtitlán lived in such a household. Interpersonal conflict, in-migration, and social class (with the existence of some type of underclass) would mean that some percentage of the population lived in other settings: in smaller households, as "renters," or even by themselves. I only argue here that the culturally preferred form in Tenochtitlán was the multifamily household.

169

were not mutually exclusive bound these multifamily groups together: generational ties; lateral ties (between adult siblings or cousins, most often of the same sex); and marital bonds, including polygynous marriages.

Several lines of evidence indicate that the multifamily household provided both the cultural norm and numerically most dominant household type in Tenochtitlán. While chroniclers gathered little systematic information about pre-Hispanic household size or structure, a few scattered clues point to the prominence of multifamily households. Fray Bartolomé de Las Casas, for example, mentioned the existence of households with from three to ten adult men (1967: I:50:265; also see Herrera 1601: I:243). Another source notes that siblings resided together to keep property holdings intact (López de Gómara 1943: II:222–23, 246). Certain references to households in the *Florentine Codex* also suggest that kin beyond the nuclear family commonly lived together (V: App., chap. 33, chap. 34: 194).

There are also a significant number of references in early colonial demographic sources that point to the continued presence and importance of a multifamily structure across the Valley of Mexico and beyond. Woodrow Borah and S. F. Cook's analysis (1960: 97) of the *Suma de visitas* (written ca. 1547–1550) for the region of Mexico-Hidalgo shows the mean number of persons per household was 6.34 (with a range of 2.70 to 10.10). The mean number of *casados* (married men) per household was 2.93 (with a range of 0.78 to 5.71) (ibid., 97–98). Other sixteenth-century sources reinforce this picture of large and complex households as common (see, e.g., *CK* 1912: 13 and the *Relación geográfica* of Tequixixtlan in Paso y Troncoso 1905–6: VI:211; also see Offner 1983: 218–21).

Nonetheless, research on specific locales reveals regional variation in household composition. Carrasco (1966, 1976a Tepoztlan, Yautepec), Jerome A. Offner (1983, 1984; Tepetlaoztoc area), and H. R. Harvey (1986b

Tepetlaoztoc area) identified areas where nuclear family forms predominated over multifamily forms;[13] yet even in these regions, multifamily households appeared in significant numbers. Households under the authority of nobles were larger and had a greater tendency toward a multifamily structure in all three cases.[14]

These findings raise the question of why Tenochtitlán, the most complex and urbanized area in the Valley of Mexico, had larger and more complex households than other nearby regions. Ethnic differences may explain some variation (Offner 1983: 202–21). Varying economic and political organizational forms may also have played a substantial role in shaping household structures. For example, households directly subject to caciques, or nobles, were often larger than nonsubject households (Harvey 1986*b:* 284–87, 291–92; Offner 1983: 219; Carrasco 1964: 190).

The most likely explanation is that Tenochtitlán's economy exerted a strong influence on household composition. Elizabeth M. Brumfiel (1987) draws a distinction between more rural regions in which populations tended to combine part-time specialization with subsistence agriculture (104–7), and Tenochtitlán, where there was a very high level of full-time occupational specialization (pp. 109–10; also see Calnek 1972). While there is some disagreement about whether these crafts were primarily utilitarian (see, e.g., Calnek 1978: 98–99) or whether craft production was oriented toward luxury items for elites (Brumfiel 1987: 110), it is clear that the vast majority of Tenochtitlán's nonelite population pro-

[13]But see Cline (1986: 78–79) and Lockhart (1992: 62) who hypothesize that the nuclear family form may have been the predominant family form. For discussions of Aztec period household structure from archaeological remains, see Evans (1989, 1993) and Smith (1993).

[14]As I finished the final revisions for this book, S. L. Cline's important new work, *The Book of Tributes: Early Sixteenth-Century Nahuatl Censuses from Morelos,* came to my attention. Her findings for the communities investigated are consistent with those of Carrasco and Harvey. She finds both a tendency toward joint-family households and variation (Cline 1993*a:* 58–69).

171

duced goods that fed into an extensive network of relations with and obligations to palaces, temples, and markets (Carrasco 1978: 32–49; Calnek 1978) in which nobles exercised authority over non-nobles in a variety of ways. In addition, a significant number of Tenochtitlán's male population frequently engaged in warfare and therefore did not contribute directly to production at those times (Brumfiel 1987: 109). These factors would have created intense needs for labor within nonelite households—needs that could have been met through bearing larger numbers of children, attracting new household members through marriage, and allowing other kin (or even friends or possibly renters) to move into households when space became available.

Extra-Familial Kin Units

Among the most contentious issues in Aztec ethnohistory is whether the Mexica had extrahousehold kin groups. Nineteenth-century scholars regarded the calpulli as clans around which a warlike but egalitarian society took shape (Morgan 1877; Bandelier 1877, 1878, 1879). A number of later scholars considered class, not kinship, the fundamental principle of Mexica social organization; consequently, they largely ignored kinship as a structuring principle (see, e.g., Moreno 1931; Soustelle 1961). Still others attempted to reconcile these two viewpoints by arguing that the calpulli were ambilateral, stratified, endogamous clans (Monzón 1949; Kirchhoff 1959; Carrasco 1971).

Recent scholarship has tended to reject the notion that the calpulli, especially in the Valley of Mexico, was a kin group (Reyes García 1975; Calnek 1974a: 296; Offner 1983: 168–72; Kellogg 1986b). One set of scholars emphasizes the household as the only significant kin-based grouping (Offner 1983; Lockhart 1992: 59–73), while others hold that chiefly households constituted significant kin-based units (teccalli or tecpan) (Carrasco

172

1976*b;* Hicks 1986) but that these were limited to elites. The evidence described here suggests that there were indeed other kin-based groupings beyond the level of the household but that these units existed throughout the economic and social levels of Tenochcan Mexica society (Calnek 1974*a,* n.d.; Kellogg 1980, 1986*b*).

These differences of interpretation will not easily be resolved. The family historian Andrejs Plakans has explained why it is inherently difficult to reconstruct the nature of extrahousehold kin units. "By definition historians are not able to observe any groups at all nor interview any members of them. All that exists is evidence from which inferences have to be drawn . . . though this evidence is entirely a matter of written record" (1984: 166). Plakans also usefully reminds us that even field anthropologists "do not expect to see kinship groups as if these groups were military units on parade" (164).[15] And in this particular case, the relevant sources are fragmentary, ambiguous, and few in number.

Nevertheless, I believe that a variety of sources indicate that kinship was indeed a significant cultural category for the Mexica. Ethnohistorical evidence suggests that there were three key kin units or categories.[16] The

[15]Plakans goes on to point out,

What will be seen are fragments of such groups, and what will be heard are the reports by members of such fragments that they conceive of themselves as belonging to large kin-based units with a membership that may include substantial proportions of the community. . . . The doubts that historians have about groups, because they cannot witness them in operation, have to be softened by the observation that anthropologists do not see such groups either. (165–66)

[16]It is helpful to recognize distinctions among three terms: unit, category, and group. Anthropologists have drawn a useful distinction between "cultural categories" and "social groups." This distinction can be defined in the following way:

A cultural category is a set of entities in the world . . . that are classed as similar for some purposes, because they have in common one or more culturally relevant atributes. . . . As categories, they exist in people's conceptual worlds. . . .

A social group, on the other hand, consists of actual warm-blooded human beings who recurrently interact in an interconnected set of roles. . . .

Mexica described these units with the following general terms (though these may be found in texts or documents in related but alternative forms): *huanyolcayotl, tlacame-cayotl,* and *teixhuihuan.* Each was fundamentally bilateral, though in certain contexts patrifilial or patrilocal links may have been emphasized.

The term *huanyolcayotl* and its variants (including, most commonly, *huanyolque* or *tehuanyolque*) appear frequently in kinship contexts in the *Florentine Codex.* Molina defines the term as referring to *pariente por sangre* or "kin through blood" (1977: Pt. I:fol.92v). The root of this term, *yoli,* is both a noun ("cosa que biue"; "something that lives") and a verb ("biuir, resuscitar, abiuar, o empollarse el hueuo"; "to live, to resuscitate or revive, to quicken, enliven or animate, or to hatch an egg" [Pt. II: fol.39v]). While the predominant meanings of *yoli* have simply to do with life, there is a suggestion or connotation of engendering life (or life coming into being) that seems to be expressed by this word and its alternative forms. When modified by the prefix *cihua-* (woman), it could also refer to kin through marriage.

This term denotes an Ego's circle of kin, however culturally defined and bounded (the precise nature of this definition and delimiting remains obscure). As a kinship category, huanyolque embraced kin beyond the household; it was an important category through which the kin who celebrated life-cycle events were brought together. This category of relatives appears to have been Ego-defined and would therefore have been theoretically different for each person within a nuclear or extended

---

Members of a social group need not all interact face-to-face. . . . What defines a group is its internal organization, the articulation of its members in a set of interconnected roles. (Keesing 1975: 10)

I add to these terms "unit" as a covering term by which to refer to both categories and groups because it may be useful at times to be able to talk about both of these forms together. But the term "unit" is also useful as, in fact, we may be in an ambiguous area with these data because of their fragmentary nature. Thus, where it can be demonstrated that some kinship entity *is* a category, it may be more difficult to ascertain whether it is a group or not.

family grouping. Anthropologists classify this kinship category as a "personal kindred."

A second term that appears both in the *Florentine Codex* and in sixteenth-century legal documents is *tlacamecayotl*. *Tlacatl* means man or person, *mecatl* refers to rope or cord, and the suffix *-yotl* turns a noun into an abstract concept (Sullivan 1976: 35). The verb *mecauia* can refer to tying something with cords and in its reflexive form carries the implication of falling—perhaps metaphorically implying birth and/or descent. *Mecayotl*, according to Molina, means "*abolorio, o parentesco de consanguinidad*" (ancestry or relationship by consanguinity) (Pt. II: fol.55r). The use of ropes as an artistic symbol of genealogy is found commonly in early colonial genealogical drawings in legal cases and chronicles as well as elsewhere in Mesoamerica.[17] The symbolic connection between ropes and the umbilical cord is clearly implied in both the terminology and its pictorial representations. The concept of "rope of people" expressed, then, a number of linked ideas about birth, consanguineal relationship, *and* descent.

What kind of descent unit was the tlacamecayotl? No definitive answer is possible because we are forced to rely on a limited number of texts and documents. Both Edward Calnek (1974*a*, n.d.) and I (1980, 1986*a*) have argued that the term may denote a cognatic descent group through which the Mexica recognized kinship and descent, structured household organization to some degree, and acknowledged certain common social and legal obligations.[18] Others have argued that it was not a descent group, preferring to interpret it either as a kindred that could be used to "establish a culturally recognized kinship relationship that could then be uti-

---

[17]See Miller (1974) for Mayan examples.

[18]The reader should be aware that Calnek qualified his discussion of the concept in the following way: "The question of whether stocks or kindreds or both played important roles in social organization can, of course, be answered only on empirical, not theoretical grounds" (1974*a*: 200).

lized for various practical purposes" (Offner 1983: 200; also see Lockhart 1992: 59, 72, 495 n.60) or as a term that merely refers to lineal consanguineal kin (Lockhart 1992: 495 n.60).

What seems clear from a careful review of the evidence is that the Tenochcan Mexica used the term to refer to a significant kinship category and that the concept of tlacamecayotl combined certain features of both bilateral kindreds and cognatic descent groups. It was kindredlike in two respects. First, according to Sahagún's informants, the unit clearly was Ego oriented. They described this bilateral group of kin (including the father, mother, child, uncle, aunt, nephew, niece, grandfather, grandmother, great-grandfather, great-grandmother, great-great-grandparent, and grandchild) as radiating out from a defining Ego rather than down from a founding ancestor or up from the youngest generation.

Second, as used in some cases, the term could be pluralized and employed to refer to a group of relatives. In one document, for example, a grandparent and her siblings were listed and designated as *his tlacamecayohua* (*itlacamecayohua*, [BNP 112, 1593: fol.28v]). Here the usage implies multiple relatives as defined by an Ego (also see Kellogg 1980: 144–46; but see Carrasco 1976*b:* 21). Still, it is noteworthy that in the Spanish translations of the Nahuatl texts in this lawsuit the term appeared as *deudos muy cercanos* ("very close kin" [fol.26v]), not simply as *deudos* or *parientes*. This translation suggests the Mexica perceived this group of kin as holding some type of collective position or relationship to the Ego through whom rights were transmitted.

In other contexts, the term *tlacamecayotl* clearly stresses the significance of descent through a distinct line of ancestors.[19] For example, the description of tlacame-

[19]Note Anderson and Dibble's translation of the following Nahuatl phrase from the *FC* (1950–82: VI:30:168): "cujx ymjxco, imjcpac titlachiaz in mocolhvan,

cayotl in the *Florentine Codex* uses that term, rather than *huanyolque,* to describe a group of relatives. Apparently, Sahagún's informants themselves chose the term (López Austin 1974: 141). They selected *this* term because it allowed them to emphasize the importance of antecedent relatives, ancestors who came before, from or through whom certain rights could be inherited but to whom certain obligations were owed.

In sixteenth-century legal documents, the term also appeared in ways that imply a category reference. In one document a witness testified about the previous owners of a house site, stating, "I also do not know his *tlacamecayotl*" (*amo no nicmatic yn itlacamecayo* [AGNT 55–5, 1564: fol.3v]). Clearly, the witness was explaining that he did not know the ancestral kin of one of the litigants and was using the term in a way that is suggestive of a descent category rather than a personal kindred. In another document from the same case, the opposing party, Ana Xoco, explained that she had inherited the land of a house site (*tohuehuetlal*) from ascendant relatives:

And as to our *tlacamecayotl,* our grandfather named Tocuiltecatl had children, he engendered ten, but only one had children, called Tlacochin, and he was the father of me, Ana Xoco, and other grandchildren who exist. (AGNT 55–5, 1564: fol.7r)[20]

This use of the term strongly implies the existence of a descent category since Ana included herself within this entity through which she expected certain rights to flow.

---

in mocioan, in moncaoan, in mecaoan" (Perhaps thou wilt know thy grandfathers, thy grandmothers, thy kinsmen, thy lineage).

In book 4, they translate the related term *jtlacaiooan* as "blood relations" (34:111). Finally, when Sahagún's informants were describing how certain high priests were chosen, they explained that the individual's ancestry was not considered and used the term *tlacamecaiotl* in that context as well (*FC* 1950–82: III:9:69).

[20]"Auh yn ica in totlacamecayo in tocol ytoca tocuiltecatl mopilhuati matlactinq̄nchiuh auh ça ce in mopilhuati ytoca tlacochin auh totatzin in nehautl anna xoco yhuā hoc ceq̄ntin teyxhuihua ōcate."

The translator employed the Spanish word *linaje* as a synonym for *tlacamecayotl* in his translation (fol.11r). While *linaje* does not carry all the same connotations as the anthropological term "lineage," in the sixteenth century, it did imply people who traced common lineal descent.[21]

There are also documents in Spanish in which the term *linaje* is employed in ways that suggest that it was used as a translation of the Nahuatl term *tlacamecayotl*. For example, in one document, a witness stated that he

> does not know that the said Magdalena and Juan and Martín are related to the said María Xoco because if they were this witness should know it because he knows them and their lineages as neighbors of the said *barrio* of Yopico. (AGNT 20–2–2, 1563: fols.114r)[22]

In another case, a witness stated that certain houses only belonged to one man of a particular "linaje" (AGNT 23–2–4, 1568: fol.214r).[23]

The term *tlacamecayotl* therefore appears to refer to a kinship concept, combining features of kindreds and descent groups, that expressed a relationship between ascendant relatives and descendant relatives with the focus upward from a given Ego to a bilateral and flexibly defined set of ascendant relations. Whatever this concept's precise characteristics, Sahagún's Mexica informants

[21] In translations of religious texts from Latin to Nahuatl, the term *itlacamecaio* (his *tlacamecayotl*) is used to describe descent and filiation (e.g., Anunciación 1577: fol.187v or Sahagún 1583: fol.55r, 123r [Louise Burkhart, pers. commun.]). The term *linaje* referred to "descent from houses and families." A seventeenth-century Spanish dictionary further explained that the etymology of the word lay in the concept of "line" (*linea*) because people descend from parents, children, and grandchildren in a straight line (Covarrubias Orozco 1611: fol.525v).

[22] . . . no sabe este tº q los dhos madalena e juº e myn tengan parentesco alguno con la dha maria xoco porque si lo tubieron este testigo lo supiera porque los conoce a ellos y a sus linajes como vzºs del dho barrio de yopico.

[23] Also see a similar use of the Spanish term *parentela* in Juan Cano's *Información* (LAL/FSC AGI Patronato 181–8: fols.53v–55v).

clearly associated it with bilateral kinship. Consider their description of those sharing in the distribution of food at a particular feast: "only the relatives, the people of the household—his family, they of the same parentage, of the same womb, those of the same lineage" (*FC* 1950–82: I:21:49).[24] This statement suggests that the Mexica considered individual households as parts of larger kin units, based on a relationship between living kin and ancestors, and that the household domain and kinship were often identified with women, that is, with "those of the same womb" (as also suggested in chap. 3).

If the concept "huanyolcayotl" described relationships among living relatives and the concept "tlacamecayotl" conveyed a relationship between living relatives and their ancestors, a third concept—"teixhuihuan"—denoted filiation and connection between older generations and those who followed with a downward focus on those of younger generations. The term *teixhuihuan* derives from the word for grandchild, *ixhuiuhtli*. The literal translation of *teixhuihuan* would be "someone's grandchildren," implying the designation of a group of cousins. The use of the prefix *te-* may be significant, suggesting a group of people (also see Carrasco 1966: 155). An expanded use of this term beyond merely grandchildren is further intimated by the Spanish translations for this term. While *noxhuihuan* ("my grandchildren") and *iixhuihuan* ("his/her grandchildren") were always translated literally as "grandchildren" (though this would naturally include cousins, i.e., children of siblings [see Kellogg 1980: 127–28, for examples]), *teixhuihuan* rarely was. It might be rendered either as *parientes* (e.g., AGNT 56–8, 1592: fol.3r,8r) or *descendientes* (e.g., AGNT 42–5, 1579: fol.8v, 12r; also see Carrasco 1976*b:* 27). The term *pilli* (child) might occasionally also be translated in this extended fashion as well (AGNT

[24]"yn ioaniolque, in vel icalloc, in centlaca, cemeoa, in vel icujtlaxcolloc, yn vel imecaioc."

22–1–4, 1576: fol.102r, 105r; AGNT 39–1–2, 1578: fol. 11v, 17v).[25]

Of the three Mexica kinship categories, huanyolcayotl and tlacamecayotl were the most significant. The Mexica used these terms most frequently, signifying that they drew a consistent contrast between one's living circle of kin with whom one interacted in a variety of contexts and one's ascending or descending circle of kin through whom one inherited a variety of rights and obligations. The term *tlacamecayotl* most closely resembles what contemporary anthropologists would call a descent line (Periano 1961) and bears functional similarities to cognatic descent groups.

FUNCTION, PROCESS AND ARTICULATION

Let us now examine how three distinct kinship units— the households, the huanyolcayotl, and the tlacamecayotl—functioned and how they were connected to other units of social organization.

Households

Tenochcan Mexica family life took place in discrete architectural units called calli, which could refer to rooms within a larger multifamily unit. Early colonial legal cases occasionally contained plans describing calli (see Calnek 1974*b;* Kellogg 1993). These generally show several rooms, commonly three, grouped around a large, open patio area (the ithualli). Each room housed a separate nuclear family, with certain shared activities— especially rituals—taking place in the common area. We do not know whether other activities—such as production, cooking, and eating—took place in the common

[25]Also see Sullivan (1987: 57 [n. 15]) on the use and meaning of the term *teixhuihuan* in Tlaxcala, where it could refer to minor nobles who were closely allied to higher-ranking nobles and who might be kin *or* supporters.

area. As an architectural unit, calli were easily modified. An upper level might be constructed, rooms added on or torn down, and existing rooms subdivided by walls, with or without doors (see fig. 9).

House plans and wills indicate that the Mexica drew distinctions among particular types of rooms. Frequently, however, surviving documents make no attempt to distinguish among types, identifying rooms simply with the term *calli* or with the designation "first," "second," or "third." Sometimes, Mexica testators or litigants labeled rooms "small" or "walled" or as a shrine or work area. Upper levels would be labeled as such, and so would the "women's" area or room (the cihuacalli).[26]

Quite naturally, then, children raised in such multiple-family units frequently interacted from their earliest days with a variety of kin: parents, siblings, cousins, aunts and uncles, and sometimes grandparents or others of older generations. Co-residents participated in infants' "bathing" ceremonies, which took place in the household's patio area, and in the many calendrical ceremonies throughout the year which had a household component (Broda 1976: 45–50). Children, both girls and boys, also began their socialization into work tasks within the household among family members (*CM* 1992: III:fols.58r–60r).[27]

In performing their ceremonial, political, and economic functions, households interacted with higher-level social units. Two units played a particularly important role in connecting households to broader urban and imperial economic, political, and religious institutions: the tlaxilacalli and the calpulli. Tenochtitlán's four great

---

[26]The term *cihuacalli* was sometimes translated as "kitchen," though whether this area functioned solely as a cooking area is not clear. It may also have served as an area where women's work and/or family-related tasks were performed (Cline 1986: 100–101).

[27]Children, especially sons, were said to learn crafts and other skills from their fathers (thus, within the household) (Durán 1967: II:44:476–77; Zorita 1942: 66).

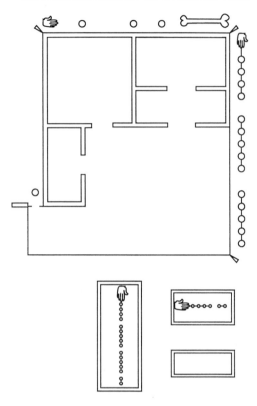

Fig. 9 A late sixteenth-century house plan, redrawn from BNP 112: fol. 13r. See also Calnek 1974*b:* 31-43 for other plans of house sites.

quarters were divided into smaller districts called tlax-ilacalli which appear to have provided the "internal administrative organization of the Aztec state" (Calnek 1976: 296). Tlaxilacalli probably consisted of groupings of as many as one hundred households through which tribute payments and service for public works were overseen (Durán 1967: II:42:313).

Local rituals and craftwork may have been organized through calpulli (Monzón 1949: 47–51) which were "corporate, localized social group[s]" and bore names identical to those used for tlaxilacalli (Calnek 1976: 296). Households, neighborhoods and even tlaxilacalli were also enmeshed in webs of material obligation to palaces and temples as well (*FC* 1950–82: IX:20:91).[28]

Households not only provided an arena and personnel for work groups and ritual practice but also partially structured Mexica inheritance and marriage practices. Extant sources suggest that marriage generally involved movement of one spouse to the other spouse's parents' household. In other words, marriage tended to be either patrilocal or matrilocal rather than neolocal, at least in its early stages. Early proscriptive sources tend to describe marriage as patrilocal (especially among nobles). The discussion of affinal relations in the *Florentine Codex,* for example, addresses the relationship between an in-marrying spouse (who was always depicted as a female) and her new household and states that a woman's natal family should not interfere in the affairs of her household by marriage (e.g., ibid., X:2:7; Motolinía 1971: 314). Early court records show a nearly equivalent number of patrilocal and matrilocal marriages during the sixteenth century (Kellogg 1980: 160–62).[29]

The *Florentine Codex* describes marriage as a lengthy process set in motion by the groom's parents (VI:23: 127–33). Both the parents of the bride and the groom played a role in the nuptial process, which was especially elaborate among noble families. Prior to the wedding, banquets were held in both the bride's and the groom's households, and speeches were given stressing the obligations assumed by the married couple. The parents also appear to have kept lists of property brought to the marriage in case of divorce (Durán 1967: I:5:57).

[28]Goods produced at local levels—households and neighborhoods—also made their way into markets though the mechanisms by which this occurred are not clear (Calnek 1978).

[29]Pre-Hispanic marriages described in these legal cases were predominantly patrilocal (Kellogg 1980: 161).

The disbursal of property through inheritance involved the household and kin group. In theory, the bilateral sibling group had equal inheritance rights; in practice, however, men and those children (often male but sometimes female) who remained within the households had greater access to residential rights and to land. The disposition of various kinds of movables was sex linked but again influenced by who remained in the household over the course of its developmental cycle (see chap. 4).

Huanyolcayotl and Tlacamecayotl

The forms of interaction between other units, especially those designated here by the terms *huanyolcayotl* and *tlacamecayotl* are less apparent because they were not directly overseen by either the tlaxilacalli or calpulli. Instead, they apparently functioned informally to regulate certain aspects of household organization. How, or if, the huanyolcayotl and tlacamecayotl interacted with higher-level units is not clear. However, they did articulate with households in a variety of ways.

The term *huanyolcayotl* appears primarily in the context of a variety of calendrical and life-cycle ceremonies (*FC* 1950–82: II, III, VI). The *tehuanyolque* were the people with whom individuals, families, and households celebrated the important events through which families and households grew and replicated and through which the Mexica stated and reinforced their values and beliefs. While we do not have data that allow us to examine the range and limits of kin who would typically be included as tehuanyolque (someone's relatives), we do know that this unit included affines. This was one way it differed from the tlacamecayotl.

The tlacamecayotl played an important role in inheritance, household recruitment and organization, and certain types of legal obligations. One context in which the term shows up is in discussions of inheritance. Dur-

184

ing the late pre-Hispanic era, it appears that only limited bequests of material property, or rights to its use, flowed between spouses. Kin who received inheritance rights included children, grandchildren, siblings, and nephews and nieces. While precise genealogical links are difficult to trace because of the extension of kin terms, the kin who received property rights were related through the concept of tlacamecayotl, that is, they could trace common ancestors back between three to five generations (Kellogg 1980: 100–105).

The concept of tlacamecayotl also served to define and delimit household residence rights. The Mexica's complex, multifamily households, in which residence rights were transmitted through bilateral inheritance of residence rights by sibling groups, faced a potential problem. Over the course of two to three generations, too many individuals might have potential claims (Calnek n.d.; Kellogg 1986*a*, 1993). Polygynous marriages further exacerbated this problem (with still more problems of interpersonal conflict often accompanying these structural issues). Moreover, increasing population density in central Mexico during the late postclassic era aggravated the problem of too many potential residents (Sanders, Parsons, and Santley 1979: 184–86).

This unit also defined the outer genealogical limits of those who might share potential residence rights. Evidence from early colonial legal cases suggests a number of other, more immediate and practical ways of limiting actual residence rights including site partition and household exogamy (Calnek 1976: 298, n.d.; Kellogg 1980: 165–70, 1993). In addition, the telpochcalli and calmecac may have served a demographic function as well as one of socialization; that is, they took young people, especially males, out of the household for some period of time (Zorita 1942: 67). Therefore, household organization reflected a pattern in which potential recruitment was circumscribed by the limits of the category tlacamecayotl as defined by Sahagún's informants.

It is also possible that there were sentiments of shared legal obligation within the tlacamecayotl. Surviving documents describe kin of offenders as holding mutual legal responsibility across a variety of kinds of behavior. Types of offenses for which kin were liable for shared responsibility, or even punishment, included stealing, traitorous acts, or a priest's breaking the rule of chastity (Motolinía 1971: 51:367–78). This joint culpability may have extended to relatives of the "fourth generation" (Las Casas 1967: II:382; Conquistador Anónimo 1941: 33). Likewise, the kin of a slave might share responsibility for providing someone to fill the status. Motolinía states that consanguineally related descendants shared this obligation.

> When the one who had been appointed and had then served some years, wishing to rest or marry, said to the others who were jointly obligated with him and *who had enjoyed the price,* that another should enter to serve for some time; but he was not freed from the obligation by this, neither he nor whomever he [she] married, whether male or female; but those who at first had been obligated, *with their descendants, contracted that obligation, and of this manner, four or five houses happened to be obligated, or the inhabitants of them were obligated for a slave to an owner and his heirs.* (1971: 369 [my emphasis]; also see Durán 1967: I:20:183)[30]

Legal liability cut across kin and households; these obligations based on shared filiation and descent rested on the Mexica concept of tlacamecayotl.

[30]Cuando aquel que habían señalado, había ya servido algunos años, queriendo descansar o casar, decía a los otros que juntamente con él estaban obligados y habían gozado del precio, que entrase otro a servir algún tiempo; pero no por esto se libraba de la obligación él ni con quien casaba, ahora fuese varón, ahora hembra; mas los que de primero se habían obligado, con los dellos descendientes, contraían aquella obligación, y desta manera de obligados acontecía estar cuatro o cinco casas, o los moradores dellas ser obligados por un esclavo a un amo y a sus herederos. There is also an interesting reference to "house clusters" (*calla onoca*) in the *FC* (XII:40:121.)

FAMILY AND KIN RELATIONS
DURING THE EARLY COLONIAL PERIOD

How did Mexica kinship concepts and units change in the transition to colonial subjugation? How did the connections between kinship units and administrative, economic, and ritual units evolve? Let us begin by examining the kinds of family and kin forms that existed during the early colonial period.

Tenochcan Mexica family and kin forms gradually changed over the period from 1521 to 1700. The structures that emerged cannot be understood simply as imitations of Spanish family and kinship practices. Instead, they arose as reactions to new material and social circumstances that profoundly altered the interactions within families and within larger kinship units.

It is possible to identify four fundamental transformations. The first and most obvious change involved the gradual decline during the sixteenth century of certain larger kin categories that had structured inheritance and property ownership. Social interaction eventually was no longer shaped by these preconquest categories. A second transformation involved the multifamily household structure. Complex households ceased to be the cultural norm and appear to have decreased in number. Over time, household structure and composition grew simpler and smaller, though this process was neither linear nor continuous.

A third key development involved a new emphasis on the spousal relationship. This shift in emphasis tended to reinforce relationships within the nuclear family and reduce the importance of other kinship relationships. Fourth and finally, the preferred virilocal marriage forms (in which the bride moves to the household of her husband's family) of the late pre-Hispanic period gave way to a more mixed pattern of virilocal marriages, uxorilocal marriages (in which the groom moves to the household of the bride's family) and neolocal marriages

187

(in which the bride and groom establish a new residence). Underlying these broad transformations were changes in cultural patterns and cognitive structures whose causes will be discussed later in this chapter.

Shifting Kinship Categories and Conceptualizations

Between the sixteenth and seventeenth centuries, a transformation occurred in the way Nahuas conceptualized kinship. The cognatic kinship system in which rights, responsibilities, and inheritance were passed through either the father or the mother did not survive into the seventeenth century. By the 1580s, a different kind of structure was beginning to emerge.

The impact of this new system was clearly evident in the texts of seventeenth-century property suits, especially those dated after 1650. It can be seen in the new ways that Indians determined inherited rights. During the sixteenth century, especially in those lawsuits during the years 1550 to 1585, the most common form for inheritance of rights of residence, use, or ownership was to trace them back two to four generations, through sibling groups, to a "founding" male or couple, who were described as the root or foundation of ownership. Thus, genealogies provided both by litigants and by testators often comprised four or five generations and were strongly cognatic as the Mexica frequently used sisters, mothers, aunts and/or grandmothers as links through whom rights were traced (Kellogg 1980: 99–105). Not only was it relatively common for genealogies to span three to five generations and include women as genealogical links through whom inheritance rights were traced, these generations were often described as sibling groups so that the kin relations depicted were both lineally and laterally complex (see figs. 10, 11; also see figs. 1, 2, 3, 5). In their testimony, early colonial litigants and witnesses tended to stress joint ownership and rights held by successive sibling groups. The evidence they provided

Fig. 10
Source: AGNT 30-1, 1570

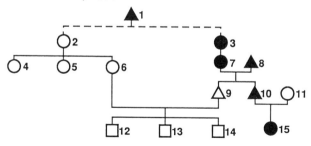

1 Cuaquile (*d. ca.* 1520)
2 Ana Papan
3 Juana (*d. ca.* 1550)
4 Petronila
5 Marina Tlaco
6 Ana Xoco
7 Magdalena (*d. ca.* 1550)
8 Martín Aca (*d. ca.* 1544)

9 Pedro Nali
10 Juan Bautista Yecapitza (*d. ca.* 1569)
11 María Tiacapan
12 unnamed
13 unnamed
14 unnamed
15 Mariana Martina (*d. ca.* 1569)

Fig. 11
Source: AGNT 48-4, 1583

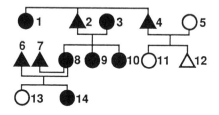

1 Ana Mocel
2 Luis Epcoatl
3 Isabel Juana
4 Bernardino Alonso
5 Ana Mocel
6 Miguel Quicen
7 Mateo

8 Juana Francisca (*d. ca.* 1575)
9 Marta Telolo
10 Magdalena
11 María Tiacapan
12 Juan Baltasar
13 Ana María Tepi
14 María Tlaco (*d. ca.* 1582)

traced ownership rights upward through ascending generations, placing a strong emphasis on antecedent generations.

By 1585, however, another form of argument began to appear in legal texts. A number of litigants presented less complex genealogies and described inheritance of rights as rooted in ownership only one or two generations above a litigant. The rights traced through these shallower, less complex genealogies tended to stress patrifilial ties, that is, the flow of rights from grandfathers and/or fathers. Only rarely did these litigants seek to establish their rights through mothers or to grandmothers. Also, these genealogies placed little emphasis on ascending generations of siblings through whom inheritance rights flowed.

The litigants who offered shallow, simplified genealogies frequently came from consanguineal or nuclear households (see figures 12, 13). Unlike the litigants from multifamily households, who often traced property rights back to the pre-Hispanic period, these litigants based their rights on a father or grandfather who had bought the property, not inherited it.

Over time, an increasing number of indigenous litigants described the range of kin through whom rights were inherited in a narrower fashion. At the same time, the focus upward through ascending sibling groups was transformed into expressions of kinship relations that placed a greater emphasis on succeeding and future generations. A 1576 lawsuit, which contains Nahuatl testimony given in 1563, suggests that part of the reason for this shift has to do with the way that Spaniards understood, translated, and expressed Mexica kinship concepts. In these texts, which described the ownership rights of don Luis de Santa María, governor of México-Tenochtitlán from 1563 to 1565, and his brother, don Martín Momauhtin, to a tecpan, or palace site, in San Sebastían Coatlan, both don Luis de Santa María and his witnesses stressed the relationship of the brothers to

Fig. 12
Source: AGNT 17-2-4, 1559

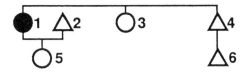

1 Magdalena Tiacapan (*d. ca.* 1546)
2 unnamed
3 Juana Teicuh
4 Bernardino Cozcaquauh
5 Marina
6 unnamed

antecedent relatives including the tlatoani Ahuitzotl and his son Acamapichtli, the father of don Luis and his brother (AGNT 22–1–4, 1576: fols.101r–103r; also see the *Crónica mexicáyotl* 1975: 145). The Nahuatl texts emphasize that this property was huehuetlalli and was inherited from the grandfather and father. The Spanish translations, in contrast, stress that don Luis and don Martín were children and descendants (AGNT 22–1–4, 1576:fols.104r–106v). While the genealogical relationships described were equivalent, the concepts used and the means of tracing them were not.

A similar shift away from inheritance transmitted along genealogical ties can be seen in documents included in the records of a 1585 case (AGNT 49–5), which involved a dispute over an eight-braza-square plot of land outside Mexico City, which Angelina Martina, a wealthy merchant, left to two of her great-grandchildren. She had purchased this property in 1551 from don

Fig. 13
Source: AGNT 42-5, 1579

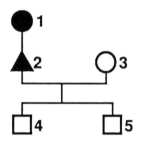

1 Juana Papan
2 Juan Totoca (*d.* 1582)
3 Juana Tlaco
4 unnamed
5 unnamed

Baltasar Tlilancalqui. The text of the letter of sale was
included in the Nahuatl documents offered as evidence
in this lawsuit. Tlilancalqui identified the land as pillalli
and stated that he had inherited it from his grandparents
(*noculhua*) and great-grandparents (*nachcocolhua* (AGNT
49–5, 1585: fol.9r). When Angelina Martina later wrote
her will in 1580, she did not define her ownership rights
in terms of the ancestors through whom she had inherited certain holdings. Instead, she offered abbreviated
descriptions of genealogy, emphasizing rights obtained
through purchase, not inheritance.

By the seventeenth century, a significant change had
occurred in Indian concepts of kinship. Notions of *ascent*
became very broad and general. Instead of rooting
ownership rights in inheritance, Indian litigants (like

Fig. 14
Source: AGNT 101-2, 1642

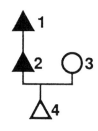

1 unnamed
2 Joséph Melchior (*d.* 1642)
3 Francisca Gerónima
4 Joséph

the barrio of San Anton Acatlan in a 1613 lawsuit) spoke of their "traditional" ownership over certain lands. In this 1613 case, the litigants based their claim simply on the ground that the property had been possessed by "*nuestros padres y abuelos y antepasados*" before the Spanish won it (*ganara* [AGNT 95–8, 1613: fol.1r]).[31]

When Indians did trace property rights through inheritance, their genealogies were precise but shallower and more lineal than those provided during the sixteenth century. By far the most common pattern for tracing inheritance rights was a three-generation genealogy tracing rights to a litigant's father or grandfather (see figs. 14, 15). These genealogies often were

[31]It is also interesting to note that the relationships among "kin" who sued each other changed. In the sixteenth century, litigation between affines was predominant (Kellogg 1980: 23) whereas by the late sixteenth century and during the seventeenth, litigation between "siblings" (generally half-siblings) was the most common form (e.g., AGNT 49–3, 1595; AGNT 155–9, 1693).

193

Fig. 15
Source: AGNT 157-7, 1694

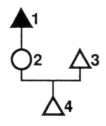

1 Sebastian Xuarez
2 Ana Francisca Xuarez
3 Nicolás de la Cruz
4 Pasqual Xuarez

patrifilial in nature and made no mention of ascending groups of siblings through whom rights were claimed.

Among the small number of cases in which litigants constructed genealogies that went back at least symbolically to the pre-Hispanic period, one had a total span of four generations and the span was created by establishing links completely lineally with a patrifilial emphasis (AGNT 183–4, 1607; fig. 16); the other traced links in three generations but again was lineal (AGNT 128–2, 1682 [see the will of Juana Agustina, 1609]; fig. 17).

As the relationships between individuals and their ascendant kin (especially ascendant collateral kin) weakened, the traditional kinship categories—especially that of tlacamecayotl—withered and ultimately disappeared. As the culturally defined unit of kin which helped shape the developmental cycle of the multifamily household became attenuated, the multifamily household structure became transformed as well.

194

Fig. 16
Source: AGNT 183-4, 1607

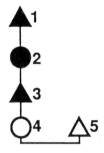

1 Chimalteuhtzin
2 Juana Xoco
3 Miguel Jacobo
4 Beatriz Francisca
5 Francisco Pablo

A Changing Household Structure

During the sixteenth century, especially in the years preceding 1585, certain continuities with the late pre-Hispanic period were still apparent in Tenochcan Mexica household patterns. One of these was a tendency for early colonial Indians to live in multifamily households.

Lawsuits provide a valuable source of information about colonial household composition. The suits from the period stretching from 1540 to 1595 offer the most detailed descriptive information about residential patterns. By examining residential histories offered by litigants and witnesses in thirty-four cases, I have recon-

Fig. 17
Source: AGNT 128-2, 1682

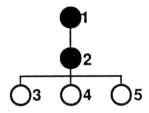

1 Macario
2 Juana Agustina
3 Juana Agustina
4 María Geronima
5 Juana Francisca

structed the composition of eighty-two households across this period.[32]

I divided households into four categories: single person, consanguineal family, nuclear family, and complex family. Consanguineal family households are defined as including *a* parent and child or children, *or* groups of co-resident unmarried siblings. Nuclear family households included married couples with or without children. Complex family households encompassed at least

[32]Twenty-three of these residence sites have longitudinal data that extend over time and thus show changes in household composition. The minimum number of individuals included is 195. This figure represents a minimum because not all residents were mentioned. There was some tendency to describe residence in terms of those people directly involved in a lawsuit as well as cases where resident children were simply referred to as *hijos* without specifying numbers or sex. Readers should also note that the table that follows differs in form from tables in Kellogg 1980 and 1986*a*. It includes somewhat fewer households because I restricted the time period to include the years for which the data are most adequate.

the remnants of more than one nuclear family usually related through consanguineal ties. These ties could be lateral, through siblings or cousins, or generational, through adult children and their parents. Complex family units often combined lateral and generational ties, or they contained segments related through polygynous marriages. Table 10 summarizes these findings.

Table 10
Types of Households

	1540s–50s		1560s–70s		1580s–90s	
SPH	3	13%	5	10%	1	9%
CoFH	4	17%	9	19%	2	18%
NFH	5	22%	11	23%	3	27%
CFH	11	48%	23	48%	5	45%

Note: SPH = single-person household; CoFH = consanguineal family household; NFH = nuclear family household; CFH = complex family household.

Given the small number of households represented and the incompleteness of some of the data, these figures can do no more than suggest possible patterns. Nevertheless, certain tendencies are readily apparent. The most striking involves the relatively large numbers of complex family household units. During the middle and late sixteenth century, they made up nearly half of all households. It appears that especially during the 1540s, 1550s, and 1560s, individual Mexica attempted to reconstitute complex family households—by inviting relatives to co-reside (see, e.g., AGNT 21–1–2, 1565 or 39–1–2, 1578 [referring to events of ca. 1545]), through virilocal or uxorilocal marriages of children (see, e.g., AGNT 2729–20, 1562 [virilocal marriage] or AGNT 20–1–2, 1563 [uxorilocal marriage]), or even by buying a new house site (see, e.g., AGNT 29–5, 1570 [referring to a sale in 1563]).[33] But one must be careful not to allow

[33]Two significant issues, one sociocultural and one demographic, must be addressed in relation to these figures. The sociocultural issue is whether the large number of multifamily households represent a largely pre-Hispanic

THE SOCIAL HISTORY OF EVERYDAY LIFE

aggregate statistics to mask certain underlying trends. For example, the figures for the period from the 1560s to the 1570s hide a decline in the number of multifamily households which may be related to the spread of epidemic disease during this time. The process of disaggregation of complex households was itself intricate, as some separated into nuclear units, while others split into consanguineal units.

By the 1580s, however, other forces that I will discuss below led to the emergence of smaller households—

pattern or whether they represent a new pattern, one that developed out of the brutal conditions of conquest and the spread of disease. I believe these households represent a pre-Hispanic pattern (which may in the years up to approximately 1580 have been reinforced by the new conditions) based on several pieces of evidence. One is that across the Valley of Mexico such figures are not unusual for the mid-sixteenth century. There are variations in the proportions of nuclear vs. complex families and Mexico City does show a more intricate household pattern, with renters and single person households, for example. But the pattern described here is not out of line with other communities in the valley. Second, chronicles do point to the multifamily household as an ideal type. This does not mean that all households conformed to such a norm—but rather suggests that such a household pattern was culturally valued and would be a form that individuals and families might try to reconstitute themselves in the first turbulent decades after conquest. Finally, the organization of production and reproduction in Tenochtitlán-Tlatelolco appear to have supported such a household structure as the cultural and statistical norm. Steady population increase, high rates of male absence due to warfare, and needs to maximize food and craft production and market efficiency all may have helped sustain relatively large numbers of multifamily households.

The demographic question is whether such a household structure was possible given recent findings by paleoanthropologists of low life expectancies and of nutritional and biological stress. This literature is briefly summarized by McCaa (1992); also see Storey (1992). Ethnohistorians, however, using chronicles, have emphasized the relative health and well-being of central Mexican peoples (see Ortiz de Montellano [1990] on the Valley of Mexico; see Crosby [1972: 35–37] more generally). The new physical evidence is quite persuasive yet must be reconciled with sustained high rates of population growth and the existence of a large number of densely settled communities in the Valley, not limited to Tenochtitlán, during the late postclassic period (Sanders, Parsons, and Santley 1979). A household structure with a relatively high number of multifamily households would not only have maximized productive efforts but would have served the needs of orphans, widows, and those elderly who survived. Two other factors that would have been particularly salient in Tenochtitlán were high rates of in-migration (Calnek 1976: 288–90) and overcrowding, especially in the older central parts of the city (ibid., 298–300; FC 1950–82: XI:12:275).

198

often nuclear in form—as independent entities. Thus, by around 1585, the nuclear family household was becoming a more stable and long-lasting form in the developmental cycle of Indian families and households.

Data on household composition contained in seventeenth-century property litigation is less complete than for the sixteenth century. In part, this is because the audiencia heard far fewer cases and because litigants presented discourses less rooted in the reconstruction of kin and family histories over time. Nevertheless, when litigants referred to their households, they were less likely to describe them as complex or constituted by multiple families. Of twelve such descriptions, eight (67%) were nuclear and four (33%) were complex.[34] The

[34]There is an interesting set of corroborating data, though again they are fragmentary and problematic and can best be understood as providing a series of clues about trends in Indian household structure, not the definitive picture. These data consist of late seventeenth-century lists (collected in 1691) of Indian inhabitants, listed by family grouping, of Mexico City's central district, the traza (AGNHi 413–1). Parish priests of the Indian barrios were required to keep records about parishioners who resided in the traza. Cope states that "this particular set of censuses has been preserved because of its importance in the aftermath of the 1692 riot, when the Viceroy ordered all the Indians living in the *traza* to return to their barrios" (1994: 89). Two particular lists (one of traza residents from the parish of San Joseph, the other of traza residents from Santa María La Redonda) are helpful because not only are families listed but the names and ages of children are given and some information about the identities of other individuals is provided as well. The material is problematic for a number of reasons. The first is that it refers to families and individuals resident in the traza and whether the characteristics of their family units are identical to those family units found in the Indian barrios is unknown. Second, because the conjugal pair was the basic unit by which Spanish priests collected such information (also see Cook and Borah 1971: I:136–37), relationships between family units (which might, in some cases, have made up larger households) are impossible to trace. Nonetheless, an examination of this material suggests the growing importance of nuclear families for Indians resident in Mexico City. Using the same categories that are used in table 10, the data show the following family types and proportions (of a total of 502 families or individuals listed): single persons accounted for sixty entries or 12% of the total number of listings; conjugal families accounted for thirty-one listings or 6.2% of the total number; nuclear families (including married couples with no children) represented 359 entries or 71.5% of the total. All other entries numbered fifty-two or 10.3%. A small number, eight, consisted of either couples with an aging parent or couples, an aging parent, and the couple's children. Many of these other listings are

composition of complex family households also underwent change; these included only one or two more
consanguineal relatives beyond the nuclear family, and
in these texts the relative was always a parent or parents
of either the husband or wife (see AGNT 101–2, 1642;
155–9, 1693; 186–9, 1693; 163–2, 1695).[35]

There are, however, some noteworthy trends in the
seventeenth-century court records. The most significant
is a growing number of nuclear families, which meant
that households were experiencing a decline in size and
complexity. Another development is for non-nuclear
households to be structured around the parent-child tie,
not around sibling or cousin ties or around relationships
stemming from polygynous marriages. Adult siblings do
not appear to have resided together commonly during
the seventeenth century. Case records suggest that even
though siblings continued to inherit house sites jointly,
generally only one sibling actually remained in residence and retained possession. The records do not
reveal any clear preference based on age or gender. In a
number of cases, the legal texts indicate that *no* child
remained resident and that adult siblings rented or sold
a house site that they had inherited from a parent or
parents (AGNT 1720–7, 1633; 157–6, 1694).

Instead of envisioning the changes that occurred in
sixteenth- and seventeenth-century Mexico City as a
breakdown of Tenochcan Mexica kinship and household structures, it would be more accurate to describe

---

people who are identified as widows, widowers, single persons (*soltero/a*), or
elderly (*viejo/a*) living in various combinations, sometimes with children. It is
likely that a variety of kin types and relationships were represented among these
people but they cannot presently be reconstructed. But also see Haskett (1991:
146–48), who finds a greater percentage of "extended family" households
during the mid-seventeenth century in the Cuernavaca region though his data
appear to refer primarily to Indian elites.

[35]This pattern is also seen in the nature of bequests in wills dating from the
latter half of the seventeenth century, as described in chap. 5. Note also Cope's
description of the short genealogical span for the inheritance of second names
among Mexico City's seventeenth-century casta and Indian population (1994:
59–63).

them as a fundamental transformation. By the seventeenth century, colonial urban Indian households were more likely than before to be nuclear. When they were complex, they were usually structured around parent-child ties rather than sibling ties; indeed, the complex phase appears to have been short-lived.[36]

Changes in the Meaning and Patterns of Marriage

While chroniclers tended to describe postmarital residence patterns as virilocal (which may partly be a result of concentration on elite practices), sixteenth-century legal texts show an almost equal number of uxorilocal (27) and virilocal marriages (25), with only three clear examples of neolocal marriages.[37] Both chronicles and legal texts indicate that when a couple married, the expectation was for the new couple to reside with either the groom's family or the bride's family.

This postmarital residence pattern was part of a developmental cycle that emphasized multifamily households as the cultural and likely statistical norm during the late pre-Hispanic period. But this residence pattern also suggests that while the Mexica viewed marriage as an important and significant event, the married *couple* itself received no great cultural or structural emphasis. Rather, larger household and kin units to which individuals belonged subsumed the married couple.

[36]Studies of contemporary Nahuatl-speaking peoples suggest that these trends continued into the twentieth century. Sandstrom (1991: 157–88) has a particularly clear discussion of kinship and household patterns among such a group. Also see Nutini (1968), Arizpe Schlosser (1973), Dehouve (1978), Taggart (1975, 1976), and Slade (1976, 1992).

[37]Legal texts suggest a high number of uxorilocal marriages, especially during the period prior to 1585. While uxorilocal marriages may have been more common during the pre-Hispanic period than chronicles depict, during the mid- to late sixteenth century, these marriages appear to have been associated with two factors: households that were pressured by a lack of males and therefore were struggling to remain *viable* (Stenning 1958) and marriages between Indian women and Spanish men and are likely overrepresented in these documents.

This multifamily residence pattern persisted through much of the sixteenth century. While there are no indications of a rapid trend toward neolocality, neither were postmarital residence patterns immutably fixed. Descriptions of household histories indicate that married couples or widows or widowers could and did change residence. Those who were widowed might return to natal sites (see, e.g., AGNT 2729–20, 1562) or activate residual residence rights through close consanguineal ties (see, e.g., AGNT 20–1–2, 1572). Some couples who had resided uxorilocally later returned to the husband's natal site (see, e.g., AGNT 30–1, 1570). The fluidity of postmarital residence patterns reinforced the looseness and flexibility of Mexica kinship structures.

During the latter part of the sixteenth century, however, the meaning of marriage began to undergo a significant transformation.[38] According to Motolinía, Christian marriage ceremonies began in Mexico City in 1526 when don Hernando, brother of the ruler of Texcoco, along with seven of his "*compañeros*" (probably kin and very close supporters) were married in a Christian marriage ceremony (1971: 146). Two members of Cortés's army, Alonso de Avila and Pero Sánchez Farfán and their wives, along with other notable Spaniards, served as *padrinos* (godparents) for the couples (147). The early priests hoped to use the Christian marriages of high elites, along with those of their children of marriageable age, as examples for the indigenous population (also see Gruzinski 1980, 1982; Ragon 1992; Cline 1993*b*).

As described by Motolinía, early efforts to promote Christian marriage foundered on the fact that many Indians, especially nobles, had "five, ten, fifteen, twenty, or thirty or more" wives, with rulers having "100, 150, even 200" (1971: 148). Motolinía further observed that

[38]The tremendous importance historically placed by the Catholic church on the institution of marriage and the conjugal bond is discussed in the entries on marriage in the *NCE* (1967–79: IX:265–90). Also see the discussion of matrimony as a sacrament and its liturgical aspects in the same source (468–73).

some men had so many wives that others, especially poor men, could not marry at all. Polygyny left priests "perplexed," but they hoped that nobles could be convinced by Catholic doctrine to content themselves with only one wife (1971: 148–49).

Other priests stressed different obstacles to the triumph of Christian marriage ceremonies. Durán, for example, suggested that because Indians mourned for their "rulers and ancient gods" (1967: I:5:56), they were not satisfied by the Catholic ceremony and sought more traditional ones. "After I married some young men and women, with all the solemnity and ceremony the sacrament demands, after leaving the church, they were taken to a house of the old people and were married again, with the ancient ceremonies and rites."[39]

Nevertheless, by the end of the sixteenth century, the Mexica increasingly enacted the Catholic emphasis on monogamous marriage and the sanctified tie between husband and wife. In legal records, litigants stated that they had undergone a proper Christian marriage as a sign of their good character and their willingness to cooperate with the colonial system (see chap. 2). A new emphasis on conjugal ties also appeared in Indian wills, which reveal that husbands and wives were regularly bequeathing property to each other and were increasingly designating specific bequests so that masses would be said in honor of the deceased partner. In wills, one also finds a heightened stress on lineal ties and a reduced cultural emphasis on lateral ties among aunts, uncles, nephews, nieces, and cousins.

The growing importance of conjugal bonds is also reflected in changing residence patterns. While extended kin might sometimes be attached to nuclear family households, it was the nuclear family, not the

[39]"Después de haber casado yo unos mozos y mozas, con toda la solemnindad y ceremonias que el sacramento demanda, acabados de salir de la iglesia, los llevaron a casa de los viejos y viejas y los tornaron a casar, con las ceremonias y ritos antiguos."

multifamily household, that became the norm for domestic life in late sixteenth- and early seventeenth-century colonial Mexico City. The emerging independence of the conjugal couple and nuclear family is reflected in the residence histories presented in seventeenth-century legal texts, which show that neolocal postmarital residences constituted an increased number of those marriages described. Five of eighteen [28%] were neolocal, nine of eighteen [50%] were uxorilocal, and four of eighteen [22%] were virilocal.[40]

It appears that during the sixteenth and seventeenth centuries, Spanish and indigenous families were evolving in different directions. While Mexica families decreased in size and structural complexity between 1521 and 1700, Spanish families did the opposite (Cook and Borah 1971: I:158–78). Thus, it seems clear that while indigenous kinship and family organization were influenced by Spanish law, religion, and family organization, Indian family patterns should not be understood simply as an imitation of a Spanish model. Rather, colonial Mexica family patterns reflected their own distinctive dynamics and historical circumstances.

The Causes and Significance of Changes in Family Life

Several factors help to explain the emergence of a colonial Indian family and kinship system, whose structures, practices, and ceremonies differed radically from those of the precolonial period. I believe that four factors were critical to this process: demographic upheaval; the imposition of tribute payments; the introduction of the Spanish legal system; and the introduction of Catholicism. Together, these factors created a strong set of pressures on individuals and families that caused them

[40]Again the number of uxorilocal marriages appears high and during the late seventeenth century appears associated with status such that the daughters of high-status men (when there were no living or co-resident sons) were likely to marry in this fashion.

to make different kinds of decisions, take alternative actions, and strategize in new and different ways. As individual Mexica did this, new kinds of cultural beliefs and institutions came into being: some were based on similarities and continuities with pre-Hispanic institutions, some were based on syncretisms; and some were truly new. For the sake of clarity, I will distinguish between the material factors and the cultural and ideological factors promoting change.

MATERIAL FACTORS INFLUENCING CHANGE

The impact of demographic upheaval is readily discernible in the court records of the Real Audiencia. For example, the case records frequently allude to the needs of children reared in other than their natal households (see, e.g., AGNT 17–2–4, 1559; 22–1–5, 1567). Many cases involved disputes over abandoned house sites (often, as we have seen, involving conflicts between nonresidents, who claimed ownership rights, and squatters; see, e.g., AGNT 22–1–3 and 22–1–4, 1576; 20–1–2, 1572).[41] Furthermore, the case records contain numerous references to residents fleeing Mexico City and the subsequent hardships they encountered (see, e.g., AGNT 23–2–4, 1568: fol.214r–214v). The conspicuous absence of both younger and older men in the mid-sixteenth-century legal cases offers another striking commentary on the impact of the conquest and subsequent waves of epidemic diseases (also see Gibson 1964: 141).[42] This sex difference is clearly demonstrated in legal cases in that many households were left with few or no middle-aged men. Differential sex ratios were related to other consequences of demographic decline.

[41]These demographic pressures would have been reinforced by physical changes occurring in the city as houses were torn down and new buildings took their place (see, e.g., AC 1889–1916: VIII:357).

[42]For a discussion of social disruption focusing on vagrancy rather than disease and death, see Martin (1957: chap. 4).

205

Within the sixteenth-century court records, one encounters vivid descriptions of families and households struggling to survive. Households adopted a number of strategies; these included uxorilocal marriage, the renting of rooms in house compounds to nonrelatives (e.g., AGNT 20–1–3, 1573, in which part of a house site was rented to "hat makers") or to distant relatives (e.g., AGNT 23–2–4, 1568), and the reactivation of residual kinship and property rights. One finds reference in the case records, for example, to female members of a multifamily household fleeing to "the patrimony and inheritance of their mothers" following their fathers' and brothers' deaths (AGNT 20–1–2, 1572: fol.131r).

Issues of household authority also grew increasingly problematic as a result of demographic disruption and economic pressure (see chap. 2). In the court records, one frequently encounters efforts by in-married spouses, usually wives, to inherit residence rights and rights of ownership that they would not have received in the pre-Hispanic period. Because households were frequently left with women and children struggling to survive economically, maintaining authority and personal relations amid such disruptions and irregular family configurations proved overwhelmingly difficult. The emphasis on age and seniority in Mexica culture (which reinforced kinship and household structuring) was another casualty of the disruption and ultimate transformation of authority relations. Early friars often lavished their attentions on children, especially elite children, pitting them against their elders and thereby further undermining lines of authority (Motolinía 1971: 38, 439; Trexler 1982; also see Gutiérrez 1991: 75–76).

Colonial tribute obligations, which grew increasingly burdensome over the course of the sixteenth century, further weakened both Nahua and Tenochcan Mexica households (Miranda 1952: 155–65, 223–24; 240–48; Gibson 1964: 196–206). Tribute grew more oppressive for a variety of reasons. The change from community assessments in kind to uniform assessments in money and maize (Gibson 1964: 197–200; Hassig 1985: 227–28), the tendency to include increasing numbers of people who had been exempt during the pre-Hispanic period and/or the earliest years of the colonial period (Gibson 1964: 200–2), and the overall population decline left many communities with too few people to labor to meet the assessments (ibid., 203). Among the new types of tribute that added to the Indian burden during the sixteenth and seventeenth centuries (Gibson 1964: 204–205) was a special tax, the *medio real de ministros,* which required Indians to pay the costs of their litigation (also see Borah 1983: 104–5), some proportion of which originated in the need to lower tribute assessments!

These processes fell heavily on the native population of Tenochtitlán. In the early years after the conquest, they paid no tribute on the grounds that the residents provided labor services for the many new needs of Cortés's capital. Silvio Zavala (1984–87) has documented in excruciating detail the many "personal services" provided by the city's indigenous population to the first Spanish rulers, viceroys and other officials. But in 1564, the native population of the city became liable for tribute payments in money (assessed at one peso and three *reales*) (Gibson 1964: 390).[43]

The imposition of monetary tribute payments provoked several reactions: the most immediate was a violent protest against Tenochtitlán's gobernador during which he was nearly killed. Yet soon thereafter, this same man was imprisoned for his "failure to collect the tax and maintain order" (ibid.). Indigenous governing elites wrote letters to the king of Spain in which they pleaded with him to withdraw the new tribute payments.[44] Such

[43]See the brief but intriguing discussion of the need for (and consequences of the use of) money and the development of a cash economy by both *forasteros* and *ayllu* members in the Cuzco region (Wightman 1990: 126–28).

[44]See, e.g., the 1574 letter by don Antonio Valeriano and his councillors in

letters express, in a muted but clear way, the misery of colonial native officials who knew that to stay in power, they had to carry out such demands but in doing so became delegitimized in the eyes of many of the indigenous population. A third response provoked by the new policy was the selling, renting, or pawning of significant amounts of Indian-held property in the city, which then had the effect of further destabilizing households economically and, in turn, led to increased interpersonal strains and litigation.

CULTURAL AND IDEOLOGICAL FACTORS INFLUENCING CHANGE

Material influences were strengthened and reinforced by ideological influences. Spaniards articulated new values designed to impose different models for structures, practices, and beliefs. Cultural influences on family life can be seen particularly clearly in Spanish law as applied to the indigenous population of New Spain, in particular, to Mexico City's indigenous population, and in divergent religious beliefs and practices as introduced by Spanish priests (also see Gruzinski 1988; Klor de Alva 1991).[45]

The new legal system exerted a powerful influence on colonial Mexica family life. Spanish property laws, especially inheritance laws, introduced a narrower, more lineal range of kin among whom property rights were to

---

which they tried, unsuccessfully, to persuade the king to exempt the city's residents from tribute payments (AGI Mexico 282; a copy of this document may also be found in "Selected documents, collected by France Scholes," Tozzer Library [Rare Book Room], Harvard University).

[45]Another arena in which these new values were expressed and reinforced was work. Working as domestic servants or apprentices, Indian women and men were exposed to an exploitative yet paternalistic work regime. One Spaniard advised Spanish employers, presumably especially artisans, to assure Indian parents — in Nahuatl — that they would treat the Indian youth as if he were their own child (Arenas 1611: 75). The Arenas vocabulary is filled with terms for instruction, work, and discipline. Also see Cope (1994: 94–105) on the importance of work as a site of paternalistic discipline.

be shared. Where the pre-Hispanic Mexica inheritance system had assigned rights to a wide range of kin, Spanish law emphasized relations within the nuclear family and did not subsume it legally or culturally within any larger kinship unit. By the end of the sixteenth century, Spanish judges had proven themselves increasingly unwilling to recognize ownership claims based on extended kin ties. Unrecognized by Spanish law, the Mexica kinship system began to wither away. Likewise, colonial authorities did not perceive multi-family households as structural units. In compiling records of birth, marriage, and death, priests focused exclusively on nuclear family relationships (see below).

The Spanish legal system also influenced Mexica family life through the emphasis that it placed on the marital relationship and on relations between parents and children. Under the Spanish legal system, property rights tended to flow lineally, usually from a parent to his or her offspring. By the seventeenth century, Indian litigants increasingly relied on this way of thinking about ownership (see chap. 4). Moreover, Spanish law promoted new ways of conceptualizing Indian women's legal status. While these legal codes did afford women, especially widows, certain protections, they also treated women as minors and dependents and subsumed their legal identity under that of their husbands' (see chap. 3).

Catholic belief and practice worked hand in hand with Spanish legal codes to promote new ideas about the family and gender roles, sanctifying the nuclear family, rejecting polygynous relationships as sinful, and upholding hierarchical relations between men and women within the family (also see Cuevas 1946–47: II:385–88). The Mexica encountered Catholic dogma in a variety of ways: in sermons (Burkhart 1989), through rituals celebrating events in the life cycle (Molina 1569; León 1611; Pérez 1713), and through religious plays that were major public events from the mid-sixteenth century on (Ravicz 1970; Horcasitas 1974; Trexler 1984; Burkhart 1991).

Priests also communicated with their urban Indian parishioners in a more individualistic way. León recommended asking questions about superstitious practices, family relations, and sexual relations in his advice to other priests (1611: fols.111v–115v; also see Pérez 1713).

But of equal significance to specific dogma, however, was the way that Catholic priests actually went about their record-keeping tasks related to their work with indigenous populations. Here we can consider Church activities, "not as a medium for fiscal administration, but as a day-to-day, working religious machine" (Cook and Borah 1971: I:136). After the mid-sixteenth century, for record keeping, the indigenous household—as a structural unit—was virtually completely ignored (Gibson 1964: 151; Carrasco 1975: 197). Nuclear family ties between couples and their children became the primary means of compiling the records of birth, marriage, and death that priests so copiously kept.[46]

The implications of this style of record keeping for Nahua family life were significant, not because record keeping directly influenced Indians in how they lived and organized their family lives and kinship relationships, but because it offered yet another point at which Spanish belief and practice emphasized the marital bond and the nuclear family. The variety of ways in which law and religion articulated a clear representation of family relations provided a model that elite Nahuas as well as others who used the Spanish system might, in part, emulate or at least *say* they were emulating. This articulation, which took place through the enactment of social dramas, rooted in real material and social conflicts, played a role in shifting family patterns. But these patterns did *not* change simply because Indians were forced or decided to *copy* Spanish behavior and norms. They

[46]This is absolutely clear in all surviving birth, marriage, and death records for the Indian parishes of Mexico City. For a listing of those records microfilmed by the Church of Jesus Christ of Latter Day Saints, see Robinson (1980).

shifted because the material and cultural processes, practices, and values—many of the underpinnings—of the pre-Hispanic kinship and family system, indeed cultural system, had themselves shifted.

CONCLUSION

Any thorough account of the consolidation of Spanish hegemony in central Mexico must take account of far-reaching changes that occurred in everyday life. The sixteenth and seventeenth centuries saw the gradual acceptance by Mexico City's indigenous population of substantially new notions of property, inheritance, gender, family, and kinship. By the end of the seventeenth century, multifamily households had been increasingly replaced by nuclear families. A conception of gender roles that viewed women and men as parallel and complementary sources of authority had been replaced by a new conception stressing husbands' authority. A cognatic kinship system, emphasizing sibling and intergenerational ties, had been supplanted by a more patrifilial system. And a more rigid differentiation had emerged between domestic and public domains, as mediating institutions, rooted in extended kinship and ritual practices, broke down.

In recent years, it has become common among ethnohistorians to stress the strength of native resistance in the face of colonial authority. While the indigenous population of sixteenth- and seventeenth-century Mexico City did occasionally violently resist Spanish authorities and their Indian collaborators, rebellion proved less long-lasting than in other areas, notably in Maya regions and in the Andes.[47] The dominant theme in Mexico City

[47]On resistance in Maya regions, see Bricker (1981), Wasserstrom (1983), Farriss (1984), Clendinnen (1987), Jones (1989), and Gosner (1992). On the Andes, see Wachtel (1977), Spalding (1984), Stern (1982, 1987), and O'Phelan Godoy (1985). On patterns of resistance in central Mexico, see Gonzáles Obregón (1952), Huerta and Palacios (1976), Taylor (1979), and Katz (1988).

is not open conflict but a complex, uneven process of cultural accommodation and negotiation.

Anyone who advances this argument runs the risk of being interpreted as implying that the Indian population of Mexico City collaborated in their own subordination. Such an interpretation misses the point. In Mexico City, unlike the Yucatán, Chiapas, Guatemala, or the Andes, a strong Spanish presence succeeded in establishing successful mechanisms for channeling and neutralizing Indian resistance. In part, this was the product of material conditions, such as the devastating demographic upheavals that followed the conquest in combination with the concentration of the Indian population in a carefully bounded urban area. Equally important were the imposition of a new legal system and Spanish evangelization, both of which subtly undercut more encompassing kinship units, transformed property relations, and reshaped basic Mexica cultural values and practices. By 1700, it was clear that the Mexica impulse for self-determination was to be asserted through two primary Spanish colonial institutions: the courts and the Church. Yet in these arenas this impulse was subject to constant acculturative pressures and coercion.

Conclusion

Compared to other regions in New Spain or Peru, resistance to Spanish colonial rule was less violent, less well organized, and less millenarian in the Valley of Mexico. While there are a variety of possible explanations for this pattern, this book has suggested a largely ignored factor: Spain's success in this region in establishing a legal system that influenced indigenous cultural beliefs and behavior and channeled and defused Nahua discontent and altered cultural beliefs and behavior.

I have argued that the Tenochcan Mexica experienced cultural changes at once real and deep, altering a variety of domains or realms of Mexica life. When ethnohistorians have focused on change, they have generally emphasized broader structural developments made manifest in political organization and economic activities (e.g., Gibson 1964; Stern 1982; Spalding 1984; Chance 1989). But the work of Lockhart and others suggests that, at least in the Nahuatl-speaking portions of New Spain, continuities of political and economic organization allowed a relatively peaceful and profitable transition to Spanish rule to take place (Lockhart 1992; Haskett 1991; Gruzinski 1992). But when ethnohistorians consider cultural change, they focus almost solely on religion (Farriss 1984: chap.10; Clendinnen 1987; Chance and Taylor 1985).

I have looked elsewhere—to the patterns of everyday life, especially as these shaped gender relations, property transmission, and family and kinship organization—to examine issues of change and continuity, power, coercion and consent, and, ultimately, the experience of colonial rule. In these realms of life, change was manifest. Sometimes new behavioral patterns were voluntary or consensual; sometimes they were coerced; sometimes they resulted simply from the human capacity to adapt to rapidly changing social and material environments and circumstances. Seemingly small changes in behavior patterns led to different kinds of cognitive patterns that, in turn, ultimately further shaped behavior and the structuring of society.

The interplay of behavior and cognitive patterning was especially clear in the texts of legal cases that, when considered as narratives, showed significant transformation in the terms, concepts, and strategies employed in making narrative arguments and legal points. These changes had less to do with changes in the legal system itself than with the development of a colonial Indian culture that had to adopt a new and alien language for conflict. Law also provided new models of belief and behavior and a highly malleable language for the expression of multiple levels of dialogue and conflict within indigenous society and between Indians and Spaniards. Wherever Spaniards ruled in the core areas of Spanish America, law proved to be a formidable tool of cultural hegemony.

During the early colonial period, the court system served as a critical arena of cultural conflict and transformation. The courts served both as an instrument of cultural resistance—through which the Mexica contested colonial authority, sought redress for political and economic grievances, resisted tribute and labor demands, and opposed Spanish encroachment on Mexica lands—and as an instrument of cultural conversion and acculturation.

If, on the one hand, the court system helped to shape and limit the authority of the Spanish colonial state, on the other hand, it also played a pivotal role in consolidating Spanish cultural hegemony. It performed this critical function in two distinct ways. First, Mexica reliance on colonial legal institutions undercut the authority of indigenous officials, tied the Mexica to Spanish authorities, and weakened any sense of a separate Mexica sovereignty.

Second, the law played a critical role in defining and disseminating new conceptions of property, family and kinship, and gender relationships. While many cases heard by the colonial courts represented communal efforts to challenge Spanish actions or authority, others dealt with more mundane disputes over inheritance, land, and house sites. But these property disputes should not be regarded as trivial as they embodied cultural issues of great importance. Embedded within these lawsuits, as we have seen, were a series of "hidden transcripts." These cases often pitted two opposing conceptions of property, family and kinship organization, and gender relationships against each other—one rooted in pre-Hispanic practices and beliefs (however shaped by intervening realities); the other reflecting Hispanic cultural values.

Out of these legal clashes emerged a hegemonic system of values that melded the structures and realities of colonial Mexica everyday life with Hispanic conceptions of authority, property, gender, and kinship. The colonial legal system fostered a novel distinction between crime and sin, largely unknown in the pre-Hispanic period, and it promoted a more rigid cultural distinction between the political realm of men and the domestic realm of women. At the same time, nuclear families rose to a privileged position over the multifamily units that were preeminent prior to the conquest. Heading these nuclear families, in turn, were men who functioned as the go-betweens between Church and state apparatus and families, which inevitably intruded on the positions and authority of women.

Although colonial law proved to be a formidable instrument of cultural hegemony throughout the core areas of Spanish America, it had its greatest impact in the central regions of New Spain and particularly in the Valley of Mexico. Four factors are especially important in understanding the impact of Spanish law on the Tenochcan Mexica. First, although while the Spanish legal system differed in some crucial ways from that of the Mexica and Nahuas more generally (see the introduction), the Spanish system was building on an already deeply rooted and highly developed legal system (Offner 1983). Second, the demographic and social disarray of the conquest itself and the immediate postconquest years undermined traditional authority relations within polities, families, and kin groups. The broad-based indigenous turn toward the Spanish legal system as a legitimate arbiter of disputes came largely out of a vacuum of authority and was marked by both nobles and commoners and men and women seeking to use the Spanish legal system to their individual, familial, or communal advantage (see chaps. 1 and 2).

Third, in the Valley of Mexico, a range of individuals and families was actively engaged in using the legal system. Perhaps this occurred because the Nahua kinship system was more bilateral, flexible, and less corporate in nature than those found among the lowland or highland Maya and among the Inca and other Andean peoples, among whom communities appear to have been the most active legal participants. Thus, whatever acculturative tendencies the legal system had were experienced particularly widely across central Mexico.

A fourth reason why these acculturative influences (and hegemonic effects) were more deeply experienced in the valley and central regions is that the Catholic clergy powerfully reinforced them through their preachings, teachings, and parochial administrative apparatus. New, more hierarchical styles of gender relations, new forms of property transmission, will making, and the legal and clerical emphasis on the conjugal bond and nuclear family all were introduced and reinforced in mutually sustaining ways. These factors worked together to shape the development of a colonial Indian culture that, while conditioned by indigenous cultural beliefs and practices in deep and significant ways and marked by important continuities with the pre-Hispanic era (Lockhart 1992; Kartunnen 1992), was nonetheless acculturative and flexible in nature.

These factors may also help explain why indigenous peasant groups across the central region tended to make "good rebels but poor revolutionaries" (Taylor 1979: 145). In urban areas, Indian and other working- and lower-class groups were not even particularly active rebels, as the sporadic timing of early colonial uprisings in Mexico City—which occurred in 1564, 1624, and 1692— suggests (Chimalpahin 1963–65: II:18; Guthrie 1937, 1945; Gibson 1964: 384).[1] Why were these more "proletarianized" Indians[2] less likely to riot or rebel than their rural counterparts? And why did both urban and rural riots in central Mexico tend to be less revolutionary in their goals and less millenarian in nature (Taylor 1979; Coatsworth 1988)?

Eric Van Young emphasizes the special, fluid character of colonial Latin American urban life, especially for the lower strata of urban society, when he argues that the urban environment was one in which

> sharp differences in wealth and status were not underwritten by a clear class structure, inviolable ethnic barriers or spatial segregation; in which associational forms for the majority of the population were probably quite weak; in

[1] Accounts of uprisings in Mexico City suggest some differences between urban and peasant uprisings. One was the ability and willingness of urban rioters to attack symbols of high colonial authority; another was the use by Spaniards of much more stringent punishments including a high number of executions. For a very thorough description and analysis of the 1692 riot, see Cope (1994: chap.7). On the riot of 1624, in addition to Chester Guthrie's (1937) work, see Stowe (1971: esp. chaps. 4–6) and Israel (1975: chap. 5). Also see Cope's (1994: 17) references to several revolts by enslaved Africans in Mexico City in the 1530s and 1540s.

[2] The term "proletarian" is used by Taylor (1979: 25) to describe villages in the Valley of Mexico but applies well to urban Indians also.

217

which a high degree of social fluidity existed; and in which much of the population was reduced to penury and homelessness. (1988: 154; also see Haslip 1986)

The weaker communal institutions and fluid character of colonial urban life certainly influenced the ability of Indians and others to organize concerted political action. The presence of stronger forms of colonial authority also militated against such action. But this authority was less martial in nature (Archer 1986: 200–2), especially during the early colonial period, than civil and religious, operating through police, sites of work, and churches and parishes to maintain social order, relying on a combination of coercion and compliance, labor, and corporal punishment to keep defiance and deviance to levels low enough to avoid serious unrest.

Urban Indians, especially in Mexico City, looked to other means to express their discontent and resistance. More often than not, they turned to the law. Lawsuits, however ultimately counterproductive as a form of protest, did express resistance against individual Spaniards and others whom Nahuas viewed as overstepping the bounds of legitimate relations. Crime also served as an individual expression of criticism and dissatisfaction, which, while seemingly nonpolitical, may reflect a relative lack of communal institutions through which political grievances could be expressed and political behavior shaped and organized (Haslip 1980: 276–78; Van Young 1988: 144). The ability of urban Indians to maintain the vestiges of some communal practices (especially those having to do with life-cycle rituals)[3] may also have been an expression of resistance, which further weakened motivations toward more overt political expressions.

[3]Priests were given explicit advice about superstitious practices for which they should look. León, for example, advised priests to ask questions about the use of fire at birth ceremonies (1611: fol.111v) and Pérez mentioned birth and marriage as points at which Mexico City's Indian population might engage in such practices (1713: 161, 170).

Of all Nahuatl-speaking peoples, the highly urbanized Tenochcan Mexica experienced the conquest and colonial rule in the most severe and direct ways. They made what Gibson (1964: 368) termed "unique adjustments" in the organization of labor and tribute, and this book shows they made unique adjustments in other realms of life as well. Their engagement with the colonial legal system brought many of the most far-reaching changes in the Mexica cultural system. Yet this same engagement served as a model for other Nahuas and other indigenous communities and groups to struggle to preserve their land base and to develop a special legal status. For the law alone could offer concrete protections in the increasingly racially charged atmosphere and economically trying circumstances of the later colonial period.

Glossary

Note: "(S)" stands for Spanish, and "(N)" stands for Nahuatl. In the text and glossary, for terms that come from the *Florentine Codex,* I follow that spelling. Nahuatl words used in the plural in the text appear in the plural in the glossary; the singular form (with the spelling regularized) is also provided.

Abogado (S)—attorney, lawyer

Acocalli (N)—upper story of a house

Acocalo (N)—see *acocalli*

Albaceas (S)—(sing., *albacea*) executors of a will

Alcalde (S)—local official with judicial and administrative responsibilities, including *cabildo* membership

Alcalde del crimen (S)—judicial official who heard criminal cases for the *audiencia*

Alcalde mayor (S)—administrative official holding both administrative and judicial responsibilities, equivalent to the *corregidor* or *gobernador*

Alguacil (S)—low-level judicial position, generally attached to councils

Amatlacuilo (N)—scribe, writer (or painter) on paper

Aposento (S)—room

Audiencia (S)—court, usually for appeal, and advisory body to the Viceroy

Autos y méritos (S)—sentences or decrees, and (their) reasoning

Ayllu—Andean social and kinship grouping, based on descent, often coterminous with the community or political grouping

Barrio (S)—ward, neighborhood, quarter

Braza (S)—Spanish measurement of length, equivalent to 1.67 m

Cabecera (S)—head town

Cabildo (S)—municipal or city council

Çaçan ie calli (N)—ordinary house

Cacique—Arawakan term that came to refer in New Spain to high-status, indigenous men holding important offices

Callejon (S)—narrow, small street or alley

Calli (N)—house or room

Calmecac (N)—school, primarily for noble youths (mostly boys), that offered religious training

Calnepanolli (N)—two-story house

Calpullalli (N)—"calpulli land"

Calpulli (N)—"big house"; community or subdivision within larger Nahua political entities

Caltepiton (N)—small house

Caltontli (N)—small house

Caltzintli (N)—small (or honored) house

Casa (S)—house; can also refer to the household

Casado/a (S)—a married person

Casas de comunidad (S)—(sing., *casa de comunidad*) houses of the community

Casta (S)—an individual of mixed-race descent

Censo (S)—annual payment

Chalchihuitl (N)—precious stone, especially precious green stone

Chinampa (N)—from the Nahuatl word *chinamitl;* refers to raised garden plots built into canals and the lake system surrounding Mexico City

Chino (S)—could refer to a mixed-race individual often of Indian and African descent, a slave, or a person of Asian descent

Cihuacalli (N)—"woman house," or "woman room"; may have constituted a common area (associated particularly with female activities) in Mexica house compounds

Cihuacoatl (N)—"woman serpent"; used to refer to the second highest political office in the Tenochcan Mexica political structure, after the *tlatoani;* it was also the name of a deity, an earth mother

Cihuaquacuiltin (N)—(sing., *cihuacuacuilli*) female priests, older and of higher status

Cihuatecuhtli (N)—"female-lord"

Cihuatepixque (N)—(sing., *cihuatepixqui*) female, lower-ranking officials

Cihuatetiachcahuan (N)—(sing., *cihuatetiachcauh*) "mistresses of women"; female leaders

Cihuatlamacazque (N)—(sing. *cihuatlamacazqui*) priestesses of lower rank

Cihuatlanque (N)—(sing., *cihuatlanqui*) matchmakers

Cihuatlatoque (N)—(sing., *cihuatlatoani*) "women rulers"

Cihuatlatquitl (N)—"woman property"; women's goods

Cofradía (S)—lay religious association

Comadre (S)—godmother

Compañero (S)—comrade, companion

Contador de cuentas (S)—chief accountant

Cuicacalli (N)—"house of song"; school for the teaching of songs, dances, and instrumental playing

Defendiente (S)—defendant

Demandante (S)—plaintiff

Deudo (S)—relative, kin

Don (S)—(female form, *doña*) noble title held by Spanish men of very high rank, used more widely among Indians to signify high status

Echura (S)—figurine, statuette

Echuras de bulto (S)—(sing., *echura de bulto*) figurines, statuettes

Estancia (S)—dependent, indigenous community

Fiscal (S)—crown attorney; also refers to colonial Indian religious official who oversaw Indian church officers and acted as an aide to priests

Forastero (S)—"stranger"; term commonly used to refer to indigenous migrants in Peru

Fuero (S)—written body of customary laws and rights

Gobernador (S)—Spanish term used for highest-ranking colonial Indian civil officials during the sixteenth century; often coterminous with *tlatoani* (i.e., both terms referred to the same office holder)

Huanyolcayotl (N)—the Mexica concept for consanguineal relationships with an emphasis on bilateral ties of ascent and descent

Huehuecalli (N)—"old house"; inherited (and inheritable) house(s)

Huehuetlalli (N)—"old land"; inherited (and inheritable) land

Ichpochtiachcauh (N)—"mistress of young women," female leader

Ichpochtlaiacanqui (N)—female matron (of young women)

Icnocalli (N)—"humble house"; house of a poor person

Iixhuihuan (N)—his/her grandchildren

Inquieto (S)—restless, noisy, troublesome

Interrogatorio (N)—written list of questions to which witnesses responded

Ithualli (N)—patio, interior courtyard within a house compound

Ixhuiuhtli (N)—grandchild

Jacal (S)—loanword from Nahuatl (*xacalli*); refers to a hut

Juez gobernador (S)—"judge-governor"; term used for indigenous colonial administrators, often an outsider to the area for which he had judicial responsibility

Juzgado General de Indios (S)—General Indian Court; as of 1591, in New Spain, had the responsibility to hear most Indian lawsuits, either in first instance or on appeal

Letrado (S)—lawyer with the highest university training

Lienzo (S)—canvas

Linaje (S)—lineage, kin (with an emphasis on lineal descent)

Macehual (S)—from the Nahuatl word *macehualli;* refers to Indian commoners

Mantas (S)—(sing., *manta*) cloaks, blankets

Mayorazgo (S)—entailed estate; can refer also to rights of inheritance and succession held by a firstborn son

Medio real de ministros (S)—tax levied on New Spain's indigenous population to pay the costs of the Juzgado General de Indios

Mejora (S)—special bequest to a specific, lawful heir

Merced (S)—grant

Merino (S)—low-level indigenous community official

Mestizo (S)—individual of Indian-Spanish descent

Metate (S)—from the Nahuatl word *metlatl;* refers to a grinding stone

Metl (N)—maguey plant

Mexicatlalli (N)—"Mexica land"

Milli (N)—field

Mocihuaquetzque (N)—(sing., *mocihuaquetzqui*) souls or spirits of women who died in childbirth

Mujer legítima (S)—legitimate wife

Nahuatlato (N)—translator

Obraje (S)—workshop using forced labor, usually for the production of textiles

Oidor (S)—"hearer"; high judge who sat on the *audiencia*

Olla (S)—pot, large kettle

Oratorio (S)—chapel, or altar area within a household

Padrino (S)—godfather

Panes (S)—(sing., *pan*) loaves

Parcialidad (S)—the two major subdivisions of Indian Mexico City, further divided into *barrios*

Pariente (S)—kin, relative

Peso (S)—Spanish monetary unit, the equivalent of eight *reales*

Petate (S)—from the Nahuatl word *petlatl;* a reed mat

Pillalli (N)—private land owned by nobles (i.e., not office lands)

Pilli (N)—"child"; term used to refer to members of the noble class

Pobre (S)—poor

Principal (S)—important, illustrious; term often used by Spaniards to refer to Indian nobles

Probanza (S)—the questions of the *interrogatorio* along with witness testimony

Procurador general de los indios (S)—General Attorney for Indians

Pueblo (S)—town, village

Quacuiltin (N)—(sing., *cuacuilli*) priests, relatively high in rank

Quinto (S)—one-fifth; fifth

Real (S)—Spanish monetary unit, equivalent to one-eighth of a peso

Real Audiencia (S)—royal audience; functioned as both a high court and an advisory body to the chief administrator, such as a viceroy

Rebeldía (S)—default, nonappearance, or failure to comply with deadlines

Recaudo (S)—documentary evidence submitted to bolster claims in a lawsuit

Receptor (S)—a trained notary who recorded testimony outside of Mexico City for the Juzgado General de Indios

Regidor (S)—a member of a *cabildo,* a councilman

Relator (S)—a lawyer who read and summarized cases for judges

República de los Naturales (S)—Republic of the Natives; quasi-legal designation, referring to the Indian *parcialidades*

Sentencia definitiva (S)—final decision

Solar (S)—plot of land that was part of a house site

Solicitador (S)—low-level legal functionary whose training came through service to *procuradores* or *abogados,* not through formal education

Soltero/a (S)—single person

Suerte (S)—plot of land

Sujeto (S)—subject community

Teachcahuan (N)—(sing., *teachcauh*) "older brothers;" masters of youths

Teccalli (N)—"noble house"; refers both to a noble's palace and lands and the social and kinship group related to the noble; term commonly used in the Puebla-Tlaxcala region; the term also refers to a high court where commoner legal cases were heard by noble judges

Tecomatl (N)—clay jar or vessel

Tecpan (N)—palace, noble house

Tecpantlalli (N)—"palace land"

Tecuhtlalli (N)—"lord's land"

Tehuanyolque (N)—(unpossessed sing., *-huanyolqui*) someone's relatives, bilateral kin unit

Teixhuihuan (N)—(sing., *teixhuiuh*), "someone's grandchildren"; may have referred also to a social unit of descent

Telpochcalli (N)—school for commoner youths, primarily boys, emphasizing military affairs and public works

Telpochtlatoque (N)—(sing., *telpochtlatoani*) "leaders of youths"; refers to a position of leadership within the *telpochcalli*

Teotlalli (N)—"god land"; refers to land of gods or temples

Tepixque (N)—(sing., *tepixqui*) low-level officials of the *tlaxilacalli*

Tequitlato (N)—"tribute speaker"; official charged with assessing tribute

Terrazguero (S)—low-status indigenous agricultural workers, primarily on rented lands

Tianquizpan tlaiacanque (N)—(sing., *tianquizpan tlayacanqui*) marketplace administrator or judge

Tianquiztlaqualli (N)—"market food"; semiprepared and prepared foods sold in the market

Tianquiztli (N)—(often rendered in Spanish accounts as *tianguis*), marketplace

Tierras de cacicazgo (S)—lands associated with cacique rule

Tilmatli (N)—cloak

Tlacamecayotl (N)—"rope of men, people"; used to refer to kin relationships of ascent and descent, possible social unit

Tlacochcalcatl (N)—one of the highest Mexica officials serving under the *tlatoani* and *cihuacoatl,* with military and administrative responsibilities

Tlacuilo (N)—scribe or painter

Tlacxitlan (N)—highest court where nobles and the most serious crimes were judged

Tlaiacanque (N)—(sing., *tlayacanqui*) guides, leaders

Tlalcohualli (N)—"bought land"

Tlalli (N)—land

Tlalmantli (N)—leveled or flat land

Tlalmilli (N)—plots of cultivable land

Tlaltenamitl (N)—fence or barricade

Tlamacazqui (N)—priest, generally lower-level

Tlatoani (N)—"speaker"; supreme ruler

227

Tlatocatlalli (N)—office lands of the ruler

Tlaxilacalle (N)—citizen (or perhaps leader) of the *tlaxilacalli*

Tlaxilacalli (N)—local subdivision of larger indigenous communities

Tohuehuetlal (N)—"our old land," our inherited land

Tomines (S)—(sing., *tomin*) a Spanish monetary unit, a coin equivalent to a *real*

Topileque (N)—(sing., *topile*) low-level, constablelike official

Tornillo (S)—screw, clamp, vise

Traza (S)—the central portion of Mexico City, where most Spaniards lived

Vara (S)—Spanish measurement of length, equivalent to 0.84 m

Viejo/a (S)—old man or woman

Universal heredero (S)—Spanish designation for an inheritor who might inherit an entire estate or residual portions of an estate

Útil dominio (S)—"use right"

Xacalli (N)—hut

Xacaltotli (N)—(correct spelling, *xacaltontli*) small hut

Bibliography

Actas de Cabildo
  1889–1916 *Actas de cabildo de la Ciudad de México*. 54 vols.
      Title and publisher vary. México.
Adamson, Walter L.
  1980 *Hegemony and Revolution: A Study of Antonio Gramsci's
      Political and Cultural Theory*. Berkeley, Los Angeles,
      and London: University of California Press.
Adorno, Rolena
  1986 *Guaman Poma: Writing and Resistance in Colonial Peru*.
      Austin: University of Texas Press.
Adorno, Rolena, ed.
  1982 *From Oral to Written Expression: Native Andean Chroni-
      cles of the Early Colonial Period*. Syracuse: Maxwell
      School of Citizenship and Public Affairs, Syracuse
      University.
Alberro, Solange
  1988 *Inquisition et société au Mexique, 1571–1700*. México:
      Centre d'etudes mexicaines et centramericaines.
Altman, Ida
  1989 *Emigrants and Society: Extremadura and America in the
      Sixteenth Century*. Berkeley, Los Angeles, and Lon-
      don: University of California Press.
Anderson, Arthur, Frances Berdan, and James Lockhart
  1976 *Beyond the Codices*. Berkeley, Los Angeles, and Lon-
      don: University of California Press.
Anderson, Karen L.
  1991 *Chain Her by One Foot: The Subjugation of Native Women
      in Seventeenth-Century New France*. New York: Rout-
      ledge.

Anderson, Perry
1976–77 "The Antinomies of Antonio Gramsci." *New Left Review* 100: 5–78.

Anunciación, Fray Juan de la
1577 *Sermonio en lengva Mexicana. . . .* México: Antonio Ricardo.

Archer, Christon I.
1986 "Military." In *Cities and Society in Colonial Latin America,* ed. Louisa Schell Hoberman and Susan Migden Socolow, 197–226. Albuquerque: University of New Mexico Press.

Archivo General de la Nación
Documents cited by *ramo* and *expediente* or volume number.

Arenas, Pedro
1611 *Vocabulario manval de las lengvas castellana, y mexicana.* México: Emprenta de Henrico Martínez.

Arizpe Schlosser, Lourdes
1973 *Parentesco y economía en una sociedad nahua.* México: Instituto Nacional Indigenista y Secretaría de Educación Pública.

Arrom, Silvia Marina
1985a *The Women of Mexico City, 1790–1857.* Stanford: Stanford University Press.

1985b "Changes in Mexican Family Law in the Nineteenth Century: The Civil Codes of 1870 and 1884." *Journal of Family History* 10(3): 305–17.

Baird, Ellen T.
1993 *The Drawings of Sahagún's Primeros memoriales: Structure and Style.* Norman: University of Oklahoma Press.

Balandier, Georges
1966 "The Colonial Situation: A Theoretical Approach." In *Social Change: The Colonial Situation,* ed. Immanuel Wallerstein, 34–61. New York: John Wiley and Sons.

Ballesteros, Pío
1945 "Los indios y sus litigios, según La Recopilación de 1680." *Revista de Indios* 6(22): 607–33.

Bancroft Library
  Mexican Manuscripts, cited by MS. number and date.
Bandelier, Adolph F.
  1877 "On the Art of War and Mode of Warfare of the Ancient Mexicans." *Tenth Annual Report of the Trustees of the Peabody Museum of American Archaeology and Ethnology,* 95–161. Cambridge, Mass.
  1878 "On the Distribution and Tenure of Lands, and the Customs with Respect to Inheritance among the Ancient Mexicans." *Eleventh Annual Report of the Peabody Museum of Archaeology and Ethnology,* 385–448. Cambridge, Mass.
  1879 "On the Social Organization and Mode of Government of the Ancient Mexicans." *Twelfth Annual Report of the Peabody Museum of Archaeology and Ethnology,* 557–699. Salem, Mass.: Salem Press.
Behar, Ruth
  1987 "The Visions of a Guachichil Witch in 1599: A Window on the Subjugation of Mexico's Hunter-Gatherers." *Ethnohistory* 34(2): 115–38.
  1989 "Sexual Witchcraft, Colonialism, and Women's Powers: Views from the Mexican Inquisition." In *Sexuality and Marriage in Colonial Latin America,* ed. Asunción Lavrin, 178–206. Lincoln: University of Nebraska Press.
Berdan, Frances F.
  1982 *The Aztecs of Central Mexico: An Imperial Society.* New York: Holt, Rinehart and Winston.
Bernal de Bugeda, Beatriz
  1975 "Situación jurídica de la mujer en las Indias Occidentales." In *Condición jurídica de la mujer en México,* ed. Sara Bialostosky de Chazán, 21–40. México: Universidad Nacional Autónoma de México, Facultad de Derecho.
Biblioteca Nacional de México
  Archivo Franciscano documents cited by box and *expediente* number.
Bibliothèque National de Paris
  Documents cited by MS. number, followed by date.

Bilinkoff, Jodi

1989 *The Avila of Santa Teresa: Religious Reform in a Six-teenth-Century City.* Ithaca: Cornell University Press.

Borah, Woodrow

1951 *New Spain's Century of Depression. Ibero-Americana,* vol. 35. Berkeley: University of California Press.

1983 *Justice by Insurance: The General Indian Court of Colonial Mexico and the Legal Aides of the Half-Real.* Berkeley, Los Angeles, and London: University of California Press.

1991 "Yet Another Look at the Techialoyan Codices." In *Land and Politics in the Valley of Mexico: A Two-thousand-Year Perspective,* ed. H.R. Harvey, 209–21. Albuquerque: University of New Mexico Press.

Borah, Woodrow and S. F. Cook

1960 *The Population of Central Mexico in 1548: An Analysis of the Suma de visitas de pueblos. Ibero-Americana,* vol. 43. Berkeley: University of California Press.

Bourdieu, Pierre

1978 *Outline of a Theory of Practice.* Translated by Richard Nice. Cambridge: Cambridge University Press.

Boyer, Richard

1973 Mexico City and the Great Flood: Aspects of Life and Society, 1629–1635. Ph.d. diss. University of Connecticut.

Bricker, Victoria Reifler

1981 *The Indian Christ, the Indian King: The Historical Substrate of Maya Myth and Ritual.* Austin: University of Texas Press.

Broda, Johanna

1976 "Los estamentos en el ceremonial mexica." In *Estratificación social en la Mesoamérica prehispánica,* ed. Pedro Carrasco, Johanna Broda, et al., 37–66. México: CIS-INAH.

Brown, Betty Ann

1983 "Seen But Not Heard: Women in Aztec Ritual—The Sahagún Texts." In *Text and Image in Pre-Columbian Art: Essays on the Interrelationship of the Verbal and*

Visual Arts, ed. Janet Catherine Berlo, 119–54. Oxford: BAR Press.

Brumfiel, Elizabeth M.

1987 "Elite and Utilitarian Crafts in the Aztec State." In *Specialization, Exchange and Complex Societies,* ed. Elizabeth Brumfiel and Timothy Earle, 102–18. Cambridge: Cambridge University Press.

1991 "Weaving and Cooking: Women's Production in Aztec Mexico." In *Engendering Archaeology: Women and Prehistory,* ed. Joan Gero and Margaret Conkey, 224–51. Oxford: Basil Blackwell.

Burkhart, Louise M.

1988 "Doctrinal Aspects of Sahagún's *Colloquios.*" In *The Work of Bernardino de Sahagún: Pioneer Ethnographer of Sixteenth-Century Mexico,* ed. J. Jorge Klor de Alva, H.B. Nicholson, Eloise Quiñones Keber, 65–82. Albany: SUNY, Institute for Mesoamerican Studies.

1989 *The Slippery Earth: Nahua-Christian Moral Dialogue in Sixteenth-Century Mexico.* Tucson: University of Arizona Press.

1991 "A Nahuatl Religious Drama of c. 1590." *Latin American Indian Literatures Journal* 7(2): 153–71.

1992 "The Amanuenses Have Appropriated the Text: Interpreting a Nahuatl Song of Santiago." In *On the Translation of Native American Literatures,* ed. Brian Swann, 339–55. Washington, D.C.: Smithsonian Institution Press.

In press "Mexica Women on the Home Front: Housework and Religion in Aztec Mexico." In *Indian Women of Early Mexico: Identity, Ethnicity, and Gender Differentiation,* ed. Susan Schroeder, Stephanie Wood, and Robert Haskett. Norman: University of Oklahoma Press.

Burkholder, Mark A., and D. S. Chandler

1977 *From Impotence to Authority: The Spanish Crown and the American Audiencias, 1687–1808.* Columbia: University of Missouri Press.

Calnek, Edward

1972 "Settlement Pattern and *Chinampa* Agriculture."
American Antiquity 37(1): 104–15.

1974*a* "The Sahagún Texts as a Source of Sociological
Information." In *Sixteenth-Century Mexico: The Work of
Sahagún,* ed. Munro S. Edmonson, 189–204. Albu-
querque: University of New Mexico Press.

1974*b* "Conjunto urbano y modelo residencial en Tenochtitlán." In *Ensayos sobre el desarollo urbano de México,* ed. Edward E. Calnek, Woodrow Borah, et al., 11–
65. México: SepSetentas.

1976 "The Internal Structure of Tenochtitlán." In *The
Valley of Mexico: Studies in Prehispanic Ecology and
Society,* ed. Eric Wolf, 287–302. Albuquerque: Uni-
versity of New Mexico Press.

1978 "El sistema de mercado de Tenochtitlán." In *Economía política e ideología en el México prehispánico,* ed.
Pedro Carrasco and Johanna Broda, 95–114. México: CIS-INAH and Editorial Nueva Imagen.

n.d. "Kinship, Settlement Pattern, and Domestic Groups in
Tenochtitlán." Unpublished MS.

Carrasco, Pedro

1966 "Sobre algunos términos de parentesco en el náhuatl
clásico." *Estudios de Cultura Náhuatl* 6: 149–66.

1971 "Social Organization of Ancient Mexico." In *Archaeology of Northern Mesoamerica,* Part 1, ed. Gordon F. Ekholm and Ignacio Bernal, 349–75. Vol.
10. *Handbook of Middle American Indians,* gen. ed.,
Robert Wauchope, Austin: University of Texas
Press.

1975 "La transformación de la cultura indígena durante la
colonia." *Historia Mexicana* 25: 175–203.

1976*a* "The Joint Family in Ancient Mexico: The Case of
Molotla." In *Essays on Mexican Kinship,* ed. Hugo G.
Nutini, Pedro Carrasco, and James M. Taggart, 45–
64. Pittsburgh: University of Pittsburgh Press.

1976*b* "Los linajes nobles del México antiguo." In *Estratificación social en la Mesoamérica prehispánica,* ed.

Pedro Carrasco, Johanna Broda, et al., 19–36. México: Instituto Nacional de Antropología e Historia.

1978 "La economía del México prehispánico." In *Economía política e ideología en el México prehispánico,* ed. Pedro Carrasco and Johanna Broda, 13–76. México: CIS-INAH and Editorial Nueva Imagen.

1984 "Royal Marriages in Ancient Mexico." In *Explorations in Ethnohistory: Indians of Central Mexico in the Sixteenth Century,* ed. H. R. Harvey and Hanns Prem, 41–81. Albuquerque: University of New Mexico Press.

Carter, Constance
1971 "Law and Society in Colonial Mexico: *Audiencia* Judges in Mexican Society from the Tello de Sandoval *Visita General,* 1543–1547." Ph.D. diss., Columbia University.

Caso, Alfonso
1958 *The Aztecs: People of the Sun.* Translated by Lowell Dunham. Norman: University of Oklahoma Press.

1963 "Land Tenure Among the Ancient Mexicans." *American Anthropologist* 65(4): 863–78.

Cedulario indiano
1596 *Cedulario indiano recopilado por Diego de Encinas.* 4 vols. Madrid: Imprenta Real.

Certeau, Michel
1984 *The Practice of Everyday Life.* Translated by Steven Rendall. Berkeley, Los Angeles, and London: University of California Press.

Cervantes de Salazar, Francisco
1953 *Life in the Imperial and Loyal City of Mexico in New Spain.* Translated by Minnie Barrett Shepard. Austin: University of Texas Press. Originally published 1554.

Ceynos, Francisco
1866 "Cartas del Licenciado Francisco Ceynos." In *Colección de documentos para la historia de México,* ed. J. G. Icazbalceta, Tomo 2, 158–64, 237–43. México: Antigua Librería. Originally written 1532, 1565.

Chance, John K.
    1978 *Race and Class in Colonial Oaxaca*. Stanford: Stanford
          University Press.
    1989 *Conquest of the Sierra: Spaniards and Indians in Colonial
          Oaxaca*. Norman: University of Oklahoma Press.
Chance, John K., and William B. Taylor
    1985 "Cofradías and Cargos: An Historical Perspective on
          the Mesoamerican Civil-Religious Hierarchy." *Ameri-
          can Ethnologist* 12(1): 1–26.
Chevalier, François
    1963 *Land and Society in Colonial Mexico: The Great Hacien-
          da*. Translated by Alvin Eustis. Berkeley and Los
          Angeles: University of California Press.
Chimalpahin, don Domingo Francisco de San Antón Muñón
    1963–65 *Die Relationen Chimalpahin's zur Geschichte Mex-
          ico*. Edited by Günter Zimmermann. 2 vols. Ham-
          burg: Cram, De Gruyter. Originally written ca.
          1600–20.
Ciudad de México
    1978 *Ciudad de México: Ensayo de construcción de una histo-
          ria*. México: SEP-INAH.
Clavijero, Francisco Javier
    1976 *Historia antigua de México*. México: Editorial Porrua.
          Originally published 1780–81.
Clendinnen, Inga
    1987 *Ambivalent Conquest: Maya and Spaniard in Yucatán,
          1517–1570*. Cambridge: Cambridge University
          Press.
    1991 *Aztecs: An Interpretation*. Cambridge: Cambridge
          University Press.
Clifford, James, and George E. Marcus, eds.
    1986 *Writing Culture: The Poetics and Politics of Ethnography*.
          Berkeley, Los Angeles, and London: University of
          California Press.
Cline, S. L.
    1984 "Land Tenure and Land Inheritance in Late Six-
          teenth-Century Culhuacan." In *Explorations in Eth-
          nohistory: Indians of Central Mexico in the Sixteenth*

Century, ed. H. R. Harvey and Hanns Prem, 277–309. Albuquerque: University of New Mexico Press.

1986 *Colonial Culhuacan, 1580–1600: A Social History of an Aztec Town.* Albuquerque: University of New Mexico Press.

1993a *The Book of Tributes: Early Sixteenth-Century Nahuatl Censuses from Morelos.* Translated and edited by S. L. Cline. Los Angeles: UCLA Latin American Center Publications.

1993b "The Spiritual Conquest Reexamined: Baptism and Christian Marriage in Early Sixteenth-Century Mexico." *Hispanic American Historical Review* 73(3): 453–80.

Cline, S. L., and Miguel León-Portilla, eds.

1984 *The Testaments of Culhuacan.* Los Angeles: UCLA Latin American Center Publications.

Coatsworth, John H.

1988 "Patterns of Rural Rebellion in Latin America: Mexico in Comparative Perspective." In *Riot, Rebellion, and Revolution: Rural Social Conflict in Mexico,* ed. Friedrich Katz, 21–62. Princeton: Princeton University Press.

Codex Magliabecchiano

1903 *Codex Magliabecchiano. The Book of Life of the Ancient Mexicans.* Edited by Zelia Nuttall. Berkeley: University of California Press. Originally written ca. mid-sixteenth century.

Codex Mendoza

1992 *Codex Mendoza.* Edited by Frances Berdan and Patricia Anawalt. 4 vols. Berkeley, Los Angeles, and London: University of California Press. Originally written 1541–1542.

Códice Kingsborough

1912 *Códice Kingsborough: Memorial de los indios de Tepetlaoztoc al monarca español contra los encomenderos del pueblo. . . .* Edited by Francisco del Paso y Troncoso. Madrid: Hauser y Menet. Originally written ca. 1555.

Códice Osuna

1947 *Códice Osuna: Reproducción facsimilar de la obra del mismo titulo, editada en Madrid, 1878.* México: Ediciones del Instituto Indigenista Interamericano. Originally written ca. 1560s.

Cohn, Bernard S.

1987 "History and Anthropology: The State of Play." In *An Anthropologist Among the Historians and Other Essays,* ed. Bernard S. Cohn, 18–49. Delhi, N.Y.: Oxford University Press.

1989 "Law and the Colonial State in India." In *History and Power in the Study of Law: New Directions in Legal Anthropology,* ed. June Starr and Jane F. Collier, 131–52. Ithaca: Cornell University Press.

Collier, Jane F.

1973 *Law and Social Change in Zinacantan.* Stanford: Stanford University Press.

Comaroff, Jean, and John Comaroff

1991 *Of Revelation and Revolution: Christianity, Colonialism, and Consciousness in South Africa.* Vol. 1. Chicago: University of Chicago Press.

Conquistador Anónimo, El

1941 *Relación de algunas cosas de la Nueva España y de la gran ciudad de Temestitlán, México.* México: Editorial América. Originally published 1556.

Cook, S. F., and Woodrow Borah

1971 *Essays in Population History.* Vol. 1, *Mexico and the Caribbean.* Berkeley, Los Angeles, and London: University of California Press.

Cope, R. Douglas

1994 *The Limits of Racial Domination: Plebian Society in Colonial Mexico City, 1660–1720.* Madison: University of Wisconsin Press.

Cortés, Hernán

1932 *Cartas de relación de la conquista de Mejico.* 2 tomos. Madrid: Espasa-Calpe. Originally written 1519–1526.

Couturier, Edith Boorstein

1978 "Women in a Noble Family: The Mexican Counts of

Regla, 1750–1830." In *Latin American Women: Historical Perspectives,* ed. Asunción Lavrin, 129–49. Westport, Conn.: Greenwood Press.

1985 "Women and the Family in Eighteenth-Century Mexico: Law and Practice." *Journal of Family History* 10(3): 294–304.

Covarrubias Orozco, Sebastián de

1611 *Tesoro de la lengva castellana, o española.* Madrid: Luis Sánchez, impressor del Rey.

Coy, P. E. B.

1968 "Justice for the Indian in Eighteenth-Century Mexico." *American Journal of Legal History* 12(1): 41–9.

Crónica mexicáyotl

1975 *Crónica mexicáyotl,* by Fernando Alvarado Tezozómoc. México: Universidad Nacional Autónoma de México e Instituto de Investigaciones Históricas. Originally written ca. early seventeenth century.

Crosby, Alfred

1972 *The Columbian Exchange: Biological and Cultural Consequences of 1492.* Westport, Conn.: Greenwood Press.

Cuevas, Mariano

1914 *Documentos inéditos del siglo XVI para la historia de México.* México: Museo Nacional de Arqueología, Historia y Etnología.

1946–47 *Historia de la Iglesia en México.* Vol. 2, *1548–1600.* México: Editorial Patria.

Cunningham, C. H.

1919 *The Audiencia in the Spanish Colonies as Illustrated by the Audiencia of Manila, 1583–1800.* Berkeley: University of California Press.

Davenport, William H.

1959 "Nonunilinear Descent and Descent Groups." *American Anthropologist* 61(4): 557–72.

Davies, Nigel

1980 *The Aztecs: A History.* Norman: University of Oklahoma Press. (1st ed., 1973).

Davis, Natalie Zemon

1987 *Fiction in the Archives: Pardon Tales and Their Tellers in*

Sixteenth-Century France. Stanford: Stanford University Press.

Dehouve, Danièle
    1978 "Parenté et mariage dans une communauté nahuatl de l'état de Guerrero (Mexique)." *Journal de la Société des Américanistes,* n.s., 65: 173–208.

Derrida, Jacques
    1976 *Of Grammatology.* Translated by Gayatri Spivak. Baltimore: Johns Hopkins University Press.

Devens, Carol
    1992 *Countering Colonization: Native American Women and Great Lakes Missions, 1630–1900.* Berkeley, Los Angeles, and London: University of California Press.

Díaz del Castillo, Bernal
    1955 *Historia verdadera de la conquista de la Nueva España.* México: Editorial Aramor. Originally written 1568.

Dirks, Nicholas B.
    1987 *The Hollow Crown: Ethnohistory of an Indian Kingdom.* Cambridge: Cambridge University Press.

Dollimore, Jonathan, and Alan Sinfield, eds.
    1985 *Political Shakespeare: New Essays in Cultural Materialism.* Ithaca: Cornell University Press.

Durán, Diego
    1967 *Historia de las indias de Nueva España e islas de tierra firme.* 2 vols. México: Editorial Porrua. Originally written 1581.

Durand-Forest, Jacqueline
    1962 "Testament d'une indienne de Tlatelolco." *Journal de la Société des Américanistes,* n.s., 52: 129–58.

Enciclopedia universal ilustrada Europeo-Americana
    1958–68 *Enciclopedia universal ilustrada Europeo-Americana.* 70 vols. Madrid: Espasa-Calpe.

Ensayos sobre el desarrollo urbano de México
    1973 *Ensayos sobre el desarrollo urbano de México.* México: SepSetentas.

Errington, Shelly
    1989 *Meaning and Power in a Southeast Asian Realm.* Princeton: Princeton University Press.

Estas son las leyes

    1941 Estas son las leyes que tenían los Indios de la Nueva España. *Nueva colección de documentos para la historia de México,* ed. Joaquin García Icazbalceta, Vol.3, 280–86. México: Editorial Chávez Hayhoe. Originally written 1543.

Evans, Susan

    1989 "House and Household in the Aztec World: The Village of Cihuatecpan." In *Households and Communities,* ed. Scott MacEachern, David J. W. Archer, and Richard D. Garvin, 430–40. Calgary: Archaeological Association of the University of Calgary.

    1993 "Aztec Household Organization and Village Administration." In *Prehispanic Domestic Units in Western Mesoamerica: Studies of the Household, Compound and Residence,* ed. Robert S. Santley and Kenneth G. Hirth, 173–89. Boca Raton: CRC Press.

Fanon, Frantz

    1963 *The Wretched of the Earth.* Translated by Constance Farrington. New York: Grove Press.

    1967 *Black Skin, White Masks.* Translated by Charles Markman. New York: Grove Press.

Farriss, Nancy M.

    1984 *Maya Society under Colonial Rule: The Collective Enterprise of Survival.* Princeton: Princeton University Press.

Femia, Joseph V.

    1981 *Gramsci's Political Thought: Hegemony, Consciousness and the Revolutionary Process.* Oxford: Clarendon Press.

Fernández de Oviedo y Valdés, Gonzalo

    1851 *Historia general y natural de las Indias.* 4 vols. Madrid: Imprenta de la Real Academia de la Historia. Originally published 1535–57.

Firth, Raymond W.

    1963 "Bilateral Descent Groups: An Operational Viewpoint." In *Studies in Kinship and Marriage,* ed. Isaac Schapera, 22–37. London: Royal Anthropological Institute Occasional Paper 16.

Florentine Codex
  1950–82 *Florentine Codex.* Compiled by Bernardino de
       Sahagún. Translated and edited by Arthur J. O.
       Anderson and Charles E. Dibble. No. 14, 13 parts.
       Salt Lake City: School of American Research and
       University of Utah Press. Originally written by 1569.
Foster, George M.
  1960 *Culture and Conquest: America's Spanish Heritage.* Chi-
       cago: Quadrangle Books.
Foucault, Michel
  1970 *The Order of Things: An Archaeology of the Human
       Sciences.* New York: Pantheon.
Fuller, Lon L.
  1967 *Legal Fictions.* Stanford: Stanford University Press.
Galarza, Joaquín
  1980 *Estudios de escritura indígena tradicional (Azteca-Náhuatl).*
       México: Archivo General de la Nación y Centro de
       Investigaciones Superiores del Instituto Nacional de
       Antropología e História.
Gallagher, Ann Miriam
  1978 "The Indian Nuns of Mexico City's *Monasterio* of
       Corpus Christi, 1724–1821." In *Latin American Wom-
       en: Historica Perspectives,* ed. Asunción Lavrin, 150–
       72. Westport, Conn.: Greenwood Press.
Gardner, Brant
  1982 "A Structural and Semantic Analysis of Classical
       Nahuatl Kinship Terminology." *Estudios de Cultura
       Náhuatl* 15: 89–124.
Gaventa, John
  1980 *Power and Powerlessness: Quiescence and Rebellion in an
       Appalachian Valley.* Urbana: University of Illinois Press.
Genette, Gerard
  1980 *Narrative Discourse: An Essay in Method.* Translated by
       Jane E. Lewin. Ithaca: Cornell University Press.
Genovese, Eugene D.
  1972 *Roll, Jordan, Roll: The World the Slaves Made.* New
       York: Random House.

Gibson, Charles
1964 *The Aztecs under Spanish Rule.* Stanford: Stanford University Press.
Gillespie, Susan D.
1989 *The Aztec Kings: The Construction of Rulership in Mexica History.* Tucson: University of Arizona Press.
Gómez de Cervantes, Gonzalo
1944 *La vida económica y social de la Nueva España al finalizar del siglo XVI.* México: Antigua Librería Robredo de J. Porrua e Hijos. Originally written 1599.
Góngora, Mario
1951 *El estado en el derecho indiano: Época de fundación, 1492–1570.* Santiago: Instituto de Investigaciones Histórico-Culturales, Facultad de Filosofía y Educación, Universidad de Chile.
Gonzalbo, Pilar
1987 *Las mujeres en la Nueva España: Educación y vida cotidiana.* México: Colegio de México.
González Echevarría, Roberto
1990 *Myth and Archive: A Theory of Latin American Narrative.* Cambridge: Cambridge University Press.
Gonzales Obregón, Luis
1900–1903 *Epoca colonial: México viejo, noticias históricas, tradiciones, leyendas y costumbres.* México: C. Bouret.
1952 *Rebeliones indígenas y precursores de la independencia mexicana en los siglos XVI, XVII, XVIII.* México: Ediciones Fuente Cultural. Originally published 1906–1908.
Goodenough, Ward H.
1955 "A Problem in Malayo-Polynesian Social Organization." *American Anthropologist* 57(1): 71–83.
Goody, Jack
1986 *The Logic of Writing and the Organization of Society.* Cambridge: Cambridge University Press.
Gosner, Kevin
1992 *Soldiers of the Virgin: The Moral Economy of a Colonial Rebellion.* Tucson: University of Arizona Press.

Gramsci, Antonio
  1971 *Selections from the Prison Notebooks of Antonio Gramsci.* Translated and edited by Quintin Hoare and Geoffrey Nowell Smith. New York: International Publishers.
Greenblatt, Stephen J.
  1988 *Shakespearean Negotiations.* Berkeley, Los Angeles, and London: University of California Press.
  1991 *Marvelous Possessions: The Wonder of the New World.* Chicago: University of Chicago Press.
Greenleaf, Richard E.
  1969 *The Mexican Inquisition of the Sixteenth Century.* Albuquerque: University of New Mexico Press.
Gruzinski, Serge
  1980 "Matrimonio y sexualidad en México y Texcoco en los albores de la conquista." In *Seis ensayos sobre el discurso colonial relativo a la comunidad doméstica: matrimonio, familia y sexualidad a través de los cronistas del siglo XVI, el Nuevo Testamento, y el Santo Oficio de la Inquisición,* 17–59. México: Instituto Nacional de Antropología e História.
  1982 "La conquista de los cuerpos." *Familia y sexualidad en Nueva España: Memoria del primer Simposio de Historia de las Mentalidades — "Familia, Matrimonio y Sexualidad en Nueva España,"* 177–206. México: Fondo de Cultura Economica.
  1988 *La Colonisation de l'imaginaire: Sociétés indigènes et occidentalisation dans le Mexique espagnol, XVIᵉ–XVIIIᵉ siècle.* Paris: Gallimard.
  1989a *Man-Gods in the Mexican Highlands: Indian Power and Colonial Society, 1520–1800.* Stanford: Stanford University Press.
  1989b "Individualization and Acculturation: Confession among the Nahuas from the Sixteenth to the Eighteenth Century." In *Sexuality and Marriage in Colonial Latin America,* ed. Asunción Lavrin, 96–117. Lincoln: University of Nebraska Press.
  1992 *Painting the Conquest: The Mexican Indians and the*

European Renaissance. Translated by Deke Dusin-
berre. Paris: UNESCO and Flammarion.

Guthrie, Chester

1937 "Riots in Seventeenth-Century Mexico City: A Study
in Social History with Special Emphasis upon the
Lower Classes." Ph.D. diss., Berkeley: University of
California.

1945 "Riots in Seventeenth-Century Mexico City: A Study
of Social and Economic Conditions." In *Greater America: Essays in Honor of Herber Eugene Bolton*, ed. Adele
Ogden and Engel Sluiter, 243–58. Berkeley: University of California Press.

Gutiérrez, Ramon

1991 *When Jesus Came, the Corn Mothers Went Away: Marriage, Sexuality, and Power in New Mexico, 1500–1846*.
Stanford: Stanford University Press.

Hall, Stuart

1991 "Introductory Essay: Reading Gramsci." In *Gramsci's
Political Thought: An Introduction*, by Roger Simon, 7–
10. London: Lawrence and Wishart.

Hanke, Lewis

1949 *The Spanish Struggle for Justice in the Conquest of
America*. Philadelphia: University of Pennsylvania
Press.

Haring, C. H.

1963 *The Spanish Empire in America*. New York: Harcourt,
Brace and World. (1st ed., 1947).

Harvey, H. R.

1986a "Techialoyan Codices: Seventeenth-Century Indian
Land Titles in Central Mexico." In *Ethnohistory*, ed.
Ronald Spores, 153–64. Vol. 4. *Supplement to the
Handbook of Middle American Indians*, gen. ed. Vic-
toria Reifler Bricker. Austin: University of Texas
Press.

1986b "Household and Family Structure in Early Colonial
Tepetlaoztoc: An Analysis of the Códice de Santa
Maria Asunción." *Estudios de Cultura Náhuatl* 18:
275–94.

Haskett, Robert
  1988 "Living in Two Worlds: Cultural Continuity and Change among Cuernavaca's Colonial Indigenous Ruling Elite." *Ethnohistory* 35(1): 34–59.
  1991 *Indigenous Rulers: An Ethnohistory of Town Government in Colonial Cuernavaca.* Albuquerque: University of New Mexico Press.
Haslip, Gabriel
  1980 "Crime and the Administration of Justice in Colonial Mexico City, 1696–1810." Ph.D. diss., Columbia University.
  1986 "The Underclass." In *Cities and Society in Colonial Latin America,* ed. Louisa Schell Hoberman and Susan Migden Socolow, 285–312. Albuquerque: University of New Mexico Press.
Hassig, Ross
  1985 *Trade, Tribute and Transportation: The Sixteenth-Century Political Economy of the Valley of Mexico.* Norman: University of Oklahoma Press.
  1988 *Aztec Warfare: Imperial Expansion and Political Control.* Norman: University of Oklahoma Press.
Hellbom, Anna-Britta
  1967 *La participación cultural de las mujeres indias y mestizas en el México precortesano y postrevolucionario.* Stockholm: Ethnographical Museum.
Herrera, Antonio de
  1601 *Historia general de los hechos de los castellanos en las islas i tierra firme del mar oceano.* 8 vols. Madrid: Emprenta Real.
Hicks, Frederic
  1986 "Prehispanic Background of Colonial Political and Economic Organization in Central Mexico." In *Ethnohistory,* ed. Ronald Spores, 35–54. Vol. 4 *Supplement to the Handbook of Middle American Indians,* gen. ed. Victoria Reifler Bricker. Austin: University of Texas Press.
Hill, Robert M.
  1991 "The Social Uses of Writing among the Colonial Cakchiquel Maya: Nativism, Resistance, and Innova-

tion." In *Columbian Consequences,* ed. David Hurst Thomas, 3: 283–99. Washington, D.C.: Smithsonian Institution Press.

Historia de los Mexicanos por sus pinturas

1941 Historia de los Mexicanos por sus pinturas. *Nueva colección de documentos para la historia de México,* ed. Joaquin García Icazbalceta. Vol. 3, xxxiv–xxxvi, 207–40. México: Editorial Chávez Hayhoe. Originally written ca. 1535.

History and Anthropology

1985 *History and Anthropology* 1(2). Special Issue: The Discourse of Law, ed. Sally Humphries.

Horcasitas, Fernando

1974 *El teatro náhuatl: Épocas novohispana y moderna.* México: Universidad Nacional Autónoma de México, Instituto de Investigaciones Históricas.

Horn, Rebecca

1989*a* "Postconquest Coyoacan: Aspects of Indigenous Sociopolitical and Economic Organization in Central Mexico, 1550–1650." Ph.D. diss., University of California, Los Angeles.

1989*b* "Indian Women in Mexican Parish Archives: Naming Patterns in Seventeenth-Century Coyoacan." Paper read at the Pacific Coast American Historical Association Meetings, August 1989, Portland, Ore.

Huerta, Maria Teresa, and Patricia Palacios, eds.

1976 *Rebeliones indígenas de la época colonial.* México: Secretaría de Educacíon Publica y Instituto Nacional de Antropología e Historia.

Hulme, Peter

1986 *Colonial Encounters: Europe and the Native Caribbean, 1492–1797.* London and New York: Methuen.

Humboldt, Alexander von

1966 *Political Essay on the Kingdom of New Spain.* Translated by John Black. 4 vols. New York: AMS Press. Originally published 1811.

Israel, Jonathan I.
1975 *Race, Class and Politics in Colonial Mexico, 1610–1670.* New York: Oxford University Press.

Ixtlilxochitl, Don Fernando de Alva
1975–77 *Obras históricas.* 2 vols. México: Instituto de Investigaciones Históricas y Universidad Nacional Autónoma de México. Originally written ca. early seventeenth century.

Jameson, Fredric
1972 *The Prison-House of Language: A Critical Account of Structuralism and Russian Formalism.* Princeton: Princeton University Press.

Johnson, Lyman L.
1986 "Artisans." In *Cities and Society in Colonial Latin America,* ed. Louisa Schell Hoberman and Susan Migden Socolow, 277–50. Albuquerque: University of New Mexico Press.

Jones, Grant D.
1989 *Maya Resistance to Spanish Rule: Time and History on a Colonial Frontier.* Albuquerque: University of New Mexico Press.

Journal of Legal Education
1990 *Journal of Legal Education* 40 (1, 2). Special Issue: Pedagogy of Narrative: A Symposium, ed. James R. Elkins.

Kagan, Richard L.
1974 *Students and Society in Early Modern Spain.* Baltimore: Johns Hopkins University Press.
1981 *Lawsuits and Litigants in Castile, 1500–1700.* Chapel Hill: University of North Carolina Press.

Kartunnen, Frances
1992 "After the Conquest: The Survival of Indigenous Patterns of Life and Belief." *Journal of World History* 3(2): 239–56.

Kartunnen, Frances, and James Lockhart, eds.
1987 *The Art of Nahuatl Speech: The Bancroft Dialogues.* Los Angeles: UCLA Latin American Center Publications.

Katz, Friedrich, ed.
1988 *Riot, Rebellion, and Revolution: Rural Social Conflict in Mexico.* Princeton: Princeton University Press.
Keesing, Roger M.
1975 *Kin Groups and Social Structure.* New York: Holt, Rinehart and Winston.
Kellogg, Susan
1980 "Social Organization in Early Colonial Tenochtitlán-Tlatelolco: An Ethnohistorical Study." Ph.D. diss., University of Rochester.
1984 "Aztec Women in Early Colonial Courts: Structure and Strategy in a Legal Context." In *Five Centuries of Law and Politics in Central Mexico,* ed. Ronald Spores and Ross Hassig, 25–38. Nashville: Vanderbilt University Publications in Anthropology.
1986a "Kinship and Social Organization in Early Colonial Tenochtitlán," in *Ethnohistory,* ed. Ronald Spores, 103–21. Vol. 4. *Supplement to the Handbook of Middle American Indians,* gen. ed. Victoria Reifler Bricker. Austin: University of Texas Press.
1986b "Aztec Inheritance in Sixteenth-Century Mexico City: Colonial Patterns, Prehispanic Influences." *Ethnohistory* 33(3): 313–30.
1988 "Cognatic Kinship and Religion: Women in Aztec Society." In *Smoke and Mist: Mesoamerican Studies in Memory of Thelma Sullivan,* ed. J. K. Josserand and Karen Dakin, 2:666–81. Oxford: BAR Press.
1992 "Hegemony Out of Conquest: The First Two Centuries of Spanish Rule in Central Mexico." *Radical History Review* 53(Spring): 27–46.
1993 "The Social Organization of Households Among the Mexica Before and After Conquest." In *Prehispanic Domestic Units in Western Mesoamerica: Studies of the Household, Compound, and Residence,* ed. Robert S. Santley and Kenneth G. Hirth, 207–24. Boca Raton: CRC Press.
Kicza, John E.
1984 "The Legal Community of Late Colonial Mexico:

Social Composition and Career Patterns." In *Five Centuries of Law and Politics in Central Mexico,* ed. Ronald Spores and Ross Hassig, 127–44. Nashville: Vanderbilt University Publications in Anthropology.

Kirchhoff, Paul

    1954–55 "Land Tenure in Ancient Mexico, A Preliminary Sketch." *Revista Mexicana de Estudios Antropológicos* 14(1): 351–61.

    1959 "The Principles of Clanship in Human Society." In *Readings in Anthropology,* ed. Morton Fried, 2: 259–70. New York: Thomas Y. Crowell.

Kleffens, Eelco Nicolas van

    1968 *Hispanic Law until the End of the Middle Ages; With a Note on the Continued Validity after the Fifteenth Century of Medieval Hispanic Legislation in Spain, the Americas, Asia, and Africa.* Edinburgh: Edinburgh University Press.

Klein, Cecelia

    1988 "Rethinking Cihuacoatl: Aztec Political Imagery of the Conquered Woman." In *Smoke and Mist: Mesoamerican Studies in Memory of Thelma Sullivan,* ed. J. K. Josserand and Karen Dakin, 2:237–77. Oxford: BAR Press.

Klor de Alva, J. Jorge

    1982 "Spiritual Conflict and Accommodation in New Spain: Toward a Typology of Aztec Responses to Christianity." In *The Inca and Aztec States, 1400–1800: Anthropology and History,* ed. George Collier, Renato Rosaldo, and John Wirth, 345–66. New York: Academic Press.

    1991 "Colonizing Souls: The Failure of the Indian Inquisition and the Rise of Penitential Discourse." In *Cultural Encounters: The Impact of the Inquisition in Spain and the New World,* ed. Mary Elizabeth Perry and Anne J. Cruz, 3–22. Berkeley, Los Angeles, and London: University of California Press.

Konetzke, Richard

    1953–62 *Colección de documentos para la formación social de Hispanoamérica, 1493–1810.* 3 vols. in 5 pts. Ma-

drid: Consejo Superior de Investigaciones Cientif-
icas.

Kubler, George
1948 *Mexican Architecture of the Sixteenth Century*. New Ha-
ven: Yale University Press.

Laclau, Ernesto
1979 *Politics and Ideology in Marxist Theory: Capitalism—
Fascism—Populism*. London: Verso.

Ladd, Doris M.
1976 *The Mexican Nobility at Independence, 1780–1826*. Austin: University of Texas Press.

Laitin, David D.
1986 *Hegemony and Culture: Politics and Religious Change
among the Yoruba*. Chicago: University of Chicago
Press.

Larson, Brooke
1988 *Colonialism and Agrarian Transformation in Bolivia:
Cochabamba, 1550–1900*. Princeton: Princeton University Press.

Las Casas, Fray Bartolomé de
1967 *Apologética historia sumaria*. 2 vols. México: Instituto
de Investigaciones Históricas y Universidad Nacional
Autónoma de México. Originally written 1555–59.

Latin American Library (Tulane)
Documents from the France Scholes Collection, cited
by *ramo* and volume number.

Lavrin, Asunción
1978 "In Search of the Colonial Woman in Mexico: The
Seventeenth and Eighteenth Centuries." In *Latin American Women: Historical Perspectives*, ed. Asunción Lavrin, 23–59. Westport, Conn.: Greenwood Press.

Lavrin, Asunción, and Edith B. Couturier
1979 "Dowries and Wills: A View of Women's Socioeconomic
Role in Colonial Guadalajara and Puebla, 1640–1790."
Hispanic American Historical Review 59(2): 280–304.

Lears, T. J. Jackson
1985 "The Concept of Cultural Hegemony: Problems and
Possibilities." *American Historical Review* 90(3): 567–93.

León, Martín de

    1611 *Camino del cielo*. México: Emprenta de Diego Lopez Daualos.

León-Portilla, Ascensión H. de

    1988 *Tepuztlahcuilolli—Impresos en náhuatl: Historia y bibliografía*. 2 vols. México: Universidad Nacional Autónoma de México, Instituto de Investigaciones Históricas e Instituto de Investigaciones Filólogicas.

León-Portilla, Miguel

    1963 *Aztec Thought and Culture: A Study of the Ancient Nahuatl Mind*. Norman: University of Oklahoma Press.

Lipsett-Rivera, Sonia

    1992 "Indigenous Communities and Water Rights in Colonial Puebla: Patterns of Resistance." *Americas* 48(4): 463–83.

Lira-González, Andrés

    1982 "Indian Communities in Mexico City: The Parcialidades of Tenochtitlán and Tlatelolco (1812–1919)." Ph.D. diss., State University of New York, Stony Brook.

Lockhart, James

    1968 *Spanish Peru, 1532–1560: A Colonial Study*. Madison: University of Wisconsin Press.

    1985 "Some Nahua Concepts in Postconquest Guise." *History of European Ideas* 6:465–82.

    1991 "Charles Gibson and the Ethnohistory of Postconquest Central Mexico." In *Nahuas and Spaniards: Postconquest Central Mexican History and Philology*, 159–82. Stanford: Stanford University Press.

    1992 *The Nahuas after the Conquest: A Social and Cultural History of the Indians of Central Mexico, Sixteenth through Eighteenth Centuries*. Stanford: Stanford University Press.

Lockhart, James, Frances Berdan, and Arthur J. O. Anderson

    1986 *The Tlaxcalan Actas: A Compendium of the Records of the Cabildo of Tlaxcala (1545–1627)*. Salt Lake City: University of Utah Press.

Loera y Chávez, Margarita

    1977 *Calimaya y Tepemaxalco: Tenencia y transmisión hereditaria de la tierra en dos comunidades indígenas (ép-*

oca colonial). México: Departamento de Investigaciones Históricas del Instituto Nacional de Antropología e Historia.

López, Geronimo
1984 Letter to the King. Reprinted in *New Iberian World,*
ed. John Parry and Robert Keith, 3:446–53. New
York: Times Books and Hector and Rose. Originally
written 1545.

López Austin, Alfredo
1974 "The Research Method of Fray Bernardino de
Sahagún: The Questionnaires." In *Sixteenth-Century
Mexico: The Work of Sahagún,* ed. Munro S. Edmonson, 111–49. Albuquerque: University of New Mexico Press.

1980 *Cuerpo humano e ideología: Las concepciones de los anti-
guos nahuas.* 2 vols. México: Universidad Nacional
Autónoma de México e Instituto de Investigaciones
Antropológicas.

López de Gómara, Francisco
1943 *Historia de la conquista de México.* 2 tomos. México:
Editorial Pedro Robredo. Originally published 1552.

Lozano Amendares, Teresa
1987 *La criminalidad en la Ciudad de México, 1800–1821.*
México: Universidad Nacional Autónoma de México.

McCaa, Robert
1992 "Courtship, Marriage, and Concubinage in Mexico
and Spain, 1500–1800." Paper presented at the Social Science History Association Annual Meetings,
Chicago, Ill., 1992.

McCafferty, Sharisse, and Geoffrey McCafferty
1988 "Powerful Women and the Myth of Male Dominance
in Aztec Society." *Archaeological Review from Cambridge* 7:45–59.

1991 "Spinning and Weaving as Female Gender Identity in
Post-Classic Mexico." In *Textile Traditions of Mesoamerica and the Andes: An Anthology,* ed. Margot Schev-
ill, Janet Catherine Berlo and Edward Dwyer, 19–44.
New York: Garland Publishers.

MacLachlan, Colin M.
  1974 *Criminal Justice in Eighteenth-Century Mexico: A Study of the Tribunal of the Acordada.* Berkeley, Los Angeles, and London: University of California Press.
  1976 "The Eagle and the Serpent: Male Over Female in Tenochtitlán." *Proceedings of the Pacific Coast Council of Latin American Studies* 5:45–56.
Maldonado López, Celia
  1976 *Estadísticas vitales de la Ciudad de México (siglo XI).* México: INAH-SEP.
  1988 *La Ciudad de México en el siglo XVII.* México: Departamento del Distrito Federal, Secretaría General de Desarollo Social, Comité Interno de Ediciones Gubernamentales.
Mann, Bruce H.
  1987 *Neighbors and Strangers: Law and Community in Early Connecticut.* Chapel Hill: University of North Carolina Press.
Marcus, George E., and Dick Cushman
  1982 "Ethnographies as Texts." *Annual Review of Anthropology* 2:25–69.
Markov, Gretchen Koch
  1983 "The Legal Status of Indians Under Spanish Rule." Ph.D. diss., University of Rochester.
Marroquí, José María
  1900–1903 *La Ciudad de México; contiene: El orígen de los nombres de muchas de sus calles y plazas, del de varios establecimientos públicos y privados, y no pocas noticias curiosas y entretenidas.* México: Tip. y Lit. "La Europea," de J. Aguilar Vera y Ca.
Martínez Alcubilla, Marcel
  1885 *Códigos antiguos de España.* 2 vols. Madrid: Administración (J. López Camacho, impresor).
Martin, Cheryl English
  1985 *Rural Society in Colonial Morelos.* Albuquerque: University of New Mexico Press.
Martin, Norman F.
  1957 *Los vagabundos en la Nueva España.* México: Editorial Jus.

Memmi, Albert
1965 *The Colonizer and the Colonized.* New York: Orion Press.

Mendieta, Fray Gerónimo de
1945 *Historia eclesiástica indiana.* 4 vols. México: Salvador Chávez Hayhoe. Originally written ca. 1571–96.

Mendoza, don Antonio de
1945 *Ordenanzas y compilación de leyes.* Colección de Incunables Americanos, Siglo XVI, vol. 5. Madrid: Ediciones Cultura Hispánica. Originally published 1548.

Merry, Sally Engle
1992 "Anthropology, Law, and Transnational Process." *Annual Review of Anthropology* 21:357–79.

Millares Carlo, Agustín, and José Ignacio Mantecón
1945–46 *Índice y extractos de los protocolos del Archivo de Nortarías de México, D.F.* 2 vols. México: Colegio de México.

Miller, Arthur G.
1974 "The Iconography of the Painting in the Temple of the Diving God, Tulum, Quintana Roo, Mexico: The Twisted Cords." In *Mesoamerican Archaeology: New Approaches,* ed. Norman Hammond, 167–86. Austin: University of Texas Press.

Miranda, José
1952 *El tributo indígena en la Nueva España durante el siglo XVI.* México: Colegio de México.

Molina, Alonso de
1565 *Confesionario mayor, en lengua mexicana y castellana.* México: Antonio de Espinosa.
1977 *Vocabulario en lengua castellana y mexicana, y mexicana y castellana.* México: Editorial Porrua. Originally published 1555–71.

Montemayor y Córdova de Cuenca, Juan Francisco
1787 *Sumarios de las cédulas, órdenes y provisiones reales, que se han despachado por su magestad, para la Nueva España. . . .* Published in Eusebio Bentura Beleña, *Recopilación sumaria de todos los autos acordados de la*

real audiencia sala del crímen de esta Nueva España. . . . (vol. 1). México: Don Felipe Zuñiga y Ontiveros.

Monzón, Arturo
1949 *El calpulli en la organización social de los Tenochca.* México: Universidad Nacional Autónoma de México.

Moore, Sally Falk
1986 *Social Facts and Fabrications: "Customary" Law on Kilamanjaro, 1880–1980.* Cambridge: Cambridge University Press.

Moore, Henrietta L.
1988 *Feminism and Anthropology.* Minneapolis: University of Minnesota Press.

Moreno, Manuel
1931 *La organización política y social de los aztecas.* México: Universidad Nacional Autónoma de México.

Morgan, Lewis Henry
1877 *Ancient Society.* New York: Henry Holt.

Mörner, Magnus
1967 *Race Mixture in the History of Latin America.* Boston: Little Brown.

Motolinía, Fray Toribio (de Benavente)
1971 *Memoriales o libro de las cosas de la Nueva España y los naturales de ella.* México: Universidad Nacional Autónoma de México. Written by ca. 1541.

Murdock, George P.
1960 "Cognatic Forms of Social Organization." In *Social Structure in Souteast Asia,* ed. George Murdock, 1–14. New York: Viking Fund Publications in Anthropology and Wenner-Gren Foundation for Anthropological Research.

Nader, Laura
1967 "An Analysis of Zapotec Law Cases." In *Law and Warfare,* ed. Paul Bohannan, 117–38. Garden City, N.Y.: Natural History Press.

1990 *Harmony Ideology: Justice and Control in a Zapotec Mountain Village.* Stanford: Stanford University Press.

Nader, Laura, ed.
1969 *Law in Culture and Society.* Chicago: Aldine.

Nader, Laura, and Harry F. Todd, eds.
1978 *The Disputing Process: Law in Ten Societies.* New York: Columbia University Press.

Nash, June
1978 "The Aztecs and the Ideology of Male Dominance." *Signs* 4(2): 349–62.

New Catholic Encyclopedia
1967–79 *New Catholic Encyclopedia.* 17 vols. New York: Mc-Graw-Hill.

Newberry Library
Documents from the Ayer Collection, cited by MS number.

Nicholson, Henry B.
1971 "Religion in Pre-Hispanic Central Mexico." In *Archaeology of Northern Mesoamerica,* pt. 1, ed. Gordon F. Ekholm and Ignacio Bernal, 395–446. Vol. 10, *Handbook of Middle American Indians,* gen. ed. Robert Wauchope. Austin: University of Texas Press.

Nutini, Hugo G.
1968 *San Bernardino Contla: Marriage and Family Structure in a Tlaxcalan Municipio.* Pittsburgh: University of Pittsburgh Press.

Offner, Jerome A.
1983 *Law and Politics in Aztec Texcoco.* Cambridge: Cambridge University Press.
1984 "Household Organization in the Texcocan Heartland: The Evidence in the Codex Vergara." In *Explorations in Ethnohistory: Indians of Central Mexico in the Sixteenth Century,* ed. H. R. Harvey and Hanns J. Prem, 127–46. Albuquerque: University of New Mexico Press.

O'Phelan Godoy, Scarlett
1985 *Rebellions and Revolts in Eighteenth-Century Peru and Upper Peru.* Köln: Böhlau Verlag.

Ordenanzas de Cuauhtinchán
1978 "Ordenanzas para el gobierno Cuauhtinchán." In *Documentos sobre las tierras y señorío en Cuauhtinchán,* ed. Luis Reyes García, 180–215. México: SEP-INAH. Originally written 1559.

Ortiz de Montellano, Bernard
1990 *Aztec Medicine, Health and Nutrition.* New Brunswick: Rutgers University Press.

Ortner, Sherry B.
1981 "Gender and Sexuality in Hierarchical Societies: The Case of Polynesia and Some Comparative Implications." In *Sexual Meanings: The Cultural Construction of Gender and Sexuality,* ed. Sherry B. Ortner and Harriet Whitehead, 359–409. Cambridge: Cambridge University Press.

1984 "Theory in Anthropology since the Sixties." *Comparative Studies in Society and History* 26(1): 126–66.

Osborn, Wayne
1973 "Indian Land Retention in Colonial Metztitlán." *Hispanic American Historical Review* 53(2): 217–38.

Ots Capdequí, J. M.
1941 *El estado español en las Indias.* México: Fondo de Cultura Económica.

Ouweneel, Arij and Simon Miller (eds.)
1990 *The Indian Community of Colonial Mexico: Fifteen Essays on Land Tenure, Corporate Organization, Ideology and Village Politics.* Amsterdam: Center for Latin American Research and Documentation.

Pagden, Anthony
1982 *The Fall of Natural Man: The American Indian and the Origins of Comparative Ethnology.* Cambridge: Cambridge University Press.

Parnell, Philip C.
1978 "Village or State? Competitive Legal Systems in a Mexican Judicial District." In *The Disputing Process: Law in Ten Societies,* ed. Laura Nader and Harry F. Todd, 315–50. New York: Columbia University Press.

1988 *Escalating Disputes: Social Participation and Change in the Oaxacan Highlands.* Tucson: University of Arizona Press.

Parry, J. H.
1948 *The Audiencia of New Galicia in the Sixteenth Century.* Cambridge: Cambridge University Press.

Paso y Troncoso, Francisco del
1905–06 *Papeles de Nueva España.* 2d ser. Geografía y estadística, vols. 1, 3–7. Madrid: Sucesores de Rivadeneyra.

Pastor Bodmer, Beatriz
1992 *The Armature of Conquest: Spanish Accounts of the Discovery of America, 1492–1589.* Translated by Lydia Longstreth Hunt. Stanford: Stanford University Press.

Pérez, Manuel
1713 *Farol indiano.* México: Francisco de Rivera Calderón.

Periano, Roger D.
1961 "Descent, Descent Line and Descent Group in Cognatic Social Systems." In *Symposium: Patterns of Land Utilization and Other Papers: Proceedings of the Annual Spring Meeting of the American Ethnological Society,* ed. Viola E. Garfield, 93–113. Seattle: University of Washington Press.

Perry, Mary Elizabeth
1990 *Gender and Disorder in Early Modern Spain.* Princeton: Princeton University Press.

Pescatello, Ann M.
1976 *Power and Pawn: The Female in Iberian Families, Societies and Cultures.* Westport, Conn.: Greenwood Press.

Peterson, Jeanette Favrot
1993 *The Paradise Garden Murals of Malinalco: Utopia and Empire in Sixteenth-Century Mexico.* Austin: University of Texas Press.

Phelan, John Leddy
1956 *The Millennial Kingdom of the Franciscans in the New World: A Study of the Writings of Geronimo de Mendieta (1525–1604).* Berkeley and Los Angeles: University of California Press.

1967 *The Kingdom of Quito in the Seventeenth Century: Bureaucratic Politics in the Spanish Empire.* Madison: University of Wisconsin Press.

Plakans, Andrejs
1984 *Kinship in the Past: An Anthropology of European Family*

Life, 1500–1900. Oxford and New York: Basil Black-well.

Pomar, Juan Bautista
1891 "Relación de Tezcoco." In *Nueva colección de documentos para la historia de México,* by J. García Icazbalceta, 3:1–69. México: Imprenta de Francisco Díaz de León. Originally written 1582.

Porras Muñoz, Guillermo
1982 *El gobierno de la Ciudad de México en el siglo XVI.* México: Universidad Nacional Autónoma de México, Instituto de Investigaciones Históricas.

Posner, Richard A.
1988 *Law and Literature: A Misunderstood Relation.* Cambridge: Harvard University Press.

Prem, Hanns J.
1992 "Spanish Colonization and Indian Property in Central Mexico, 1521–1620." *Annals of the Association of American Geographers* 82(3): 444–60.

Presencia y transparencia
1987 *Presencia y transparencia: La mujer en la historia de México,* by Carmen Ramos Escandón et al. México: Colegio de México.

Puga, Vasco de
1945 *Provisiones, cédulas, instrucciones para el gobierno de la Nueva España.* Facsimile ed., Colección de Incunables Americanos. Vol. 3. Madrid: Ediciones Cultura Hispánica. Originally published 1563.

Rabasa, José
1993 *Inventing America: Spanish Historiography and the Formation of Eurocentrism.* Norman: University of Oklahoma Press.

Ragon, Pierre
1992 *Les Indiens de la découverte: Evangélisation, mariage et sexualité Mexique, XVIᵉ siècle.* Paris: Editions L'Harmattan.

Rammow, Helga
1964 *Die Verwandtschaftsbezeichnungen im klassischen Azteckischen.* Vol. 1. Hamburg: Bieträge zur mittelamerikanischen Völkerkinde, Herausgegeben vom Ham-

burgischen Museum für Völkerkinde und Vorge-
schichte, VI.

Ravicz, Marilyn Ekdahl
1970 *Early Colonial Religious Drama in Mexico: From Tzom-
pantli to Golgotha.* Washington, D.C.: Catholic University of America Press.

Read, Kay
1988 "'Destruction,' 'Death,' and 'Disappearance': Mexica-
Tenochca Conceptions of Time and Sacrifice." Paper
read at the Annual Meeting of the American Anthropological Association, Phoenix, Ariz.

Representations
1990 *Representations,* no. 30 (Spring). Special Issue: Law
and the Order of Culture, ed. Robert Post.

Reyes García, Cayetano, et al., eds.
1982 *Documentos mexicanos.* 2 tomos. México: Archivo General de la Nación.

Reyes García, Luis
1975 "El término calpulli en los documentos del centro de
México." Paper presented at the Seminario de Ve-
rano sobre Organización Social del México Antiguo,
CIS-INAH, Mexico City.

Ricard, Robert
1966 *The Spiritual Conquest of Mexico.* Translated by Lesley
Byrd Simpson. Berkeley and Los Angeles: University
of California Press.

Ricouer, Paul
1984 *Time and Narrative.* Translated by Kathleen McLaugh-
lin and David Pellauer. Chicago: University of Chicago Press.

Robertson, Donald
1974 "The Treatment of Architecture in the *Florentine
Codex* of Sahagún. In *Sixteenth-Century Mexico: The
Work of Sahagún,* ed. Munro S. Edmonson, 151–87.
Albuquerque: University of New Mexico Press and
School of American Research.

Robinson, David J.
1980 *Research Inventory of the Mexican Collection of Colonial*

Parish Registers. Salt Lake City: University of Utah Press.

Rodríguez, María

1988 *La mujer azteca.* México: Universidad Autónoma del Estado de México.

1990*a El estado azteca.* México: Universidad Autónoma del Estado de México.

1990*b* "Enfoque y perspectivas de los estudios sobre la condición femenina en el México antiguo." *Mesoamérica* 19:1–11.

Rojas, José Luis de

1986 *México Tenochtitlán: Economía y sociedad en el siglo XVI.* México: Fondo de Cultura Económica; Zamora: Colegio de Michoacán.

Romney, A. Kimball

1967 "Kinship and Family." In *Social Anthropology,* ed. Manning Nash, 207–37. Vol. 6, *Handbook of Middle American Indians,* gen. ed. Robert Wauchope, Austin: University of Texas Press.

Ruiz de Alarcón, Hernando

1984 *Treatise on the Heathen Superstitions That Today Live Among the Indians Native to This New Spain, 1629.* Translated and edited by J. Richard Andrews and Ross Hassig. Norman: University of Oklahoma Press. Originally written 1629.

Ruiz Medrano, Ethelia

1991 *Gobierno y sociedad en Nueva España: Segunda audiencia y Antonio de Mendoza.* Zamora: Colegio de Michoacán.

Sahagún, Fray Bernardino de

1583 *Psalmodia cristiana y sermonio de los sanctos del año en lengua mexicana.* México: Pedro Ocharte.

1975 *Historia general de las cosas de Nueva España.* México: Editorial Porrua. Originally written 1576–77.

Said, Edward

1983 *The World, the Text, and the Critic.* Cambridge: Harvard University Press.

Sanders, William T., Jeffrey R. Parsons, and Robert S. Santley
    1979 *The Basin of Mexico: Ecological Processes in the Evolution of a Civilization*. New York: Academic Press.

Sandstrom, Alan R.
    1991 *Corn Is Our Blood: Culture and Ethnic Identity in a Contemporary Aztec Indian Village*. Norman: University of Oklahoma Press.

Scardaville, Michael Charles
    1977 "Crime and the Urban Poor: Mexico City in the Late Colonial Period." Ph.D. diss., University of Florida.

Scheffler, Harold W.
    1964 "Descent Concepts and Descent Groups: The Maori Case." *Journal of Polynesian Society* 73(2):126–33.
    1965 *Choiseul Island Social Structure*. Berkeley and Los Angeles: University of California Press.

Scheper-Hughes, Nancy
    1992 *Death Without Weeping: The Violence of Everyday Life in Brazil*. Berkeley, Los Angeles, and London: University of California Press.

Scholes, Robert, and Robert Kellogg
    1966 *The Nature of Narrative*. New York: Oxford University Press.

Schroeder, Susan
    1991 *Chimalpahin and the Kingdoms of Chalco*. Tucson: University of Arizona Press.

Schwaller, John Frederick
    1986 "Manuscritos nahuas en: The Newberry Library (Chicago), the Latin American Library, Tulane University, the Bancroft Library, University of California, Berkeley." *Estudios de Cultura Náhuatl* 18:315–83.

Scott, James C.
    1985 *Weapons of the Weak: Everyday Forms of Peasant Resistance*. New Haven: Yale University Press.
    1990 *Domination and the Arts of Resistance: Hidden Transcripts*. New Haven: Yale University Press.

Seed, Patricia
    1982 "Social Dimensions of Race: Mexico City, 1753." *Hispanic American Historical Review* 62(4): 569–606.

1988 *To Love, Honor and Obey in Colonial Mexico: Conflicts Over Marriage Choice, 1574–1821.* Stanford: Stanford University Press.

1991 "Colonial and Post-Colonial Discourse: A Review of Recent Works in Political and Cultural Criticism." *Latin American Research Review* 26(3): 181–200.

Serna, Jacinto de la

1892 "Manual de ministros de indios para el conocimiento de sus idolatrías y extirpación de ellas." *Colección de documentos inéditos para la historia de España,* vol. 104, 1–267. Madrid: Imprenta de José Perales y Martínez. Originally written 1656.

Silverblatt, Irene

1987 *Moon, Sun and Witches: Gender Ideologies and Class in Inca and Colonial Peru.* Princeton: Princeton University Press.

Slade, Doren L.

1976 "Kinship in the Social Organization of a Nahuat-speaking Community in the Central Highlands." In *Essays on Mexican Kinship,* eds. Hugo Nutini, Pedro Carrasco and James Taggart, 155–87. Pittsburgh: University of Pittsburgh Press.

1992 *Making the World Safe for Existence: Celebration of the Saints among the Sierra Nahuat of Chignautla, Mexico.* Ann Arbor: University of Michigan Press.

Smith, Barbara Herrnstein

1981 "Narrative Versions, Narrative Theories." In *On Narrative,* ed. W. J. T. Mitchell, 209–32. Chicago: University of Chicago Press.

Smith, Michael E.

1993 "Houses and the Settlement Hierarchy in Late Post-classic Morelos: A Comparison of Archaeology and Ethnohistory." In *Prehispanic Domestic Units in Western Mesoamerica: Studies of the Household, Compound, and Residence,* ed. Robert S. Santley and Kenneth G. Hirth, 191–206. Boca Raton: CRC Press

Solórzano y Pereyra, Juan de

1776 *Política indiana.* 2 Vols. Madrid: Imprenta Real de la Gazeta.

Soustelle, Jacques
  1961 *Daily Life of the Aztecs, on the Eve of the Spanish Conquest.* Translated by Patrick O'Brian. Stanford: Stanford University Press.
Spalding, Karen
  1970 "Social Climbers: Changing Patterns of Mobility among the Indians of Colonial Peru." *Hispanic American Historical Review* 50(4): 645–64.
  1984 *Huarochirí: An Andean Society under Inca and Spanish Rule.* Stanford: Stanford University Press.
Starr, Jane, and Jane F. Collier, eds.
  1989 *History and Power in the Study of Law: New Directions in Legal Anthropology.* Ithaca: Cornell University Press.
Stenning, Derrick
  1958 "Household Viability Among the Pastoral Fulani." In *The Developmental Cycle in Domestic Groups,* ed. Jack Goody, 92–119. Cambridge: Cambridge University Press.
Stern, Steve J.
  1982 *Peru's Indian Peoples and the Challenge of Spanish Conquest: Huamanga to 1640.* Madison: University of Wisconsin Press.
Stern, Steve J., ed.
  1987 *Resistance, Rebellion, and Consciousness in the Andean World, 18th to 20th Centuries.* Madison: University of Wisconsin Press.
Stone, Lawrence
  1993 *Broken Lives: Separation and Divorce in England 1660–1857.* Oxford: Oxford University Press.
Storey, Rebecca
  1992 *Life and Death in the Ancient City of Teotihuacán: A Modern Paleodemographic Synthesis.* Tuscaloosa: University of Alabama Press.
Stowe, Noel James
  1971 "The Tumulto of 1624: Turmoil at Mexico City." Ph.D. diss., University of Southern California.
Sullivan, Thelma D.
  1974 "The Rhetorical Orations of *Huehuetlatolli,* Collected

by Sahagún." In *Sixteenth-Century Mexico: The Work of Sahagún*, ed. Munro S. Edmonson, 79–109. Albuquerque: University of New Mexico Press.

1976 *Compendio de la gramática náhuatl*. México: Universidad Nacional Autónoma de México.

1982 "Tlazolteotl-Ixcuina: The Great Spinner and Weaver." In *The Art and Iconography of Late Post-Classic Central Mexico*, ed. Elizabeth Boone, 7–35. Washington, D.C.: Dumbarton Oaks.

1987 *Documentos tlaxcaltecos del siglo XVI*. México: Universidad Nacional Autónoma de México.

Taggart, James M.

1975 *Estructuras de los grupos domésticos de una comunidad nahuat de Puebla*. México: Instituto Nacional Indigenista y Secretaría de Educación Pública.

1976 "Action Group Recruitment: A Nahuat Case." In *Essays on Mexican Kinship*, ed. Hugo Nutini, Pedro Carrasco and James M. Taggart, 137–53. Pittsburgh: University of Pittsburgh Press.

Taussig, Michael T.

1987 *Shamanism, Colonialism, and the Wild Man: A Study in Terror and Healing*. Chicago: University of Chicago Press.

Taylor, William B.

1979 *Drinking, Homicide and Rebellion in Colonial Mexican Villages*. Stanford: Stanford University Press.

Todorov, Tzvetan

1977 *The Poetics of Prose*. Translated by Richard Howard. Ithaca: Cornell University Press.

1984 *The Conquest of America*. Translated by Richard Howard. New York: Harper Torchbooks.

Torquemada, Fray Juan de

1975 *Monarquía indiana*. 4 vols. México: Editorial Porrua. Originally published 1615.

Trexler, Richard C.

1982 "From the Mouths of Babes: Christianization by Children in Sixteenth-Century New Spain." In *Religious Organization and Religious Experience*, ed. John Davis, 115–35. New York: Academic Press.

1984 "We Think, They Act: Clerical Readings of Missionary Theatre in Sixteenth-Century New Spain." In *Understanding Popular Culture: Europe from the Middle Ages to the Nineteenth Century,* ed. Steven L. Kaplan, 189–227. Berlin and New York: Mouton.

Turner, Victor
1971 "An Anthropological Approach to the Icelandic Saga." In *The Translation of Culture,* ed. Thomas Beidelman, 349–74. London: Tavistock.

Tutino, John
1983 "Power, Class and Family: Men and Women in the Mexican Elite, 1750–1810." *Americas* 39(3): 359–82.

Valle-Arizpe, Artemio de
1949 *Calle vieja y calle nueva.* México: Editorial Jus.

Van Young, Eric
1981 *Hacienda and Market in Eighteenth-Century Mexico: The Rural Economy of the Guadalajara Region, 1675–1820.* Berkeley, Los Angeles, and London: University of California Press.

1984 "Conflict and Solidarity in Indian Village Life: The Guadalajara Region in the Late Colonial Period." *Hispanic American Historical Review* 64(1): 55–79.

1988 "Islands in the Storm: Quiet Cities and Violent Countrysides in the Mexican Independence Era." *Past and Present* 118:130–55.

Vigil, Ralph
1987 *Alonso de Zorita: Royal Judge and Christian Humanist, 1512–1585.* Norman: University of Oklahoma Press.

Villanueva, Margaret
1985 "From Calpixqui to Corregidor: Appropriation of Women's Cotton Textile Production in Early Colonial Mexico." *Latin American Perspectives* 12(1): 17–40.

Wachtel, Nathan
1977 *The Vision of the Vanquished: The Spanish Conquest of Peru through Indian Eyes, 1530–1570.* Translated by Ben and Sian Reynolds. New York: Barnes and Noble.

Warren, J. Benedict
1973 "An Introductory Survey of Secular Writings in the European Tradition on Colonial Middle America, 1503–1818." In *Guide to Ethnohistorical Sources, Pt. Two,* ed. Howard Cline, 42–137. Vol. 13, *Handbook of Middle American Indians,* gen. ed. Robert Wauchope. Austin: University of Texas Press.

Wasserstrom, Robert
1983 *Class and Society in Central Chiapas.* Berkeley, Los Angeles, and London: University of California Press.

White, Hayden
1978 *Tropics of Discourse: Essays in Cultural Criticism.* Baltimore: Johns Hopkins University Press.

White, James Boyd
1985 *Heracles' Bow: Essays on the Rhetoric and Poetics of the Law.* Madison: University of Wisconsin Press.

Wightman, Ann M.
1990 *Indigenous Migration and Social Change: The Forasteros of Cuzco, 1570–1720.* Durham: University of North Carolina Press.

Williams, Raymond
1977 *Marxism and Literature.* Oxford: Oxford University Press.

Wood, Stephanie
1984 "Corporate Adjustments in Colonial Mexican-Indian Towns: Toluca Region, 1550–1810." Ph.D. diss., University of California, Los Angeles.
1991a "The Cosmic Conquest: Late-Colonial Views of the Sword and Cross in Central Mexican *Títulos.*" *Ethnohistory* 38(2): 176–95.
1991b "Adopted Saints: Christian Images in Nahua Testaments of Late Colonial Toluca." *Americas* 42(3): 259–94.

Zavala, Silvio
1971 *Las instituciones jurídicas en la conquista de América.* México: Editorial Porrua.
1984–87 *El servicio personal de los indios en la Nueva España.*

3 vols. México: Colegio de México, Centro de Estudios Históricos.

Zorita, Alonso de

1942 *Breve y sumaria relación de los señores de la Nueva España*. México: Imprenta Universitaria. Originally written ca. 1570.

Zulawski, Ann

1990 "Social Differentation, Gender and Ethnicity: Urban Indian Women in Colonial Bolivia, 1640–1725." *Latin American Research Review* 25(2): 93–114.

Index

Courts. *See* Juzgado General de Indios; Real Audiencia; Teccalli; Tlacxitlan
Crafts, 171, 198n; calpulli and, 182; father-to-son instruction in, 181n.27; women and, 97, 110, 113. *See also* Artisans, Indian; Guilds, craft
Craftsmen. *See* Artisans
Cremation, 122
Creoles, 11, 13
Crime(s), 218; shared responsibility for, 186; sin and, 215
Crucifixes, as bequest, 141, 149, 151
Cruz, Cristina de la, 79–80
Cuacuilli. *See* Quacuiltin
Cuauhtemoc, 53
Cuernavaca, Mex., 200n
Cuicacalli, 91, 102, 107, 168, 223; women in, 98–99
Cuitlatenamic (pueblo), as litigant, 64–65
Culhuacan (city), 144n
Cultural category, and social group contrasted, 173n.16
Custom, litigant reliance on, 69, 76–77. *See also* Land use, customary
Cuzco, Peru, 207n.43
Cypresses, rulers as, 167

Dancing school. *See* Cuicacalli
Day signs, 95
Death. *See* Capital punishment; Drowning, death by; Funerals; Human sacrifice; Mortality
Debt, as will consideration, 136, 141, 156
Decisions, judicial, 39, 78–81
Defendants, 39, 40, 66, 67, 75, 78, 110. *See also* Litigants
Defendientes, 223. *See also* Defendants

Deities, 91, 114, 122, 123, 166, 203; female, 100, 102 (*see also* Cihuacoatl); human ties to, 163
Demandantes, 223. *See also* Plaintiffs
Deudo, 223. *See also* Kinship
Díaz Agüero, Pero, 6, 14, 19–20, 40
Diego Francisco, 6–7
Disease: death and, 122, 123; epidemic, 198, 205; as Spanish legacy, 69, 198n
Divorce: in Castilian law, 105; parent anticipation of, 183
Doçan, Pedro, 151
Documents, legal, 38–42; fraudulent, 68; oidor rejection of, 81. *See also* Bills of sale; Evidence, documentary; Interrogatorios; Testimony, expert; Wills
Don (term), 71
Dons, 25, 26, 223; as court witnesses, 34, 35
Dowries, 47, 48, 73, 93, 105, 110, 126
Drawings, evidentiary, 39, 44. *See also* House plans; Maps
Dropsy, 122
Drowning, death by, 122, 123
Durán, Diego, 96n.14, 203

Echuras [de bulto], 223. *See also* Images, religious
Education, women in, 101–102. *See also* Schools; Teachers
Elderly, 198n, 199–200n
Elites, Indian, 24–29, 34, 36, 71, 121; as audiencia witnesses, 34–35; funerals of, 122; gearing of crafts to, 171; houses of, 124; shift to Christian marriage practices, 202–203. *See also* Nobles, Indian